THE POET AS BOTANIST

For centuries, poets have been ensnared – as one of their number, Andrew Marvell, put it – by the beauty of flowers. Then, from the middle of the eighteenth century onward, that enjoyment was enriched by a surge of popular interest in botany. Besides exploring the relationship between poetic and scientific responses to the green world within the context of humanity's changing concepts of its own place in the ecosphere, Molly Mahood considers the part that flowering plants played in the daily lives, and therefore in the literary work, of a number of writers who could all be called poet–botanists: Erasmus Darwin, George Crabbe, John Clare, John Ruskin and D. H. Lawrence. A concluding chapter looks closely at the meanings, old or new, that plants retained or obtained in the violent twentieth century.

M. M. MAHOOD is Emeritus Professor of English Literature, University of Kent, Canterbury. Her main areas of interest are Shakespeare and Third World literature, and, after her retirement, she pursued her interest in biology by completing an Open University degree course. Her books include *Bit Parts in Shakespeare's Plays* (Cambridge, 1992), *Shakespeare's Wordplay* (1957) and *Poetry and Humanism* (1950), and she is the editor of *The Merchant of Venice* in the New Cambridge Shakespeare series (new edition 2003).

THE POET AS BOTANIST

M. M. MAHOOD

CAMBRIDGE
UNIVERSITY PRESS

CAMBRIDGE UNIVERSITY PRESS
Cambridge, New York, Melbourne, Madrid, Cape Town, Singapore, São Paulo, Delhi

Cambridge University Press
The Edinburgh Building, Cambridge CB2 8RU, UK

Published in the United States of America by Cambridge University Press, New York

www.cambridge.org
Information on this title: www.cambridge.org/9780521862363

First published 2008

Printed in the United Kingdom at the University Press, Cambridge

A catalogue record for this publication is available from the British Library

Library of Congress Cataloguing in Publication data

Mahood, M. M. (Molly Maureen)
The poet as botanist / M. M. Mahood.
p.   cm.
ISBN 978-0-521-86236-3
1. English poetry – History and criticism.   2. Botany in literature.   3. Nature in
literature.   4. Perception in literature.   5. Philosophy of nature in literature.   6. Darwin, Erasmus,
1731–1802 – Knowledge – Botany.   7. Crabbe, George, 1754–1832 – Knowledge – Botany.   8. Clare,
John, 1793–1864 – Knowledge – Botany.   9. Ruskin, John, 1819–1900 – Knowledge –
Botany.   10. Lawrence, D. H. (David Herbert), 1885–1930 – Knowledge – Botany.   I. Title.
PR508.N3M35 2008
821.009′364–dc22   2007051675

ISBN 978-0-521-86236-3 hardback

in memoriam
Kathleen Esther Wallace, née Mahood
(1908–2006)
who first showed me Sussex hedgerows in spring

Contents

Illustrations

Acknowledgements

In writing this book I have experienced anew the extraordinary generosity with which specialists in many fields of learning make their expertise available to a non-specialist who is so rash as to venture into their territory. I am particularly grateful to those friends and former colleagues who have found time to read and comment on portions of the typescript: to Pamela Woof, Moira Mosley, Caroline Jackson-Houlston, Martin Priestman, Louis James, Robert Heyes, Prudence Smith, Mark Kinkead-Weekes and John Worthen; and to James Cullen who has cast an expert botanic eye over the whole. Others have readily responded to questions to which they alone had the answers: Alison Andrews, James Dearden, David Ellis, Reg Foakes, Paul Foster, Richard Garnett, Cherry Gertzel, Tim Hilton, Helen Jagger Wood, John Jamieson, Desmond King-Hele, Lyn Innes and Martin Scofield, Dinah James, Bernard Lamb, Laurence and Natalie Lerner, Marion O'Connor and Bernard Sharrett, Judith Peacock, John Richards, Eric Robinson, Keith Sagar, Anne Stow, U. T. Summers, Lotte Troupp, Lawrence Wigley and Richard Wilbur.

Among the libraries I have been privileged to explore, my biggest debt is to the London Library, whose policy of never throwing out a book has made a treasure-house of its 'Science and Miscellaneous' section. I also gladly acknowledge the help I have received from staff members of the British Library, the Bodleian Library, the Radcliffe Science Library at Oxford, Cambridge University Library, the Library of Trinity College, Cambridge, the Hallward Library at the University of Nottingham, the Brotherton Library at the University of Leeds, the Poetry Library (London), the Lindley Library of the Royal Horticultural Society, the University of Sussex Library and the Ruskin Library at the University of Lancaster. Other institutions to whose staff my warm thanks are due are the Whipple Museum of the History of Science at Cambridge, the Nottingham Castle Museum, the Peterborough Museum and the Royal Botanic Gardens at Kew.

While my footnotes acknowledge my debt to a variety of printed sources, they make little or no mention of a small number of reference works to which I have had recourse so often that I want to put on record here my gratitude to their authors: A. G. Morton, for *History of Botanical Science* (1981); Geoffrey Grigson for *The Englishman's Flora* (1958) and Richard Mabey for its successor, *Flora Britannica* (1996); A. R. Clapham, T. G. Tutin and D. M. Moore for their *Flora of the British Isles* (1989 edition) together with Marjorie Blamey and Christopher Grey-Wilson for their *Illustrated Flora of Britain and Northern Europe* (1989); the contributors to *Flowering Plants of the World* (edited by Vernon Heywood, 1993); Franklyn Perring and Max Walters for their *Atlas of the British Flora* (1962); and John van Wyhe for the *Complete Works of Charles Darwin Online*.

Finally, a special word of thanks to Sarah Stanton of Cambridge University Press for her unfailing patience and encouragement while this book was in the making.

A note on quotations

In quotations from works written before 1850, spelling, use of capital letters and italics, and to a lesser degree punctuation, have all been brought into conformity with modern practice. The few quotations taken directly from manuscripts are, however, given in their original form. Two writers have presented special problems. Erasmus Darwin distinguishes the topic words of his verse paragraphs by small capitals, and these I have kept. John Clare's idiosyncrasies of spelling and punctuation are preserved by his Oxford editors, but since I share Jonathan Bate's belief that Clare expected his publishers to normalise his spelling and punctuation, I have done the same with what I hope has been a light hand, and without any interference with the poet's grammar or wording.

Introduction

This is a book about the ways in which poets see plants. More exactly it is an attempt to record something of poets' perceptions of the richness and intricacy and life-giving importance of the plant world as these have been revealed in the generations since Linnaeus made botany big science. At least, that is its field, or scope. But like a plant, a book requires a supply of energy, a driving force; and to define that force I have to have recourse to a fragment of autobiography.

Many years ago, I came round from an emergency operation to find myself in a tropical hospital. Around me were all the mysterious comings and goings that belong to such an occasion. Then, as the bustle died down, one stranger more (the matron, I was later to discover) placed a small bowl of white flowers by my bed. 'Just watch those', she said before she, too, disappeared. So I lay and watched as the flowers changed – for they were *Hibiscus mutabilis*, blushing hibiscus – from white to shell pink, thence to a deeper pink, and finally, as night fell, to red. I meanwhile, transfused with fresh blood as they with pigment, came off the danger list. Next morning the bowl had gone, leaving my mind, now re-activated, busy with two questions. What was this empathy that during those fragile hours had caused me to feel I was being brought back to life by the flowers? And what made the blushing hibiscus blush?

The second of these questions, which implies both a 'how?' and a 'why?', was to prove the less difficult to answer. Although at the time molecular biologists had only just begun to explore the inner processes involved in this kind of colour change, it had been known for over a century that the hibiscus's blushing was triggered by a rise in temperature. Moreover I soon realised, since the year was 1960 and neo-Darwinism in its heyday, that the change was part of the plant's strategy for survival. The flowers which at daybreak still had the pallor that had attracted nocturnal moths and so enabled them to become pollinated had, by evening, become so inconspicuous as to merge into the darkness: the plant's struggle to reproduce could now be taken up by those expanding flowers that were still unfertilised.

But there was a contradiction here. The colour change that had seemed to power my renewed hold on life turned out to be a sign of senescence; it heralded the death of the flower. This prompted more questions. Who was I to impose my feelings so imperiously on another organism? Was not my empathy just an instance, bred of rather dramatic circumstances, of the pathetic fallacy? On the other hand: was my curiosity about the evolutionary advantage to a flower of changing colour in its short life anything more than the intrusion of what Wordsworth called the meddling intellect into the recall of an experience that, at the time, had had about it an aura of the transcendent?

In short, my emotional response to this episode, and the intellectual curiosity it aroused, appeared to belong to what Kipling's character Kim called 'separate sides of my head'. So I should perhaps have been content, with Kim, to praise Allah for the gift of this duality. But we now know that what was a metaphor to Kipling has a basis in neurological fact, and that good, even great, things can be achieved when the separate sides of the head work together. Poetry is one of these things. A literary critic by trade, I flattered myself that the interplay of mental forces induced by my hibiscus was close to the nexus of thought and feeling poet–critics such as Coleridge and Eliot believed to be the fundamental poetic experience. But I was no poet; so there the matter had to rest.

What reactivated it, nearly three decades later, was a reading of Keith Thomas's *Man and the Natural World*. This richly documented study of the changes that, in the early modern period, overtook the ways in which human beings thought about other species fired me with the ambition to trace the effect of such changes upon literature and on poetry in particular: a project, I soon realised, to which further limits would have to be set. Writers' explorations of one of Nature's two major kingdoms would give me more than enough scope, and for two reasons I chose what poets had once called the realm of Flora. One was the realisation that the distance between the plant and the animal world gives definition and a measure of detachment to our experience of the former. However complex our perception of a plant may be, it is clear-cut in contrast with our perception of an animal, apt as that is to be mixed up with the hope (or fear) of a response and with a readiness to anthropomorphise such response if it is made. Plants do not wag their tails – even if scientists in earlier times, and pseudo-scientists in our own, have sometimes entertained the notion that they are sentient beings. But though they pay us no attention, they deserve all of ours – and this was the second reason for my choice – because we owe to them our very existence. The Book of Genesis gets the order right: some group of organisms had to evolve a way of making the atmosphere oxygen-rich, as plants can do, before animal life could radiate into its uncounted forms. And whereas it is possible to conceive of a world without animals – though there would be no place in it for Flora, since its flowers would be unremarkable – there could be no life for us and our sister-species in a world without plants.

Because these reflections brought back the questions raised long before by *Hibiscus mutabilis* I decided, though with many regrets at having to pass over such lifelong favourites as Coleridge, Hardy and Hopkins, to focus upon writers who also had some claim to be called botanists. Erasmus Darwin, typical savant of the Enlightenment, became the versifier of Linnaeus almost by accident, but he was also the author of a substantial work on plant physiology. George Crabbe, an enthusiast for the flowers of shore and salt marsh, devised his own classification of the plant kingdom – a venture not wholly lost, as I hope to show, when he put the manuscript on his garden bonfire. John Clare, whose knowledge of wild flowers earned him a place of his own in George Druce's *Flora of Northamptonshire* (1930), at one time himself aspired to write a local flora, despite his mistrust of Linnaeus's 'dark system'. John Ruskin, after years of testing painters' fidelity to nature against his own observations of trees and their foliage, wrote and illustrated a book about alpine and Arctic plants. D. H. Lawrence, whose exactitude in observing flowers shows itself as clearly in his last poems as in the first one he wrote, studied botany at university level. Chapters on these five poets (using the word in the wide sense that allows Ruskin to be included) form the core of the book, and are unabashedly biographical: for each I have constructed a *biographia botanica* in the belief that this, in as much as it is built from some of the subject's best and happiest moments, is an aspect of his personal history that surely deserves to go on record. And with specialist students of one or other of these poets in mind, I have also, at the risk of some repetition, tried to make each chapter a self-contained whole.

My first and last chapters attempt to give a framework to these five studies, partly by exploring the relationship between biological thought and the poetic process, partly by carrying the story of our perception of the green kingdom beyond the centuries covered by Thomas's book, and initially into a period when, as he writes, 'to understand that the natural world was autonomous, only to be understood in non-human terms, was still an almost impossible lesson to grasp'. Though the replacement of herbals – traditionally written for physicians – by detached and objective floras culminated in Linnaeus's *Species plantarum* of 1753, the 'natural' order that the Swedish naturalist believed to exist, and which such immediate successors as the Jussieus were soon to attempt to reveal, was almost universally understood to have been the part of the divine plan that had been put into effect on the third day of Creation and dedicated to human use on the sixth. In the next century, this confident certainty that all creatures great and small had been placed on earth for the benefit of mankind was sustained by Paley's argument from design, by the subjectivism of much Romantic poetry, and by the revivalist movements of both High and Low Church. Even in the 1920s, a child who asked why grass was green could be told, in all seriousness, that green was the most restful colour for human eyes.

That was some seventy years after *The Origin of Species* (1859), the work in which Charles Darwin was generally held to have effected the dethronement of man as lord of creation. With the famous Oxford debate in mind, we tend to think of that dethronement in terms of *Homo sapiens*' relegation to the animal kingdom. But even *The Descent of Man* (1871), in which Darwin squarely faced the human implications of his theory of descent by natural selection, was less incipiently subversive than the botanical studies by which he had already substantiated that theory. In the former, man was in the centre of the picture, so that unconvinced readers could always address an appeal to his unique powers of mind and perhaps of spirit too. But in the latter, man had been airbrushed out by the revelation that the 'beauty' he imputed to a plant, and most notably to the colour, form and scent of its flowers, was for the plant itself no more – or rather no less – than the means whereby its species might survive. It could be argued that, of all Darwin's writings, his six books of botany were the most effective prelude to a century in which evolutionary biology dominated the life sciences, in succession to the 100 years of collection and classification initiated by Linnaeus.

Plant studies in laboratory and field at first flourished in this changed context. But by the middle of the twentieth century, traditional, whole-plant botany was losing its prestige and appeal. Advances in molecular biology, which it has now become customary to symbolise by the discovery, just 200 years after *Species plantarum* had been published, of DNA's helical structure, were indeed epoch-making. But they also spelt the end of an epoch in which botany had steadily held its own, first in a systematical and later in an evolutionary context, as a science to which the man in the country lane could contribute; whereas molecular biology's exploration of organic processes, with its basis in atomic physics, was and in large part has remained a closed book to the non-scientist. Groups of field botanists may still be observed of an evening in corners of Swiss hotels, recording the names – many of them first bestowed by Linnaeus – of their day's finds; but every year they appear older and fewer. Where are their successors?

Up the mountainside, camping out to guard some clump of an endangered species, is one possible answer. Many more are poised over quadrats, sampling the diversity of plant communities. Many more again are at their computers, putting on national records the year's first unfolding of, say, oak or ash buds. Others are in the garden, planting whatever will allure bees and butterflies. For as I suggest in my closing chapter, the decline of both professional and amateur support for botany has been fully compensated for by the rise in prestige of ecology at all levels.

Here a clarification is called for. When 'ecology' is used in the following pages, it stands for the branch of biology concerned with the relationship of organisms to one another and with their physical setting. It does not mean what is sometimes distinguished as 'ethical' rather than 'scientific' ecology, namely, a concern over, or attempt to counter, man's damage to the natural world. This latter is, properly speaking, environmentalism: also a powerful force in modern poetry, as my final chapter illustrates. Of course the relationship between the two activities is close. Concern over vanishing species fuels much ecological research, and the findings of professional ecologists can lend power to the conservationist's elbow. But at the risk of seeming to cry over lexical spilt milk, I have tried on two counts to keep ecology and environmentalism distinct. One is regard for a discipline that in the last century had a hard fight for recognition from practitioners of the 'exact' sciences, because the dynamic changes to which the interrelationships of organisms are subject make quantification difficult. 'Ecology's not real science', I was once told, by the then editor of *Nature*. Ecologists were not helped in this struggle when the word was employed for an ethical or political stance that was rooted in New Age ideas about the 'unnaturalness' of scientific procedures – with the odd result that the name of one branch of biology was invoked to attack the life sciences in general.

My other reservation about the use of 'ecology', for a moral or political stance is prompted by the prominence now given to the term in literary studies. One of the first to make use of it in this context was Jonathan Bate in a book on Wordsworth called *Romantic Ecology* (1991), though this in fact turned out to be less about the poet's environmentalism than about the power of his poetry to restore us to the home in nature that we have lost: an idea that Bate has more recently, in *The Song of the Earth* (2000), developed very subtly and persuasively into an entire 'ecopoetics' – an etymologically sound term. But he has not entirely abandoned the less justifiable 'ecocriticism', and this is to be regretted, in view of the fact that there has been produced in the meantime a whole body of writing that goes by this name and that I find alarmingly prescriptive. An ecocritic, runs a definition by one of the abler claimants to the title, is 'a person who judges the merits and faults of writings that depict the effects of culture upon nature, with a view towards celebrating nature, berating its despoilers, and reversing their harm through political action'. Although, as a committed Green, I hope I can berate Nature's despoilers with the best, I am appalled at the idea of political correctness being made the standard of literary judgement, because this can only result in an overvaluing of writing that has little merit beyond worthy sentiments, in this case about the harm man is doing to his home planet. A fair number of modern anthologies are made up of poems chosen on these grounds, and I suspect that by the turn of the next century some of them will have the faint charm of Victorian flower books which, in their day, reassured their readers that they had the right attitudes towards the natural world – even though those attitudes were very differently conceived.

This is not to deny that there are Green anthologies that reveal unexpected treasures. And I feel nothing but admiration for the way that leading poets such as Ted Hughes have been ready to write on request for environmental causes, despite realising that in the process their poetry itself was bound to suffer – or have even abandoned poetry altogether in favour of campaigning on environmental issues, as Judith Wright chose to do in later life. Nor have I engaged in this book with ecocriticism as a critical method, because criticism of criticism strikes me as a narcissistic and barren pursuit. Literary studies inhabit an environment that, unlike real ecosystems, has an infinite number of niches, from none of which there is competitive exclusion. I have only sought to add a little to its diversity, and diversity, all ecologists agree, is a very desirable thing.

CHAPTER I

Primroses at Dove Cottage and Down House

Primroses grow in some surprising places, thanks to the mice and ants that pick up and then drop their seeds. Soon after Wordsworth and his sister settled in Grasmere, they noticed one on top of a boulder where it (or its progeny) was to remain safely out of human reach for the next thirty years. And as in life, so in literature. In the third part of *Modern Painters* (1856) a primrose makes a sudden appearance that is inexplicable till we realise where it has come from. The passage affords a good starting point for this study because in it Ruskin is trying to distinguish between the ways in which poets see plants.

So then, we have the three ranks: the man who perceives rightly, because he does not feel, and to whom the primrose is very accurately the primrose, because he does not love it. Then, secondly, the man who perceives wrongly, because he feels, and to whom the primrose is anything else than a primrose: a star, or a sun, or a fairy's shield, or a forsaken maiden. And then, lastly, there is the man who perceives rightly in spite of his feelings, and to whom the primrose is for ever nothing else than itself – a little flower, apprehended in the very plain and leafy fact of it, whatever and how many soever the associations and passions may be that crowd around it. And, in general, these three classes may be rated in comparative order, as the men who are not poets at all, and the poets of the second order, and the poets of the first. (*Modern Painters III*, 'Of Many Things', chapter 12, § 8[1])

The primrose so casually introduced here is of course another Wordsworthian one. Less than forty years after the publication of 'Peter Bell: A Tale', Ruskin could count on his readers recognising a flower made famous by its insignificance: the primrose by a river's brim that, to Peter Bell, was a yellow primrose 'and it was nothing more'.

The allusion works well, but in other ways Ruskin's argument, which forms part of his discussion of the pathetic fallacy, strikes the modern reader as itself weakened by fallacies about the nature of perception. First

---

[1] For an explanation of references to Ruskin's writings see p. 149.

Primula acaulis.

1 Primrose, *Primula vulgaris*, drawn and engraved by William Kilburn for William Curtis's *Flora Londinensis* (1777–8). In showing the two forms of flower and the bending back of the stalk once the flower fades it closely follows Curtis's text, which goes on to question Linnaeus's belief that primroses and cowslips are a single species, and to discuss the portrayal of both in English poetry. (Reproduced from the copy in the Victoria and Albert Museum.)

and foremost among them is the assumption that the primrose can ever be apprehended 'in the very plain and leafy fact of it', unaffected by the associations it carries and the emotions it arouses: that it is possible to see an object, as Ruskin's contemporary Matthew Arnold believed it could be seen, 'as in itself it really is', so that, in the words of the early computer slogan, 'what you see is what you get'; whereas our modern alertness to cultural conditioning makes us realise that much of what we see is what we have already got. We see, that is, what we are prepared to see, and the preparation includes not only all our past experience of the object in view but also our experience of its representations by others whether in visual form or in writing.

Admittedly, the term 'primrose' has for centuries carried for poets certain early associations that go some way towards the common ground suggested by 'the very plain and leafy fact of it'. A sudden glimpse of wayside colour; eye-to-eye contact with a pale corolla's darker centre; fingers sliding down to pinch and pluck at the base of a thin, hairy stem, while a faint yet distinctive scent hits the nostrils; then a groping towards the base of stout leaves, in search of cool wrappings for a fistful of flowers already becoming limp: primroses would have carried these connective memories even for Peter Bell, before he lapsed into the state from which the events related in Wordsworth's ballad finally redeemed him. But such basic 'folk' or childhood associations – which in any case have lost much of their evocative power for recent readers, who can no longer be assumed to share them – are inevitably overlaid by others derived from adult occupations and preoccupations, whether these are the poet's own or those of his contemporaries. The Renaissance herbalist saw a different primrose from the one seen by the maker of an emblem book or the bearer of a lover's posy. So with visual artists: the maker of religious icons does not see the same flower as the botanic illustrator or the Impressionist painter. And the plant seen by the Victorian systematic botanist ('Primroses by the river's brim / Dicotyledons were to him')[2] would appear quite otherwise to the floral biologist of the 1890s or the geneticist of more recent times.

It so happens that the greatest poet and the greatest scientist of the nineteenth century both paid much heed to primroses. Wordsworth in 1808 wrote a long poem called *The Tuft of Primroses* which, although it was unfinished (and until 1946, unpublished), was almost certainly intended to form part of his projected major work, *The Recluse*. Darwin in 1861 read to the Linnean Society a paper 'On the two forms, or dimorphic condition, in the species of *Primula*, and on their remarkable sexual relations', which would become the core of *The Different Forms of Flowers on Plants of the Same Species* (1877), in its turn one of a series of botanical works in which the author of *The Origin of Species* demonstrated the mechanism of natural

[2] May Kendall, 'Education's Martyr', in A. Leighton and M. Reynolds (eds.), *Victorian Women Poets: An Anthology* (1995), p. 635.

selection. In this chapter I want to put Wordsworth's and Darwin's observations of the primrose, together with the written outcomes of those observations, side by side in a way that will, I hope, afford a basis for the ensuing studies of writers who combined a passion for botany with their creativity. And because the primroses in the gardens of Dove Cottage and Down House were mediated to their owners through the familiarity of many generations with this 'favourite of favourites'[3] I preface my comparison with an attempt to sketch out a cultural history of the same flower. Or rather, since botanists well into the nineteenth century followed Linnaeus in believing various primulas to be a single species, a brief history of the genus *Primula*'s yellow-flowered English members – cowslips, common primroses, the oxlip of the poets which is a primrose–cowslip cross, and the very local true oxlip; and by the side of these the alpine *Primula auricula* and its descendants, called French cowslips when they arrived among the treasured possessions of French and Flemish weavers seeking asylum in Elizabethan England.

I

We have the Renaissance botanist Pierandrea Mattioli[4] chiefly to thank for the fact that botanists know cowslips and primroses by the generic name *Primula*, rather than by the medieval herbalists' names *Arthritica* and *Paralysis*, with their almost wholly misleading indications of curative powers. A diminutive, the word suggests the affection in which the flower has always been held, so that the medieval French form of the name, *primeveroles* or 'firstlings of spring', has much the effect of Dorothy Wordsworth's 'the dear dear primroses'. This simple pleasure informs the first depictions of *Primula* in Northern European art. Primrose leaves, with their goffered edge and quilted surface – 'crimp and curdled' to John Clare, 'pulled and plotted' to Gerard Manley Hopkins – have a personality which was enough, once stiff-leaf decoration had become an accepted part of Gothic carving, to make any stone mason reach for his chisel. One such mason made them part of a capital in a French cathedral as early as the

---

[3] Geoffrey Grigson, *The Englishman's Flora* (1975), p. 287. The regard in which the primrose was held led sixteenth-century botanists to identify it, wrongly, with Pliny's 'flower of the twelve gods', *Dodecatheon*: the name since given to another genus of the family *Primulaceae*, the spectacular North American shooting-stars.

[4] P. A. Mattioli, *Commentarii in libros sex P. Dioscoridis . . . de materia medica* (1554), lists all the names in learned and common use (p. 803 of the 1598 edition).

thirteenth century.[5] The flowers followed before long, blossoming in the margins of Books of Hours and springing up with other *mille fleurs* between the hooves of tapestried unicorns, or at the feet of the Virgin in her *hortus conclusus*. And then occurs, in Germany, the supreme portrayal of *Primula* in art. A tuft of cowslips drawn in gouache on vellum,[6] it bears Dürer's monogram along with the date 1526, and although its authenticity has been questioned it shows all the empathy with living plants that Dürer extends to his grasses and dandelions in *The Large Piece of Turf*. Like them, this cowslip is still growing, the clod in which its roots are intertwined with those of grasses and clovers having been lifted from the meadow (where a small predator has been at its leaves) and placed a little below eye level. The resultant effect is less of light falling on the leaves than of each leaf reaching towards the light, making almost palpable its power to capture the energy that has gone into its flowering. This is more than a drawing of a plant. It is a Renaissance portrait, and like the best of such portraits it is full of insight into the sitter's personality. This is what it must have been like to be *Primula veris* in sunshine in 1526.

In his grasp of a plant's vitality, Dürer was a man of his time. The same spirit infuses Leonardo da Vinci's plant drawings and the best of the illustrations to sixteenth-century herbals. A plant's 'habit', its distinctive form of growth, was important for medical men because a life might depend on a correct identification. This feeling for plant character increased when botany became a branch of learning in its own right, largely as the result of Europe being flooded with new species from the Discoveries. Botanic gardens were established and *lectores simplicium* appointed to demonstrate their wonders. There being as yet no hothouses, these savants had in winter to rely on dried specimens, whose preservation in herbaria was soon brought to a fine art, or on teaching aids such as the hundreds of exquisitely accurate watercolour drawings that Clutius[7] produced or commissioned at Leyden. England was behindhand in these developments: the appointment of Botanists Royal and the establishment of the Oxford Botanic Garden belong to Stuart times. The Tudors had their printed herbals, but for the most part these were illustrated by debased versions of Continental woodcuts. Nothing as inspirational as Dürer's *Tuft of Cowslips* contributed to the Elizabethan awareness of the genus *Primula*.

[5] Joan Evans, *Pattern: a Study of Ornament in Western Europe from 1180 to 1900* (1931), vol. I, p. 42.
[6] In the Armand Hammer Collection, National Gallery of Art, Washington, DC.
[7] Dirck Kluyt, not to be confused with the garden's director, Carolus Clusius (Charles de l'Écluse), who was more famous but declined to lecture. See Claudia Swan, *The Clutius Watercolors: Plants and Flowers of the Renaissance* (1998), p. 10.

But if England had no flower painters, it had plenty of artists of another kind – the gardeners. The first known book of gardening advice in English, written early in the fifteenth century, advocates the planting of primroses and cowslips.[8] Alas, garden snobbery also began early; in the early seventeenth century John Parkinson's attitude to the custom of transplanting such everyday wild flowers is one of 'all right, if you must'.[9] For what *Primula* enthusiasts had by then hunted out and propagated were mutations of all kinds, such as the Frantic or Foolish Cowslip, otherwise Jackanapes on Horseback, a mop head of partial and complete flowers mixed with streaked leaves in mad genetic disorder. A clue to the appeal of such oddities lies perhaps in the way several of their names are suggestive of clothing (Pepys was to own a jackanapes coat). The Elizabethans liked to disguise their bodies in bombast and whalebone in a way that showed the same taste for exaggeration verging on the grotesque as did the typographic decorations of their books and the architectural details of their buildings. In keeping with this spirit of the age, the knot garden of the time, clipped into an intricate geometry, became a cabinet of floral curiosities.

'Natural' primroses and cowslips were to be found, but chiefly in the kitchen garden where, besides providing salad leaves, they were raised as 'strewing herbs',[10] to add fragrance to the rushes that were the usual floor covering at the time. On an important occasion such as a masque at Court, special care would be taken to scatter sweet-smelling flowers, and Ben Jonson incorporates this action into *Pan's Anniversary* (1623), which begins with an entry of nymphs strewing primroses and cowslips. They are then sent off for other flowers with which to decorate the setting, and this gives the poet the opportunity for an exuberant descriptive passage in which flowers of spring and summer, of garden and field, commingle as they do in early Netherlandish flower-pieces painted about the same time. Did Jonson know enough about plants to compile his catalogue from experience, or did he browse some herbal with the same linguistic appetite that he brought to works of alchemy? It has been suggested that the first flower passage in English pastoral poetry, in the April eclogue of Spenser's *The Shepherds' Calendar* (1579), was composed with the help of Henry Lyte's

---

[8] See Miles Hadfield, *A History of British Gardening* (1979), p. 31.

[9] *Paradisi in sole paradisus terrestris* (1629), pp. 242 (primroses), 244 (cowslips). Parkinson names many of the anomalous varieties.

[10] Thomas Tusser, *Five Hundred Points of Good Husbandry: with an Introduction by Geoffrey Grigson* (1984), p. 90.

New Herbal, published the previous year.[11] It is certainly hard to believe Michael Drayton had no recourse to herbals for the long lists of plants with which he embellished both his pastorals and the vast historical and topographical survey of Britain that he called *Poly-olbion* (1612 and 1622).

Whatever the immediate source of such lists, they were classical-humanist in inspiration. The ceremonial use of flowers, because of its association with the worship of Greek and Roman gods, had been proscribed in Christendom for over a millennium. In consequence, whenever the Renaissance re-discoverers of Theocritus and of the Greek Anthology came across a passage about a flowery or leafy garlanding, they felt themselves to be at the heart of classical culture. Here was something worthy of being imitated and even, with the help of the favourite rhetorical device of 'copiousness', surpassed, so that the flower passages of the ancients, which in themselves are not – to use ecological jargon – very species-rich, are transformed into lavish floral displays. In the symbolic marriage of Thames and Isis in *Poly-olbion,* the groom's coronal is composed of every conceivable garden flower and the bride's of many different wild ones – among which Oxfordshire primroses have pride of place.[12]

For all their charm, these flower-passages provide a limited pleasure to the reader hoping to find the poetic equivalent of the flowers portrayed by Renaissance artists. We are hurried from plant to plant by the writers' enthusiasm for sheer profusion, for *copia,* and a similar enthusiasm for all things curiously wrought means that the flowers are for the most part transformed into garlands and headdresses. So a shepherd offers his love a 'tire' in which a pattern of differently coloured roses is assembled in a wire mesh and set round – since in Elysium everything blooms at the same time – with 'a fret of primroses'.[13] And the primroses that seem to Giles Fletcher to 'blaze' from their leafy beds and 'woo' him to pick them expect to be drenched in perfume and tied with velvet ribbon before they can become an Easter offering (*Christ's Triumph after Death,* line 53). Two further features of Renaissance poetry add to this overall impression of artifice. One is the poets' love of what the rhetoricians called figures of words, which results in the verbal equivalent of the knot garden; the other the emblemising cast of mind that burdens all objects in the physical world with a moral message. Even a fine sonnet by the recusant poet Edmund Bolton ('Palinode' in *England's Helicon,* 1600), which

[11] Agnes Arber, *Herbals, their Origin and Evolution: a Chapter in the History of Botany* (1938), pp. 126–7.
[12] Drayton, *Poly-olbion,* song XV, line 149.
[13] Drayton, *The Muses' Elysium* (1630), nymphal II, lines 218–19. Compare nymphal V, line 129, 'a course of cowslips', and the April eclogue of *The Shepherds' Calendar,* lines 59–63.

opens promisingly with a primrose by a river's brim, ends with the flower rhetorically reduced to a single motif in an elaborate pattern and conceptually reduced to a symbol of transience.

Primroses were free at least from the fixed religious connotations that many flowers carried in Mediterranean art, and English poets gave them a wide range of symbolic meanings. They are forsaken maidens in the two most famous flower passages in English poetry: 'pale primroses / that die unmarried' in *A Winter's Tale*, 'the rathe primrose that forsaken dies' in 'Lycidas'. Unfulfilled hopes, hence virginity, hence innocence; when the wicked queen in *Cymbeline* seeks a cover for her villainy she pretends she has been out with her maidens gathering cowslips and primroses. Yet despite such associations, in other contexts a hint of the voluptuous hangs about primroses. Shakespeare's Venus seduces Adonis on a primrose bank, and one translator of Ovid's Epistles[14] substitutes a primrose for the plucked rose that symbolised the deflowering of a virgin. Most startling of all are Shakespeare's images of the primrose way of dalliance (*Hamlet*, 1.3.50) and the primrose path to damnation (*Macbeth*, 2.2.19). Broad the way to destruction, says St Mark's Gospel; and Lavatch in *All's Well that Ends Well* turns this into 'the flowery way that leads to the everlasting bonfire' (4.5.54–5). The flowers, it would seem, have come in from representations of Hercules at the crossroads between Vice and Virtue, theme of a number of Renaissance paintings.[15] An English poet encountering the legend might well picture the path of Vice as a 'way / Primrosed, and hung with shade': Henry Vaughan's image in 'Regeneration' for the unregenerate life. And primroses attracted other polarised meanings. Since primrose time was also Easter time, the flower that was for Bolton a symbol of the life that fades could equally well stand, as its buds thrust through dead leaves, for life reborn. 'O primroses! Let this day be / A Resurrection unto thee' is Herrick's command to the flowers 'Upon Julia's Recovery'.

The primroses in Herrick's Devonshire bucolics, each dew-filled on its frail stalk ('yet it doth not break'), hint at an awareness of the living plant such as is displayed in only two other poets of the period: as we might expect, they are Shakespeare and Donne. Perdita's primroses may be conventionally pale and pining (though the dramatic context renders them far from conventional), but Shakespeare has looked deep into

---

[14] George Turbervile, *The Heroical Epistles of ... Ovidius Naso, in English Verse* (1567), Epistle 4, line 63.
[15] Erwin Panofsky, 'Hercules am Scheideweg', *Studien der Bibliothek Warburg* 18 (1930), surveys the theme in art. It is noteworthy that the very flowery version of the legend on a ceiling of the Palazzo di Firenze in Rome is based on a work by Giulio Romano, the only Italian artist ever named by Shakespeare.

cowslips and knows that the darker patches mark the way to their nectaries –
'in those freckles live their savours' (*Midsummer Night's Dream*, 2.1.13).
Although this may not attain the 'degree of accuracy almost botanical'[16]
that it represented for William Curtis writing in a bardolatrous age, it does
suggest alertness to plant character and the ability to capture it in a word or
two. So also with false oxlips, often bigger than cowslips on account of their
hybrid vigour ('As cowslip unto oxlip is, so seems she to the boy',
Tennyson would write of the brother and sister in 'The Talking Oak').
'Bold oxlips' in *The Winter's Tale* (4.4.125) reflects both this vigour and
another distinctive feature: the way the corollas flare back, primrose fashion, to look the beholder in the eye, whereas the flowers of their cowslip
parent, as Milton noted, hang the pensive head. Oxlips also inherit from
their primrose parent a calyx that, unlike the baggy cowslip calyx, tightly
hugs the yellow corolla, with the result that when the five petal lobes open
'they never', as Ruskin with fellow-feeling said of primroses, 'leave their old
nursery'.[17] They are, in truth, the 'oxlips in their cradles growing' scattered
before the bride at the opening of *Two Noble Kinsmen* (1.1.10).

Yet for all this sharpness of definition, Shakespeare's oxlips remain a part
of the listings that go towards a pastoral *mise-en-scène*. Only Donne,
around the time Shakespeare wrote his last plays, was able to break free
from these conventions in 'The Primrose', which begins with the real-life
experience of coming upon primroses massed below the walls of
Montgomery Castle. The poet finds counterparts for his feelings in the
Israelites' joy at discovering manna in the desert, and Galileo's excitement
when his telescope resolved the Milky Way into a host of distinct stars.
These rouse expectations that the flower will present itself vividly to this
well-stocked and enquiring mind. And momentarily, as the poem pro-
gresses, Donne seems to ask himself a question that also exercised
Sir Thomas Browne: why this five-fold radial symmetry? – a question
nineteenth-century biologists would ask of primroses and starfish and
other organisms. Donne, however, is counting petals chiefly in the hope
of finding a flower with four or six, which will indicate that his lover is true
to him. The primrose has been turned into that dire abstraction, Woman;
and the poem collapses in a muddle of misogyny and numerology. All the
same, those opening lines afford a glimpse of an encounter, of the kind
recorded in Leonardo's sketchbooks, between the creative intellect and a
form of life that is at once alien and akin to our own.

---

[16] William Curtis, *Flora Londinensis* (1777–87); pages are not numbered.
[17] *Proserpina*, vol. I, chapter 4, § 20.

Flowery rites of spring such as those Herrick celebrated were banned during the Interregnum. But in 1660 Flora returned in the train of Charles II, gathered together all the tribes of flowers, including one that comprised the different kinds of primula, and commanded them to choose their candidates for the office of her vicereine. Or so we are told by the Restoration's most renowned poet, Abraham Cowley, in the third book, written around 1663, of his *Six Books of Plants*: a work which would deserve more attention here had it not been written in Latin, and had the translations of it made piecemeal in the Restoration period not been so wayward. ('Ragwort' for *orchis*: was someone joking?) An informed translation of *Sex libri plantarum*, not omitting its notes, is a crying need, because the poem is of great interest for the way that the stages of its composition parallel the changes that occurred during the second part of the seventeenth century in people's perception of plants. The progress of its separate parts, following the poet's successive interests, from herb-garden to botanic garden to flower garden to orchard to native woodland, parallels the cultural shift of the time from an age of herbal medicine to an age of horticulture, that in its turn provided the groundwork for an age of true botanic enquiry.

In Cowley's third book, the choice of candidate by the Primula tribe falls on a beautiful *Primula auricula*. The name comes from the shape of its petals, and according to the doctrine of signatures current at the time these indicated its medical use. Hunters in its native Alps, it was said, used it as a prophylactic against dizziness (the English name 'bears' ears' appears to refer to the prey rather than the hunter), and this led to its being considered a cure-all for brain disorders. So Cowley sees its densely flowered umbel as a lighthouse, symbolic of its ability to keep the light of the mind, that *conspicuam sed fragilem Pharon*, from extinction. But it was above all its beauty that brought the auricula to the fore, in life as in Cowley's poem: beauty that, despite competition from another floristic triumph, the poly-anthus, ensured the auricula its pride of place in gardening books of the time. The alpine kind, its strong yellow centre contrasting with a deep-coloured or striped outer corolla, makes eye contact with us in many Dutch paintings. During Cowley's lifetime, in the still-life genre called *Vanitas*, it stood for earth's fading pleasures; an admonitory note abandoned in the flower pieces of the next century, where it represents the *beau idéal* by which horticulturalist and painter together transcended nature.[18]

---

[18] Compare, for example, the still life by Hendrik Andriessen (Ashmolean Museum), which places the cut heads of auriculas alongside a skull, a goblet, a globe and a mask, and Jan van Huysum's 1726 flower piece in the Wallace Collection, with its four varieties of auricula, including the prized Black Imperial.

Meanwhile, English fanciers had developed their own speciality, the 'show' auriculas, many of them green-petalled and further distinguished by the silver-white meal, or farina – the siliceous product of countless tiny glands – spread over stem, leaf and flower. These too had their portraitist: the émigré artist Georg Ehret. To set one of Ehret's auriculas side by side with Dürer's cowslips is to get the full measure of the neo-classical age's intervention in plant life: the one so earthy in the meadow soil that surrounds it, so evidently involved in the struggle for life; the other in potted isolation and rendered unearthly by the farina that gives a ghostly appearance to flowers on which rain was never allowed to fall.

Outshone by these exotica, the peeps (as growers still call individual flowers) of native primroses and cowslips scarcely got a look-in during the first three-quarters of the eighteenth century. So when Christopher Smart writes

> The grass the polyanthus checks
> And polished porphryry reflects
> By the descending rill,

readers picture a scene in keeping with the Song-of-Songs opulence of the rest of *A Song to David*: magnificent dusky-red blooms, perhaps, beside a marble fountain. It took a poet–botanist of the twentieth century, Geoffrey Grigson, to grasp that the lines are in fact Smart's touching recall, in Bedlam, of a common sight from his County Durham childhood: the bird's eye primrose, *Primula farinosa*, growing profusely among limestone boulders.[19] That the native and natural should thus linguistically disguise itself as the exotic and cultivated was a sign of the times. Admittedly, wild primroses crop up in eighteenth-century pastorals, and James Thomson's *Seasons* affords them a passing reference, but what makes his springtime borders splendid are 'polyanthus of unnumbered dyes' and 'auriculas, enriched / With shining meal o'er all their velvet leaves'.[20]

Historians of the Enlightenment often present it as a time when artists and natural philosophers were confident of man's power to master nature. Certainly there is a strongly triumphal note in Cowley's celebration, in 'The Garden', of cultivated flowers – 'God has so ordered that no other part / Such space and such dominion leaves for Art' (lines 184–5) – and of the fruit-grower's skill in grafting: 'Who would not joy to see his conquering hand / O'er all the vegetable world command?' (196–7). But there had been an alternative tradition in the Enlightenment, ever since Bacon

---

[19] *The Englishman's Flora*, p. 285.   [20] 'Spring', lines 529 and 533–4.

provided space in his ideal garden for a wilderness alive with cowslips and primroses. Cowley's ode is sometimes read as a riposte to Marvell's 'The Mower against Gardens', which lamented that men had allured flowers from the fields 'Where Nature was most plain and pure'. Marvell's poem was not in print in Cowley's lifetime, and the two works may well be separate witty variations upon different classical themes. None the less, the contrast between them strikingly parallels the contrast between the determination to master plant life through agriculture, floristry and forestry, which was one objective of the Royal Society, and the humble willingness to let Nature be their teacher that was shown by the best natural philosophers of the time. And this last approach was beginning to take them deep into her secrets.

Already in the Interregnum, at the time Marvell was creating his unique version of pastoral, the new spirit was showing itself in the researches of a young Fellow of Trinity College, Cambridge. Ordered by his doctor to leave his books for the open air, John Ray found himself inspired by the beauty of wild flowers and the 'cunning craftsmanship' of Nature that they revealed. The result of his walks and rides through the length and breadth of Cambridgeshire was the first county flora, *Catalogus plantarum circa Cantabrigiam nascentium* (1660), dedicated to 'the true philosophers whose concern is not so much to know what authors think as to gaze with their own eyes on the nature of things and to listen with their own ears to her voice'.[21] True to these principles, Ray examined each species where it grew before turning to the existing herbals and floras for help in formulating descriptive names. So when he finds *Primula veris elatior pallido flore* inside Kingston and Madingley woods, where sun-loving cowslips would not venture, we can be confident that these are not the poets' hybrid, but our first record of the true oxlip that is native to East Anglia.

Ray devoted the rest of his life to natural history, and primarily to botany. Years of plant hunting throughout the British Isles and across Europe honed his ability to perceive the natural affinities between groups of plants and from these observations to work out the system of classification on which he based his major work, the *Historia plantarum* (1686): a triumph of the inductive method and in many ways the foundation stone of our modern taxonomy.[22] In addition, its sixty or so introductory pages

[21] A. T. Ewen and C. T. Prime (eds. and translators), *Ray's Flora of Cambridgeshire* (1975), pp. 22 and 27.
[22] Classifications had been attempted by Cesalpino and Lobelius, and Ray's contemporary Tournefort worked out a system that was in general use in the first half of the eighteenth century, but modern systematists consider Ray's to be the soundest of its time.

have some claim to be called the first textbook of plant physiology. As such, they follow naturally from discoveries about the anatomy of plants made in the previous decade by Marcello Malpighi and Nehemiah Grew with the help of the recently invented microscope.

Grew's beautiful drawings of plant tissues in his *Anatomy of Plants* are, from our present point of view, of less interest than the overall conclusion he comes to about their significance. What end, he asks, is served by these interior 'elegancies'? Not to give pleasure to the human eye, since they are hidden from all but the very few:

> Wherefore, we must suppose some other ends of the same varieties, which should have their effect, and so these not be in vain whether men behold them or not. Which are, therefore, such as have respect to vegetation: that the corn might grow, *so*; and the flower, *so*: whether or no men had a mind, leisure, or ability to understand *how*.[23]

The same functional approach is felt everywhere in the 'Idea of a philosophical history of plants' that prefaces Grew's *Anatomy*. When he suggests that 'that fine white flour or powder, which lies over the leaves of some plants, as of Bears' Ear'[24] be experimentally investigated, he is looking for an answer to the question: what use is meal, or farina, *to the auricula itself*? Similarly with a plant's stamens: Grew's name for these, the 'attire', suggests their contribution to the beauty that, with any medicinal virtues, was still, in all eyes, the *raison d'être* of a flower. But he believed that they also had a more important 'primary and private use'.[25] At the time (1671) he wrote the first book of the *Anatomy* this eluded him, but the fourth book describes how he hit on it some time later, when he and a fellow-member of the Royal Society agreed, in conversation, that 'the attire doth serve, as the male, for the generation of seed' in the form of 'globulets' that fall upon the 'seed-case or womb'.[26] In this unobtrusive way was launched the study of plant sex: in itself clear evidence that botanists were beginning to accept that a plant's structure and history represented the fulfilment of its own ends.

Half a century later, Linnaeus based his botanical classification on the view that flowers are 'nothing else but the genitals of plants'.[27] The class to which a plant belonged could be determined from the number and arrangement of its stamens, or male parts, and its order within that class

---

[23] *Anatomy of Plants* (1682), p. 7.   [24] *Ibid.*, p. 11.   [25] *Ibid.*, p. 40.

[26] *Ibid.*, pp. 71–172. The fellow-member was Sir Thomas Millington: see p. 95 below.

[27] Hugh Rose, *The Elements of Botany ... Being a Translation of the* Philosophia Botanica *and Other Treatises of the Celebrated Linnaeus* (1775), p. 221.

from the number of its carpels, or female parts. The next level down – for this is a top-down, essentialist classification – was the genus, determined according to other details of the flower or subsequent fruit. Only when it came to the species within the genus were non-floral parts of the plant brought into play. On the basis of this scheme, Linnaeus's amazing industry and powers of observation enabled him to complete, in 1753, his *Species plantarum*, which, in the words of a leading botanist of the last century, 'took and held the field as the one and only comprehensive survey of the world's flora'.[28] In the case of *Primula*, though, the survey proved less than comprehensive. Linnaeus could not have known of the 400 or so species in the genus's Asian heartland; but he recorded only a handful of European species, and one of these, *Primula veris*, represents a lumping-together of primroses, cowslips and oxlips as mere varieties. It was left to William Hudson, in his *Flora Anglica* (1762), a work that supplied Linnaean names and classifications for all the English plants described by Ray, to restore the primrose's independence, and accordingly its name in full is '*Primula vulgaris* Hudson'.

Hudson's book is an indication of how quickly Linnaeus's sexual system established itself in England, where the new taste for the picturesque meant that gardeners were letting primroses stray where auriculas had once paraded. Botanising, with a compendium of the Linnaean orders and classes in the pocket, became the new rural sport:

> Thus oft did Nature's works engage,
> As oft we searched Linnaeus' page:
> The Scanian Sage, whose wondrous toil
> Had classed the vegetable race:
> And curious, oft from place to place
> We ranged, and sought each different soil,
> Each different plant intent to view,
> And all the marks minute to trace
> Whence he his nice distinctions drew.[29]

The 'Poet of the Botanists', John Scott of Amwell, who wrote this, was in fact only one of a number of poets who began from the 1770s onwards to pack their verses with the names of wild flowers. Each was accorded its Latin binominal in a footnote, and a long comment might be added if the plant had some special interest. This practice fitted in easily with the Augustan poetic; readers expected poets to be informative, as Horace had

[28] W. T. Stearn, Introduction to the Ray Society facsimile of *Species plantarum* (1957), p. 3.
[29] 'Ode XII: to a Friend', *Poetical Works of John Scott Esq.* (1795), pp. 126–7.

advocated, and Virgil exemplified in his *Georgics*. No one met their demands better than Erasmus Darwin when, in the next decade, he constructed *The Loves of the Plants* upon Linnaeus's scheme of plant genera. What is surprising, however, is to find similar botanic exactitude and similar learned annotations in poetry of the confessional kind that was beginning to reflect the late eighteenth-century cult of sensibility. *The Loves of the Plants* was rivalled in popularity by Charlotte Smith's *Elegiac Sonnets*, and not just on account of the pathos of her sentiments; the sequence appealed by a profusion of botanic detail, carried even further in the posthumously published *Beachy Head* (1807). More expectedly, the poet who was a man or woman of feeling, especially of the tender melancholy induced by solitary wanderings, was now often encouraged by the vogue for botany to devote a poem to a single flower. The primrose gets a good share of attention. Pale and not long for this world, it is likened to the cottage maid whose fate it is to 'bloom unseen and die'. Its pallor is at best 'the wan lustre Sickness bears / When Health's first feeble beam appears'. Brief as its days will be, it is invited into the poet's garden – 'And ere thou diest, pale flower, thou'lt gain the praise / To have soothed the bard and to have inspired his lays.' And *there's* glory for you, we murmur, driven to levity by these misrepresentations of the very tough, long-flowering and long-lived *Primula vulgaris*.[30]

It was the mawkishness of verses such as these that provoked Coleridge, a few years later, into one of his most famous pronouncements:

Never to see or describe any interesting appearance in nature, without connecting it by dim analogies with the moral world, proves faintness of impression. Nature has her proper interest; and he will know what it is, who believes and feels, that everything has a life of its own, and that we are all *one life*.[31]

Coleridge, who knew as much about organic chemistry as could be known at the time, has left us one prose passage that reveals astonishing insight into a plant's 'life of its own', the activities concealed beneath its outward stillness; but the passage, apart from its functioning chiefly as an extended metaphor, is itself hidden away in an appendix to a politico-moral tract, *The Stateman's Manual* (1816). His notebooks and letters are full of delicate observations of the green world, and his eye for a tree has left its mark on

---

[30] The poems instanced are W. L. Bowles, 'The Primrose' (1795); an anonymous poem, 'To a Primrose', used as a filler by Coleridge in *The Watchman* (1795); and Charles Lloyd, 'To a Primrose' (1795). Lloyd's sonnet makes an observant start. He was around this time being taught by Coleridge.

[31] E. L. Griggs (ed.), *Collected Letters of Samuel Taylor Coleridge* (1956–9), vol. II, p. 864.

several of his poems; indeed he planned at one time to devote a whole
section of a substantial autobiographical poem to 'plants and flowers – my
passion'.[32] But once he had abandoned this and other poetic projects, the
baton passed to Wordsworth, who had already declared – when seated in a
wood full of primroses – his faith that every flower enjoyed the air it
breathed.

2

'Oh! that we had a book of botany',[33] Dorothy Wordsworth wrote in her
journal on 16 May 1800. It was her first spring in Grasmere, and during a
short absence of her brothers William and John she was busying herself by
making a flower garden around their cottage at Town End. This she did
mainly by transplanting flowers from the wild: not primroses, for they
already grew in the cottage's orchard (and everywhere else – they were, she
records, 'preeminent'[34] that spring), but many others, the names of which
she did not always know. What, for example, was 'a beautiful yellow, palish
yellow flower, that looked thick round and double, and smelt very sweet'?[35]
Three weeks later she had learnt that the local name for *Trollius europaeus*
or globe flower, a characteristic plant of North Country fells, was 'lockety
goldings' – simplified to the more common 'gowans'[36] by the time, two
years later, that she and William fetched a further supply for the garden.

   That Dorothy Wordsworth should thus substitute wild plants for florists' cultivars was a sign of the times (as well, of course, as of poverty). So
too was her wish for a 'book of botany' which at that date meant a flora on
Linnaean lines, and so too the fact that it was *her* wish, rather than her poet
brother's. The study of plants had great appeal for women, both as mothers
sharing their pleasures with their children and in their newer role as a
significant proportion of the reading public. Linnaean botany gave women
their entrée to the scientific revolution.[37] Augusta, Dowager Princess of
Wales, established Kew as a botanic garden, and Queen Charlotte on
account of her botanical interests was hailed as a Scientific Wife. Women
were proving skilful botanic illustrators and some of those who

---

[32] Kathleen Coburn (ed.), *The Notebooks of Samuel Taylor Coleridge*, vol. I (1957), note 1610.
[33] Pamela Woof (ed.), *Dorothy Wordsworth: the Grasmere and Alfoxden Journals* (2002), p. 2 (hereafter
Journals).
[34] *Ibid.*   [35] *Ibid.*, p. 1.   [36] *Ibid.*, pp. 7 and 99.
[37] On women's part in the growth of botanical thought, see especially Ann B. Shtier, *Cultivating
Women, Cultivating Science; Flora's Daughters and Botany in England 1760–1860* (1996); also Jennifer
Bennett, *Lilies of the Hearth: the Historical Relationship between Women and Plants* (1991).

accompanied their husbands to the Cape or to India became pioneer plant hunters. The authors of the 'books of botany' that appeared in England in the last thirty years of the century (they included an expanded translation by the Cambridge Professor of Botany of Rousseau's charming *Lettres sur la Botanique*) thus wrote in the awareness that many, perhaps a majority, of their readers would be women. This was certainly the case with William Withering, whose *Arrangement of British Plants according to the latest Improvements of the Linnean System and an Introduction to the Study of Botany* (third edition, 1796) Wordsworth and his sister acquired in the late summer of 1800.

Along with the four volumes came a simple microscope. Coleridge owned an identical instrument, and in light-hearted verses titled 'Stanzas written in my Pocket-Copy of Thomson's "Castle of Indolence"', Wordsworth implies that his brother poet used it to study plants; but only a reference by Dorothy to 'speedwell ... with its beautiful pearl-like chives'[38] (Withering's word for stamens) suggests that the Dove Cottage one was ever used. The flora itself, however, proved a serviceable guide. By the spring of 1802, Dorothy was confidently writing the Linnaean 'lychnis' for red campion and 'anemone nemorosa'[39] for windflower. Something she describes in her journal for 28 May as 'that pretty little waxy-looking dial-like yellow flower' is identified, two days later, on the fly-leaf of Withering's first volume, as 'Lysmachia nemorum. Yellow Pimpernell of the Woods. Pimpernell Loosestrife. May 30th, 1802.' Before that, towards the end of April, brother and sister together must have turned to Withering to find a less clinical name than 'pilewort' for the flowers whose starry profusion Dorothy had already noted three times over, for on the last day of the month she records that 'William began to write the poem of the celandine'; and 'celandine' it was for her henceforth. At a slightly later date she must have brought back for identification a flower of bogbean (from a spot where it still grows today), since Wordsworth recorded the find by writing 'Low Rocks Head of Rydal Mere May 11th' against the relevant item in Withering's second volume.[40] Three days later they were both out hunting plants for the garden when Dorothy observed 'the little star plant a star without a flower'.[41] This was butterwort. Wordsworth must have known it all his life, but his note against *Pinguicula vulgaris* in

---

[38] *Journals*, p. 98.
[39] *Ibid.*, pp. 96 and 98. Dorothy's journal for the flowering season of 1801 has not survived.
[40] Withering, *Arrangement*, vol. II, p. 236. If however the note belongs to May 1801 the find may have been Wordsworth's.
[41] *Journals*, p. 99.

Withering suggests that he and Dorothy could not put a name to it until
they were able to examine its floral details and so look it up. The plant, he
complains,

is here very ill described, a remarkable circumstance belonging to it is the manner
in which its leaves grow, lying close to the ground and diverging from the stalk so
as exactly to resemble a starfish, the tall slender stalk surmounted by the blue
flower and rising from the middle of this starfish renders the appearance of this
plant very beautiful, especially as it is always found in the most comfortless and
barren places, upon moist rocks for example.[42]

The interest of this note is that it describes the kind of wild flower that
had most significance for Wordsworth. Typically it was, or resembled, an
alpine: a plant, that is, that could make a home for itself in the bleakest
spot, its roots anchored in a crevice's minute parcel of soil, its leaves spread
low in a wind-resistant rosette, its light, bright flowers free to move on their
flexible stalks – an embodiment, all in all, of the Wordsworthian virtues of
delicacy, independence and fortitude. Wherever the poet travelled in
subsequent years, he was likely to notice plants that had the same resilience,
whether they grew on rocks beside the Clyde or at the entrance to Fingal's
Cave, on a ruin in the Apennines or in the spray of a Swiss waterfall.[43] Even
more tellingly, in words addressed directly to his sister towards the end of
The Prelude, he writes of his own soul as a rock – 'But thou didst plant its
crevices with flowers' (Book XIV, line 253, 1850 text). And Dorothy was
doing this throughout the spring of 1802, drawing her brother's attention
to beauties that by his own admission he had not heeded in all his thirty
years. His interest thus quickened, Wordsworth wrote that spring a number of short poems on flowers as well as other parts of the humbler creation.
Coleridge regretted these diversions from the great philosophical poem he
looked his friend to write, but apostrophes to daisies and lesser celandines had personal value for Wordsworth. They strengthened his bond
with Dorothy in a way that, in view of his forthcoming marriage to Mary
Hutchinson, must have helped to make possible the lasting peace of the
threefold relationship.

What the best of Wordsworth's flower poems have in common is that
they all arise from a *shared* perception of plants; shared even when the other
person was not present but his or her way of seeing was a part of the poet's

---

[42] Withering, *Arrangement*, vol. II, p. 18, in possession of the Wordsworth Trust.
[43] *Memorials of a Tour in Scotland, 1814*, no. ii; *Poems Composed or Suggested during a Tour in the
Summer of 1833*, no. xxxi; *Memorials of a Tour in Italy, 1837*, no. xxiii; *Memorials of a Tour on the
Continent, 1820*, no. xiii.

awareness, with the result that (as Eliot said of the Burnt Norton garden) the flowers 'had the look of flowers that were looked at'. Wordsworth foretold this kind of sharing in a poem written early in the summer of 1802. 'Going for Mary', as Dorothy called it, is one of the most attractive among the many poems that have been written about gardens, not least for the reason that its eagerness to welcome Mary Hutchinson into 'the blessed life which we lead here' is mixed with that perennially comic anxiety of gardeners – will the garden be past its best by then? They will just have to tell her what it was like in the spring, a thought that gives Wordsworth the chance to recall for Dorothy the 'best beloved and best' spring they had enjoyed *à deux*: the way, for example, that 'Here with its primroses the steep rock's breast / Glittered at evening like a starry sky.'

When Wordsworth published this least public of poems, now called 'A Farewell', he placed it among 'Poems founded on the Affections', and clearly affection for his wife-to-be and his sister were uppermost as he wrote. But the primroses around the garden's rocky outcrops had associations with other members of the Grasmere circle. Wordsworth's sailor brother John, who had worked hard to help make the Town End garden, shared his brother's and sister's enjoyment of wild flowers. In a letter of the previous spring he had described going ashore on the Isle of Wight on the eve of departure on a long voyage and seeing primroses by an evening light.[44] Another presence was that of Coleridge: the primroses in 'Going for Mary' merge with similar flowers that Wordsworth, Dorothy and Coleridge had together noticed a month or so before the poem was begun. Dorothy's journal for 24 April records that, on a walk to Rydal, 'We all stood to look at Glow-worm Rock – a primrose that grew there and just looked out on the road from its own sheltered bower.'[45] It was a moment of communion with the flowers and with one another, for the three of them were at their most happy and harmonious, having just discovered, on the hillside, their own rocky retreats or 'bowers', which they planned to plant with flowers.

Six years later, everything had changed. John was dead, gone down with his first command, the ill-fated *Abergavenny*. Coleridge had left his home at Keswick and the harmony between him and the Wordsworth family had been broken. The two poets however were still sufficiently close for Wordsworth, in March 1808, to respond to news of the other's ill health by seeking him out in London. Summoned back by news of further illness, this time afflicting his sister-in-law Sara, he returned to Grasmere still

[44] Carl H. Ketcham (ed.), *Letters of John Wordsworth* (1969), p. 112.   [45] *Journals*, p. 91.

deeply troubled by Coleridge's condition. But Sara made a good recovery, which Wordsworth celebrated by a poem in blank verse. This begins by hailing the reappearance of the primrose on the rock, from where it adds to the happiness of the happy and brightens the wintry mood of downcast souls. The poet's own welcome to its flowers far exceeds the 'serene delight' with which he has greeted them in previous years, for he is rejoicing in his sister-in-law's recovery and looks forward to her once again climbing the Rydal road to enjoy the sight of the primrose in bloom.

In the late summer, after the growing family's move from Town End to a larger house, Wordsworth returned to the poem, now called *The Tuft of Primroses*, and expanded it by over 500 lines, possibly with the intention of its becoming part of *The Recluse*. The state of the manuscript suggests that he found it difficult to link this continuation to the 'surpassing joyance' of the original; as well he might, since the next 150 lines are elegiac to the point of lamentation.[46] Over and above coping with bereavement, estrangement and the move to a new home (life's three major traumas, according to psychologists) he was trying to come to terms with changes in the very landscape that surviving members of the original Grasmere circle had hoped to share for the rest of their lives:

> Alas how much
> Since I beheld and loved thee first, how much
> Is gone, though thou be left; I would not speak
> Of best friends dead, or other deep heart loss
> Bewailed with weeping; but by river sides
> And in broad fields how many gentle loves,
> How many mute memorials passed away.

Wordsworth is recalling from the previous year the changes that he and his family found in the views to the north and south of their cottage when they returned to it after some months' absence. 'All the trees in Bainriggs are cut down, and even worse, the giant sycamore near the parsonage house, and all the finest fir trees that overtopped the steeple tower', Dorothy wrote in a letter of July 1807.[47]

The destruction of fine trees, more durable than people and often more dominating than their buildings, is the most disturbing experience that

---

[46] My quotations are from Joseph F. Kishel's edition, in the Cornell Wordsworth, of *The Tuft of Primroses with other Late Poems for* The Recluse (1986). For the poem's background I am indebted to Kishel's introductory essay and to James A. Butler, 'Wordsworth's *Tuft of Primroses*: "an unrelenting doom"', *Studies in Romanticism* 14 (1975), pp. 237–48.

[47] E. de Selincourt (ed.), *Letters of William and Dorothy Wordsworth: the Middle Years*, revised by Mary Moorman (1969), vol. II, p. 159.

poets can have of the plant world. Cowper, Burns, Hopkins, Charlotte Mew and a host of others have recorded a shock similar to bereavement, and Wordsworth here voices just such a mixture of grief, anger and denial:

> Ah, what a welcome! When from absence long
> Returning, on the centre of the vale
> I looked a first glad look and saw them not.
> Was it a dream? The aerial grove, no more
> Right in the centre of the lovely vale
> Suspended like a stationary cloud,
> Had vanished like a cloud . . .

Because the trees round the church had served as a link between the living and the dead, Wordsworth's thoughts pass to human lives that have also been cut down, and in particular to the members of one family, the Simpsons, who had befriended Dorothy in her first months at Grasmere, helping her to transfer wild flowers to the Town End garden and supplementing them with plants from their own. Now all of them have died within two years of one another, and the garden from which they once so 'generously dispersed' flowers to their neighbours itself lies waste.

At this point, with the poem becoming the very antithesis of 'Home at Grasmere' – his 1800 celebration of his lakeside home as a source of joy and creativity – Wordsworth returns to the flower of the title in hope of finding some pledge of the stability that is proving so elusive. The tuft of flowers is visible by all lights, and at dusk appears 'Lonely and bright, and as the moon, secure'. But the unvoiced thought that the moon is more often the emblem of changefulness would seem to launch the poet into a cry for the protection, here in his home vale, of 'all growth of nature and all frame of art'. This plea or prayer, the most eloquent thing in the poem, goes unheard: 'the deafness of the world is here'

> and the best
> And dearest resting-places of the heart
> Vanish beneath an unrelenting doom.

Crushed, as it were, by the finality of these words, the primroses of the title never reappear. And although Wordsworth continued *The Tuft of Primroses* with the history of other seekers after creative self-renewal in a secluded valley – the founders of eastern monasticism, the Carthusians of the Grande Chartreuse – in the end the poem was abandoned unfinished.[48]

---

[48] Substantial passages, not concerned with primroses, were incorporated into *The Excursion* and *The Prelude*.

The poem withered, but spring after spring the real-life tuft of primroses on Glow-worm Rock flowered anew. Regretful, perhaps, that he had abandoned the poem about it, and mindful (again perhaps), that readers of 'Peter Bell', published in 1819, might wonder what a yellow primrose was to its author, Wordsworth returned to the plant over twenty years later in a lyric called 'The Primrose of the Rock' – or to give it the delightfully prolix title it bears in a copy made by Dorothy: *Written in March 1829 on seeing a primrose-tuft of flowers flourishing in a chink of a rock in which that primrose-tuft had been seen by us to flourish for twenty-nine seasons.* In keeping with the High Anglican piety of Wordsworth's later years, the plant's reappearance now carries a religious message: 'We also . . . Shall rise and breathe again.' This analogy, however, besides being both poetically threadbare and logically unconvincing, failed on doctrinal grounds to satisfy the author of *Ecclesiastical Sonnets.* The Christian hope had to be shown to rest on revelation, not on natural theology. So Wordsworth tinkered (his word) with the poem, and in its final form as it was published in 1835 the emphasis is not on the plant's survival but on the way it has kept faith with its beholders. This links it with the New Covenant which 'turned the thistles of a curse / To types beneficent'. But this flash of wordplay on *Carduus benedictus* does not save the poem's conclusion from banality. Wordsworth left too late, one feels, the celebration of his primrose, which was at one time to have been the unifying symbol of continuity in a section of the great philosophical poem he aimed to write. And he nearly left it too late in another way. The note on 'The Primrose of the Rock' that he dictated in 1843 ends with the statement: 'The tuft of primroses has, I fear, been washed away by heavy rains.'[49] This matter-of-factness, so characteristically close to bathos, can be felt at another reading to be a no less characteristic way of keeping emotion at a seemly distance. As a more recent poet has found, 'The art of losing isn't hard to master',[50] and by the 1840s Wordsworth, his greatest loss confronting him daily in the spectacle of his sister's dementia, had had plenty of practice.

3

The Isle of Wight, where the spring flowers had given such pleasure to John Wordsworth after weeks at sea, deserved, in John Keats's opinion, to be renamed Primrose Island – 'that is, if the nation of Cowslips agree

[49] Jared Curtis (ed.), *The Fenwick Notes of William Wordsworth* (1993), pp. 16–17.
[50] Elizabeth Bishop, 'One Art', *Complete Poems* (1991), p. 178.

thereto'.[51] Half a century later, Queen Victoria would send Disraeli boxes of primroses, his favourite flower, from her own retreat on the island. But primrose-picking was strongly disapproved of by her Poet Laureate, Tennyson, who had made his home near Freshwater at the western end of Wight, where the flowers grew in profusion along what he called his path of dalliance.

In any case, primrose time was over in August 1868, when Tennyson's friend and would-be biographer William Allingham slipped away from his desk in the Lymington customs house, crossed the Solent and made for Freshwater. Here his first engagement was luncheon with the pioneer photographer Julia Cameron, who introduced him to other summer visitors: three members of the Darwin family, but not Charles Darwin, whose avoidance of social occasions, Allingham noted in his diary, had led to his being known as the Missing Link. However, Darwin's close friend, 'Dr Hooker of Kew', was present and after the meal accompanied Allingham to Tennyson's house, where the three men walked round the garden, Joseph Hooker identifying flowers and recalling their overseas counterparts; he had famously hunted for plants in Australasia and the Himalayas. Now he was not only Director of the Royal Botanic Gardens, but currently President of the British Association for the Advancement of Science into the bargain. So when, the next day, Allingham paid his formal call on the Darwins he found Hooker in a downstairs room, writing his presidential address and anxious to check the accuracy of a three-line verse quotation. Allingham made sure he had got it right and then stepped upstairs to meet Charles Darwin, who struck him as 'tall, yellow, sickly, very quiet'.[52]

Darwin's poor health would in fact prevent his attending the British Association's annual meeting later in the month. Thus he missed hearing a presidential address which was in essence a celebration of his theory that new organisms came into existence through the process of natural selection: the very theory that had caused uproarious opposition at the BA's meeting in Oxford only eight years previously. Now, in 1868, Hooker declared it to be 'an accepted doctrine with almost every philosophical naturalist',[53] and went on to show that Darwin's writings subsequent to *The Origin of Species*, notably the series of papers on botanical subjects that Hooker termed his *pièces justicatives*, had played a major part in achieving

[51] Hyder Rollin (ed.), *The Letters of John Keats* (1958), vol. I, p. 131.
[52] H. Allingham and D. Radford (eds.), *William Allingham's Diary* (1907), p. 184.
[53] *Report of the British Association for the Advancement of Science, 1868*, p. lxx.

that acceptance. One paper in particular, on the fertilisation of primroses and cowslips, had astonished botanists like himself by its insights:

I felt that my botanical knowledge of these homely plants had been but little deeper than Peter Bell's to whom

> A primrose by a river's brim
> A yellow primrose was to him
> And it was nothing more.[54]

Primroses and cowslips could be said to have astonished Darwin himself in 1860, the year in which he sought relief from the toil of re-writing his 'big book' on natural selection (from which he had in the previous year abstracted *The Origin of Species*) by means of an inquiry into the fertilisation of wild orchids. As Matthew Arnold noted in 'Thyrsis', orchids consort with cowslips in May meadows (a fact, incidentally, that has its own bearing on matters of fertilisation), and it was on 7 May 1860 that Darwin took a close look at cowslips and realised that their flowers were of two kinds. Those on some plants had a long style and short stamens; those on others, a short style and long stamens. The difference had in fact always been known to auricula breeders, who called the one form pin-eyed, from the pinhead shape of the stigma, and the other thrum-eyed: 'thrums' being a weaver's term for loose ends of thread. Only pin-eyed plants were acceptable for showing – a rule that obtains to this day – and the fact that thrum-eyed flowers were considered imperfect may explain why Linnaeus and other eighteenth-century botanists overlooked this variant in their descriptions. Microscopic examination of the two forms also revealed to Darwin small differences in their pollen and in their stigmas. His mind running on possible links in the evolutionary process, he at once wrote to Hooker with a hypothesis: the two forms of cowslip could be 'a fine case of gradation between an hermaphrodite and unisexual condition'[55] – that is, an intermediate evolutionary step between flowering plants whose flowers carry male and female parts together, and plants of which every individual is either male or female.

---

[54] *Ibid.*, p. lxvii.
[55] F. Burkhardt *et al.* (eds.), The *Correspondence of Charles Darwin*, vol. VIII (1993), p. 192. In this section I am very indebted to this magnificent edition, and also to two biographies: Adrian Desmond's and James Moore's *Darwin* (1992) and Janet Browne's *Charles Darwin, the Power of Place: Volume Two of a Biography* (2002), as well as to Mea Allan's *Darwin and his Flowers* (1977) and Nicolette Scourse's *The Victorians and their Flowers* (1983). Quotations from Darwin's published works are from *The Complete Works of Darwin on Line*, http://darwin-online.org.uk.

The next day Darwin marked equal numbers of each kind of flower with a view to watching them set seed. Within a week he had discovered that primroses also had flowers of two forms, and was communicating his theory of why this might be so to John Henslow, mentor and friend since his Cambridge days. Henslow, Darwin half-remembered, had pointed out the two forms to him at some time in the past. That time could have been thirty years previously, when Darwin was an undergraduate dissecting primroses under Henslow's direction. Or it could have been some point during the years when Henslow combined being Regius Professor of Botany with teaching the basics of the subject in the village school of his country living: Darwin's remark, in his paper on the two forms of *Primula*, that 'Village children notice this difference, as they can best make necklaces by threading and slipping the corollas of the long-styled flowers into each other'[56] may represent the schoolchildren's confidence that they could still teach a thing or two to the clergyman who expected them to spell such hard words as 'gymnospermous' and 'thalamifloral' before he would admit them to his classes.

Another botanist to be told in 1860 of Darwin's new interest was Asa Gray of Harvard, chief transatlantic defender of natural selection. That was in June, by which time Darwin was disconcerted to feel ovules swelling on the short-styled plants that he had decided must be males. 'How perplexing'[57] it would be, if the two forms of flower proved equally fertile. Gray's reply was that, from long observation of many other species with two forms of flower, he would expect this outcome, but that he still believed the two forms to represent an evolutionary halfway house. And he added that when, earlier in their correspondence, Darwin had first told him of his theory of the probable necessity of cross-fertilisation – about which he himself was still sceptical – he had thought of all those two-form species 'as a pretty case of arrangement for it'.[58]

Darwin acknowledged that Gray's letter gave him valuable hints; hints that he recalled in December when he found time to weigh the seeds from his marked cowslips and primroses and report his findings to Hooker. Reminding Hooker of 'all the fuss' about the two forms that he had made in the spring, he now announced that

by Jove the Plants of Primrose and Cowslip with short pistils and large-grained pollen are rather *more* fertile than those with long pistils and small-grained pollen.

---

[56] *Journal of the Proceedings of the Linnean Society, Botany 6* (1862), p. 78.
[57] *Correspondence*, vol. VIII, p. 248.   [58] *Ibid.*, p. 284.

I find that they require the action of insects to set them, and I never will believe that these differences are without some meaning.[59]

Darwin, like many another researcher, had been on the wrong track. The notion that heterostyly – to give the phenomenon its modern 'hard word' name – was a stage towards the evolution of single-sex plants had to be abandoned. But Gray's suggestion of its being a means to achieve inter-crossing, an idea already sufficiently formed for him to have netted a few flowers on one cowslip plant and noted that they failed to set seed, now took possession of Darwin, who began to marshal his forces for a spring attack. First, the marked wild cowslips had to be transplanted from their various sites into a garden bed where they could all enjoy optimum conditions. Scarcely had the first wild primroses of 1861 appeared than Darwin was writing to Daniel Oliver, Kew's curator and newly appointed Professor of Botany at University College London, asking him to request William Hood Fitch, foremost botanic artist of the day, to draw for him a pin-eyed and a thrum-eyed primrose cut 'longitudinally with sharp scissors'.[60] Oliver, together with his propagation foreman, was also given the task of identifying any two-form species of *Primula* as it came into flower and dispatching specimens to Darwin at Down.

A small hitch now occurred: ordinary primroses, which for all their abundance can be choosy about their habitat, appeared not to grow wild at Kew. Darwin had to send some from Down, where he was already busy with Chinese primroses and auriculas in addition to the transplanted cowslips. He repeated and extended his demonstration of the dependence of these last on cross-pollination. He thrust the proboscides of dead insects down corolla tubes to satisfy himself that they would have picked up pollen from anthers at two distinct levels. And there were more elaborate proce-dures: after netting all the plants involved to prevent their pollination by insects, Darwin himself took on the insect role by hand-pollinating flowers with pollen from other individuals of both forms. He was hopeful of his results by June, but it was September before he was able to complete collecting his data and to tell Gray, beneath his drawing (hardly up to Fitch's standard) of the two forms, 'I think I have made out their good or meaning clearly'.[61] A week later, his paper for the Linnean Society was finished, and in November he made one of his very rare public appearances in order to present to the society 'a case new, as far as I know, in the animal and vegetable kingdoms'.[62]

[59] *Ibid.*, p. 532.   [60] *Correspondence*, vol. IX (1994), p. 65.   [61] *Ibid.*, p. 264.
[62] *Journal of the Proceedings of the Linnean Society, Botany 6* (1862), p. 90.

That case was that the two forms of *Primula* flowers represented a kind of double hermaphroditism. Darwin showed that 'the relative heights of the anthers and stigmas in the two forms lead to insects leaving the pollen of the one form on the stigma of the other'.[63] So pollen from the high-up anthers of 'thrums' would be transferred from the mouth-parts of a large insect (and as has since been observed, from its head and perhaps its thorax too) onto the high stigma of a 'pin', and pollen from the low-down anthers of 'pins' onto the low stigma of a 'thrum'. Such pollen would, as it were, take precedence ('prepotency' was Darwin's word) over any pollen from the same flower or from other flowers of the same form. In this way the existence of the two forms demonstrated 'how nature strives, if I may so express myself, to favour the sexual union of distinct individuals of the same species'.[64]

I have chosen to relate Darwin's discovery of the 'meaning' of hetero-styly in the words of letters he wrote in 1860 and 1861 and of the paper he read in November of the latter year, rather than in the language of his 1877 book, *The Different Forms of Flowers on Plants of the Same Species*, in order to convey his excitement over his discovery as he experienced it – and in this connection, it is worth recalling that in the 1860s 'experience' had not yet lost the meaning of 'experiment'. Darwin's investigation into two forms of *Primula* species was indeed an experience and one that brought him real joy. It was not just the joy of the chase, though his letters reveal how intense ('mad' is a recurrent word) his pursuit of heterostyly's significance had become. Nor was it just that his garden beds offered a refuge from the public fuss and bother about human descent, and also from the wearisome task of extracting the detailed evidence for natural selection from the abandoned 'big book' – 'Eheu, eheu, what much better fun observing is than writing.'[65] It was not even, in the first place, the pleasure of sharing his ideas with the circle of devoted friends who were always ready with encouragement and help. Asa Gray, though himself still sceptical about the importance of insect pollination, had directed Darwin's attention to this aspect of *Primula* survival, and was sending specimens of other dimorphic plants across the Atlantic. Darwin would affectionately dedicate *Different Forms of Flowers* to him. Hooker, the friend whose scientific opinions Darwin valued above those of all others, supplied more plants and more encouragement. Letters on the minutiae of primrose floral structure went back and forth between Oliver and Darwin. Henslow's death while the investigation was in progress was keenly felt by Darwin, but it made it

---

[63] *Ibid.*, p. 92.   [64] *Ibid.*, p. 94.   [65] *Correspondence*, vol. IX, p. 264.

easier for him to question his former teacher's belief that primroses and
cowslips were varieties of a single species, and ultimately to demonstrate
their true specific differences – sorting out true and false oxlips in the
process.

Of course not all Darwin's personal relationships at the time of his
primrose experiments were harmonious, and it is tempting to digress a
little on the adverse effect that the inharmonious ones had on this area of
his work as he continued it through the 1860s. Thomas Huxley's insistence
that the theory of natural selection could not be proved until varieties
showed themselves to have the sterility of hybrids, was a constant irritant.
Over several years, Darwin wasted much time and energy in an effort to
convince Huxley that he had found an equivalent to hybrid sterility in the
declining fertility of those *Primula* plants that had originated in self-form
pollination. Another distorting factor in Darwin's *Primula* researches was
his underlying fear that he had bequeathed to his children both his own ill
health and the debility that was believed to be a consequence of first-cousin
marriages. Family illnesses were causing him much anxiety when the 1861
paper was in the making, and he was himself prostrated by the effort of
delivering it – possibly because of the nervous excitement the subject
aroused in him. The necessity of out-breeding became an obsession,
showing itself not only in the fact that three of his six wholly botanic
books were on the subject of cross-fertilisation, but also in the use (from
1863 onward) of such give-away terms as 'illegitimate unions' and 'legit-
imate unions' and, above all, in the formulation of a law that 'Nature
abhors perpetual self-fertilisation'. For all her concern with genetic variation, Nature tolerates selfing in many plants.

But to return to the positive aspect of Darwin's discoveries: the deeper
source of his pleasure was surely the plants themselves. Readers of *The
Origin of Species* during the 1860s may have had little joy from contemplating the fact that species after species had vanished (to appropriate
Wordsworth's phrase) beneath an unrelenting doom. But by turning his
attention in the same decade to the 'various contrivances' by which orchids
and primroses, carnivorous sundews and clambering honeysuckles fought
off that doom, Darwin was putting upon his theory a wholly positive
interpretation. Plants, to which he had hitherto given limited attention,
were proving, as he put it, more wonderful than animals, and he began to
regret that he had not been a botanist.[66] Primroses in particular, which

---

[66] *Correspondence*, vol. IX, p. 344.

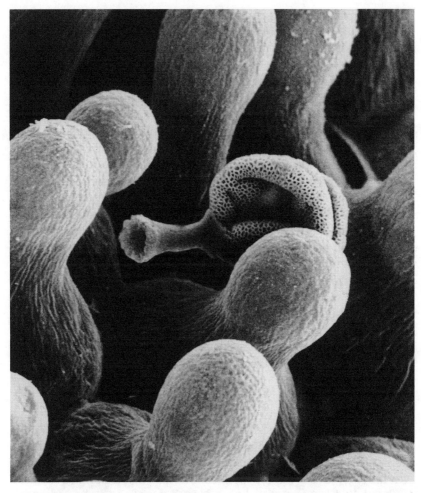

2 Pollen grain of thrum cowslip, *Primula veris*, on thrum cowslip stigma. It has germinated to produce a tube but this is unable to penetrate the stigma. (Scanning electron micrograph by Trevor Booth, © John Richards.)

'I have lately been putting the pollen of the two forms on the division of the stigma of the *same* flower, and it strikes me as truly wonderful that the stigma distinguishes the pollen; and is penetrated by the tubes of the one and not by those of the other.'

(Charles Darwin to Asa Gray, 14 July 1862)

make everyone happy, made Darwin supremely happy because they enabled him to show, with the neat simplicity praised in Hooker's address, that a fact familiar to every village child offered striking proof of the workings of natural selection. 'I do not think', he would write in his autobiography, 'anything in my scientific life has given me so much satisfaction as making out the meaning of the structure of these plants.'[67]

That satisfaction shines through the 1861 paper, thanks to the fact that, at that date, a scientific paper did not have to assume the passive-voice impersonality favoured today. Darwin concluded it, as a modern biologist would do, with suggestions for further research – but he could not resist adding that he had already begun experiments upon other dimorphic flowers, those of the garden plant *Linum grandiflorum*, and that these had shown them to be completely self-incompatible. That a plant's own pollen should produce no more effect upon it 'than so much inorganic dust'[68] was, he declared, one of the most surprising facts he had ever observed. And when, the following summer, he went on to examine *Linum grandiflorum*'s stigmas under the microscope he found yet more cause for wonder. The first step in a plant's fertilisation is the growth from a pollen grain of a tube that enters the stigma. In this species, Darwin found, only tubes emitted by 'other-form' pollen did this; 'own-form' pollen tubes, if they grew at all, were unable to penetrate. That pollen and stigmas should thus 'mutually recognise each other' was, as he told Gray, 'truly wonderful';[69] and in his presidential address Hooker called it just that. Today, an electron microscope's image of this recognition process in the flower of a cowslip – with which it all began – makes it possible for all of us to share Darwin's amazement at Nature's resourcefulness.

4

Wordsworth and Darwin both sought meaning in a primrose. Darwin found it; Wordsworth failed to do so, and his unfinished *Tuft of Primroses* did not see the light of day until the middle of the last century, long after 'On the two forms . . . in the species of *Primula*' had established itself as a landmark in the history of evolutionary biology. Of course things were not always this way round. Darwin had his failures, most notably his formulation of a 'pangenesis' theory of heredity. Wordsworth, after all, wrote *The Prelude*. But when, in contrast with these intellectual voyagings, both focused their attention on a single organism, the advantage was with

---

[67] N. Barlow (ed.), *The Autobiography of Charles Darwin, 1809–1882* (1958), p. 128.
[68] *Journal of the Proceedings of the Linnean Society, Botany* 6 (1862), p. 96.
[69] *Journal of the Proceedings of the Linnean Society, Botany* 7 (1864), p. 75; *Correspondence*, vol. X (1997), p. 321.

Darwin. The difference lay, not in observation of minute details – as Samuel Johnson said, it is no business of the poet to count the streaks of the tulip – but in the nature of each man's primary perception.

If we turn back to the passages in *The Tuft of Primroses* that directly confront the plant we find a language that is at once strained and uninformative. Praise of its 'beauty', even when reinforced as 'sacred beauty', tells us nothing, and it is hard to see how a perky cluster of primroses can ever have presented itself as 'a queen / Smiling from thy imperishable throne / ... in splendour unimpaired' or as having the luminosity and permanence of a heavenly body; indeed the crossed-out 'large as the moon' reveals the ineptness of this last image. In such inflated language, Wordsworth seems to be asking more of *Primula vulgaris* than it could give. It is as if he is seeking a visionary experience of the kind that had recently come to him when, leaving London in a deeply anxious state of mind, he had looked up Ludgate Hill and found 'an anchor of stability' in the prospect of St Paul's Cathedral in snow: an experience that, on his return to Grasmere, he was able to record in lines that have some of the power of *The Prelude*'s famous 'spots of time'. Joseph Kishel, who includes 'St Paul's' in his edition of *The Tuft of Primroses*, suggests that the poet's original sighting of the flower in 1802 may have been an experience of the same kind. But as far as we know it did not have the essential element of a Wordsworthian moment: the way that sudden release from mental or physical tension would cause the unified splendour of a wide landscape ('like workings of one mind') to sweep in upon his consciousness. One small plant was unlikely to produce that effect in 1802 and even more unlikely to do so in 1808, by which time the religious significance of a great cathedral perhaps moved Wordsworth more than anything in the natural world. The primrose, too, had by then become docketed in his mind as a symbol, with the result that he no longer really looked at it; the sole directly descriptive phrase in the entire poem, 'flower-like leaves' (because they form a rosette?) merely puzzles.

The reason why the primrose on the Grasmere boulder remained alive for between thirty and forty years was that its rootlets incessantly probed crannies in the rock, finding anchorage against winter gales and detecting every trace of moisture in summer drought. No one would have known this better than Charles Darwin who spent long hours observing such activity and recording it for his last botanic work, *The Power of Movement in Plants* (1881). Interest in tropisms, as botanists now call movements in response to stimuli, had run parallel with his interest in cross-fertilisation ever since he had detected distinct movements in the pollen-bearing organs of orchids.

From there he went on to study other tropisms that could ensure a plant's survival and so its eventual reproduction: the closing of a Venus flytrap on its victim; the elastic grip of bryony tendrils; the nightly 'sleep' of wood sorrel leaves; above all, the exploratory thrust of root and shoot. His son Francis, who was his collaborator in this last work, has left us a vivid description of the way of seeing plants that underlay his father's experiments. There ran, he wrote in his memoir, 'all through his relation to natural things a most keen feeling of their aliveness'.[70] And in his letters, especially those to Hooker, Darwin gives free rein to his empathy. A climbing plant, moved to his study table and unable to find a support, behaved 'as if it were disgusted with its failure but were resolved to try again'.[71] Even in the circumspect prose of *The Power of Movement in Plants*, Darwin's way of describing a broad bean rootlet's negotiation of the assault course he devised for it is a running commentary on its lively behaviour: behaviour indicating to him that the root tip 'acts like the brain of one of the lower animals'.[72]

'Like' is the operative word. In contrast to his grandfather who believed that plants *had* brains, Darwin, by his use of such modifiers as 'like', 'as if', even 'a poet might imagine', never lets the reader forget that he is dealing with analogies. If on the one hand he was prepared, in letters to other botanists, to play along with the family joke that he believed 'wicked dear little *Drosera*' to be a disguised animal,[73] on the other hand he found plants 'splendid for making one believe in Natural Selection *as will and consciousness are excluded*'[74] – and with them, he implied, Lamarck's theory of evolution through acquired adaptations. Even if it could be argued that giraffes might get longer necks by determined stretching, honeysuckles, having no nerve-centre to direct their twining, had to wait for their climbing skills to be selected for. But Darwin's resistance to his own vitalising turn of mind was not just scientific caution. At the root of it there lay a sense of otherness that counterbalanced the intense empathy he felt for green and growing things. 'Beautiful' is a word freely used in his letters: not to convey a pleasure in colour and form (though Francis tells us these

---

[70] Quoted by Browne, *Charles Darwin, The Power of Place*, p. 417, from Francis Darwin's manuscript. In the printed memoir Francis Darwin, hurt perhaps by Julius Sachs's scorn for what he regarded as Darwin's anthropomorphism, substituted 'He could not help personifying natural things.'

[71] Quoted by Allan, *Darwin and his Flowers*, p. 215.

[72] *The Power of Movement in Plants*, p. 573. Darwin had detected the stimuli that activate plant growth-factors such as auxin.

[73] *Correspondence*, vol. VIII, p. 491.

[74] Quoted by Browne, *The Power of Place*, p. 442. My italics.

meant much to him) but to express his delight at the utterly unexpected ways in which plants functioned. He 'never saw anything so beautiful' as the movements of orchid pollinia.[75] 'Wonderful' is another word that comes again and again; expressive both of amazement at Nature's ingenuity and of the curiosity about evolutionary causes that it prompted.

All divinity, said John Donne, is love and wonder; and if we substitute for the divinity of the orthodox a quest for the truths of the natural world, we find in the mindset of many, and perhaps the majority, of biologists just such an equipoise between empathic identification with another being and a distancing respect for that being's distinctness. Charles Kingsley had a sense of this when he wrote that the naturalist had 'obtained that great need of all men, to get rid of self'.[76] Some biologists have sought to define this cast of mind, as Francis Darwin did when he spoke of his father's feeling for the aliveness of other life forms: a social biologist has called it 'biophilia'; a plant geneticist, 'a feeling for the organism'. 'Deep ecology' is a term in fashion at the time I write this, though I find this appropriation of the name of a branch of biology misleading. Communicators in the humanities have, of course, their own equivalents to this way of seeing: Coleridge found a phrase for it when, observing his small son's absorption in the movements of much smaller creatures, he wrote of a 'Brahmin love and awe of life'.[77] To another poet, it is life delighting in life; to a novelist, life recognising itself; to a theologian, reverence for life; to a philosopher, alterity. Creative writers in particular, when they involve themselves with a life science, often find themselves in a world of rich relationships beyond the human and their own work is correspondingly enriched. In the lifetimes of Erasmus Darwin, Crabbe and Clare that science was most likely to be botany, which, writes Janet Browne, 'with all its ramifications into colonial enterprise, the plantation system, horticulture, herbarium research, agriculture, recreation and fashion, was the "big science" of its day'.[78]

Dorothy Wordsworth certainly had a feeling for the organism. Her poet brother by and large did not, though he responded to such feelings on her part. The difference is suggested in a further encounter with primroses that the two of them had at the very end of 1802, when they came across a tuft in

[75] *Correspondence*, vol. VIII, p. 286. Pollinia are sticky masses of pollen grains, peculiar to orchids.
[76] 'On the study of natural history', *Miscellanies* (1859), vol. II, p. 357.
[77] Coburn (ed.), *Notebooks*, vol. I, note 959.
[78] *The Power of Place*, pp. 172–3. On the subject's popularity see D. E. Allen, *The Naturalist in Britain: a Social History* (1978) and Lynn Barber, *The Heyday of Natural History 1820–1870* (1980).

bloom and debated whether to pick the flowers or to let them take their
chance in the winter cold. From her journal entry it can be inferred that it
was Dorothy who wanted to leave them to 'live out their day' and that she
won. She felt justified some days later when she saw them still cheerfully
blooming. A trivial episode, but for Dorothy a significant one, thanks to
her ability to enter into the life of other beings.[79] The same ability made her
respond readily to the botanic fervour of the time, whereas Wordsworth,
by his own admission, neglected the subject, 'into which neglect I was
partly seduced by having in the early part of my life, my sister almost always
at my side in my wanderings, and she for our native plants was an excellent
botanist'.[80] He even on occasion registers hostility to the fashionable
science: the savant who is capable of botanising upon his mother's grave
('The Poet's Epitaph') is surely one of those whose 'meddling intellect /
Mis-shapes the beauteous forms of things' ('The Tables Turned'). And
apart from the Trinity College ash (which Dorothy once characteristically
made an object of pilgrimage), plants are of such small account in *The
Prelude* that towards the end of the work the poet virtually apologises for
this absence of 'Nature's secondary grace' (Book XIV, line 282). It is a
telling phrase: plants, when they were not massed into a feature of landscape, were for Wordsworth of secondary importance to the large appearances of inanimate nature that stirred his imagination; secondary also in
that awareness of them tended to come to him at second hand, most often
through the responses of the sister to whom he pays high tribute in this last
book of *The Prelude*. When this happened, the result could be a memorable
lyric – as any reader knows who has been asking 'what about "Daffodils"?'
And as a lifelong devotee of Wordsworth, I am myself unable to part
company with him at this point, without a brief recall of three wholly
satisfying poems that he wrote about flowers.

'Daffodils' is not Wordsworth's title; the poem is more accurately
referred to by its first line, 'I wandered lonely as a cloud'. The line itself,
though, is far from accurate, since Wordsworth had Dorothy at his side on
the wet and windy tramp the length of Ullswater during which they came
upon a scattering of daffodils growing at the water's edge and wondered
how they came to be there. 'We fancied that the lake had floated the seeds
ashore, and that the little colony had so sprung up': these words in
Dorothy's journal suggest talk that had the effect of causing them to put
themselves, however briefly, in the place of these wholly different beings;

---

[79] *Journals*, p. 136.
[80] *The Letters of William and Dorothy Wordsworth, 1821–1850, Part IV* (1980), p. 22.

and as a result, when they came upon the main mass of the flowers, it was not just the pathetic fallacy that caused them to see and subsequently write about them as laughing and dancing. True, both were experiencing a happiness they were ready to project. Wordsworth had just returned from making arrangements with Mary Hutchinson – who, incidentally, would contribute two very good lines to the poem – for their forthcoming marriage. And though Dorothy may not fully have shared the exhilaration with which her brother fronted the wind (some of the daffodils, she noticed, lay down as if 'for weariness'), she was happy in his happiness, as is clear from her account of their subsequent evening at the inn where they put up – 'we enjoyed ourselves and wished for Mary'.[81] But beneath any tendency to anthropomorphise lay that initial speculation about how the flowers came to enter the dance of life: an illuminating flash of the curiosity that one day would drive Charles Darwin to suggest that a species could originate in this way. Seed dispersal by water was to form important evidence for the theory of natural selection.[82]

Another outstanding flower poem shows Dorothy's influence, but in a quite contrary way, because on this occasion Wordsworth, I suspect, was not responding to it but reacting against it. The two sets of verses he addressed to the lesser celandine in April 1802 present the flower very much as Dorothy recorded it in her journal that spring: bright, beautiful and abundant. Both say little more than 'how pretty!' and say it with forced sprightliness. But a third poem, 'The Small Celandine', begun in 1803 and completed the next year, suggests that Wordsworth took another look at the flower and discovered something for himself. Although a celandine's petals can close to protect it from the weather, a day comes when Nature's harsh energy plan causes them to lose this power and become blanched and lustreless. What most surprises in the poem is the 'spleen', almost vindictiveness, with which the poet contemplates this change. Dare one suggest a passing repudiation of Dorothy's way of looking – something akin to Paul's exasperation at Miriam's tenderness over flowers in *Sons and Lovers* – that left Wordsworth space for what he elsewhere calls his oversternness? The breakaway, if that was what it was, worked: 'This neither is its courage nor its choice / But its necessity in being old' convinces us that, however slight the subject might have seemed, it had an underlying significance that did indeed occasion thoughts too deep for tears. And this is even more the case with a poem of 1805, the 'Elegiac Verses' written four months after John Wordsworth was lost at sea.

[81] *Journals*, pp. 85–6.   [82] *Origin of Species* (1859), pp. 358–60.

Wordsworth had climbed to the spot at the head of Patterdale where he and Dorothy had parted from their brother five years previously, and where in consequence he 'only looked for pain and grief'. Instead, he found that he was able to take peace and comfort from the sight of 'a plant unknown, / A little one and lowly sweet'. It was a rarity: the beautiful moss campion.

> And let me calmly bless the Power
> That meets me in this unknown flower,
> Affecting type of him I mourn!
> With calmness suffer and believe,
> And grieve, and know that I must grieve,
> Not cheerless, though forlorn.

Wordsworth, who elsewhere writes of John as 'a silent poet' with a 'fine and delicate eye'[83] for natural beauties, sees the plant with the same pleasure that his brother would have felt. But over and above this, it presents itself as the type or symbol of his brother's nature because its alpine character makes it as perfectly at home in its mountain environment as John had shown himself to be. This affinity sets Wordsworth's imagination free to speak as if his brother were able to be told of the find, and brought to see it on his return from sea. One only has to remember a later poem about another loss, the sonnet beginning 'Surprised by joy', to realise the emotional risk the poet is here taking. But the calm of mind holds, and serves to bring the poem to a steady close.

When, thirty-seven years on, Wordsworth included the 'Elegiac Stanzas' among his published poems, he appended a note on the moss campion's strong-rooted sturdiness and then added that it had disappeared from the two sites where he previously found it growing. The inference is plain, and leads on to a plea to botanists not to dig up rare and beautiful plants. For the present-day reader, the poignancy and aptness of Wordsworth's encounter with the flower are deepened by the knowledge that his plea went unheard. *Silene acaulis* cannot now be found in the Lake District.

5

Sketchy as was my account of how successive generations saw primroses and their kin, it did, I hope, indicate that a surge of scientific interest in the natural world, such as occurred early in the sixteenth century or at the

---

[83] 'When first I journeyed hither' and *Letters*, vol. I, p. 548.

Restoration or in the mid-eighteenth century, did not of necessity influence the way poets saw plants. That influence made itself felt only when the biologist's blend of a vivid and observant awareness of the organism's own life with an underlying sense of somehow sharing that life spoke to the condition (in the Quaker phrase) of the individual poet. The year after Wordsworth, who had kept the poem by him some twenty years, published 'Peter Bell', John Clare's first collection appeared and in it the first of his hundreds of poems wholly or in part about primroses. Reviewers who picked out this sonnet for praise may have had Peter Bell's deficiencies fresh in their minds. What is certain is that here was a poet with as profound insight into the life of herb and tree as he had into the life of bird and mammal; insight based on intimate childhood knowledge and strengthened by the botanical enthusiasm of the age.

In Victorian painting and poetry at large, however, flowers, including a profusion of primroses, are there for the sake of their associations. A still life for example by William Hunt of an egg-filled nest beside a bunch of primroses (a subject he and his imitators painted again and again) tells, as the Victorians liked their pictures to do, a story – in this case, about a small boy and girl exploring a hedgerow. It owes, that is, its appeal to a double nostalgia, for childhood outgrown and countryside lost.[84] Children picking 'the child's flower in the childhood of the year', as a sonnet by William Allingham defines primroses, are a favourite subject of other painters, causing Ruskin to maintain, rather wishfully, that the artists were protesting 'against the misery entailed on the poor children of our great cities, – by painting the real inheritance of childhood in the meadows and fresh air'.[85] A more disturbing thought for today's viewer is that, in real life, many of these bunches were being picked for the churchyard. Primroses were planted on children's graves, and some parishes decorated all burial plots with the flowers at Easter time. No reader of James Kilvert's diary ever forgets his description of graves heaped with primroses, looking in the moonlight 'as if the people had laid down to sleep for the night out of doors, ready dressed to rise early on Easter morning'.[86] Nor can we forget the solitary child he had helped to deck four of these graves.

Cowslips too could intimate mortality. Millais, when he painted a group of young women returned from a flower-gathering, placed an abandoned

[84] The provenances of his paintings suggest industrialists were very fond of Hunt's nests and primroses. His seeming vandalism is explained by the fact he was seriously disabled. Whole chunks of primrose bank had to be transferred to his studio, where he made them convey pleasures he had probably never himself experienced.

[85] *The Art of England* (1884), § 112. [86] William Plomer (ed.), *Kilvert's Diary 1870–1879* (1944), p. 27.

scythe at the edge of his canvas, so that the eye follows the downward curve of its blade into a trug filled with drooping cowslips and thence to the heart of its owner who, dressed in the two cowslip yellows, is lying on the grass watched over by a black-clad companion or nurse. This is part of the painting's intricate symbolism, which visitors to the RA's summer exhibition in 1859 do not appear to have made out. They ought to have done better, since they had for over a generation been bombarded with similar symbolism in the immensely popular flower-books that, like the age's paintings, tell us a great deal about the average Victorian's way of looking at flowers.

Flower-books ranged from drab volumes of prayer book size intended for 'some of the labouring classes'[87] to gorgeous folios dedicated to the queen, but the plan of their contents hardly ever varied. A series of engravings or lithographs of flowers was presented in seasonal order, each accompanied by an essay that was a pot-pourri of botanical facts (limited for the most part to a classification and a few descriptive details), mythology, folklore and customs (which gave the chance to bring in mourning rites). All this would be interspersed with quotations from poets and poetasters and the whole would be liberally glued together with moral reflections. Though there would sometimes be a recall of the famous *Langage des Fleurs* of 1819 (in which *primavères* stood for the longings of puberty), the popularity of floral emblemata with Evangelicals and Tractarians alike was most likely to result in primroses being equated with modesty and innocence: meanings still alive in the 1870s to Browning, who has a rakish character visit a theatre in the hope of picking up a 'primrose' among the audience. (The hope is exceeded when he instead encounters a cultivated – and scarlet? – flower of her sex, since 'To primrose, polyanthus I prefer').[88]

A typical flower-book of the decade during which Darwin was carrying out his investigations into plant life is John Ingram's *Flora Symbolica* (1869); typical among other things for its plagiarisms. Thus Ingram repeats from one of the earliest flower-books a legend to explain primrose pallor. Paralisos was a beautiful youth who pined with grief for the loss of his beloved Melicarta until his parents, Flora and Priapus, transformed him into a primrose.[89] Next he lifts from Elizabeth Kent's *Flora Domestica*

[87] H. C. Adams, *Flowers, their Moral Language and Poetry* (1850), Preface.

[88] *Red Cotton Nightcap Country* (1873), line 1502.

[89] I have not been able to trace this further back than the *Flora Historica* of Henry Phillips (1824), but do not suspect Phillips, a Quaker botanist who advised Constable on his foregrounds, of its invention. Ingram's chapter on the primrose is on pp. 262–5 of *Flora Symbolica*.

(1824) some sentimental musing on the flower's association with childhood ('the irresistible primroses which have so often lured our young feet into the wet grass') and adds to it another favourite theme of the colonising era, the exile's home thoughts: 'Who does not remember the tremendous excitement that took place in Australia upon the arrival of the first primrose from old England?' Here however he had been anticipated by Anne Pratt, whose flower-books are among the most attractive of the genre, and who ends a chapter on the primrose with a poem of her own about Douglas (of fir-tree fame) discovering a primrose-like flower in the Rockies and reflecting that, across the sea, 'when the wild flowers blew / They sighed for him who loved them too'.[90] Ingram may also be following Anne Pratt when he includes quotations from poems by Clare, 'as thickly strewn with primroses as the woods themselves', alongside the familiar ones from Shakespeare and Milton. The final flourish to his primrose chapter, however, is a sub-Wordsworthian lyric from 'Mrs Hemans' ever-faithful muse' that in its self-absorption is representative of some ninety per cent of flower-book poetry. For the one thing that all these fairy tales and moralisings and facile sentiments tell us about what flowers were for the Victorian reader is that the writers never doubted that flowers – to twist the phrase – were for *them*: 'manifestly preordained for the excitement of delight',[91] as Paley claimed and as Mary Howitt paraphrased Paley in a poem, 'The Uses of Flowers', that is cited again and again,

> Our onward life requires them not –
> Then wherefore had they birth?
> To minister delight to man,
> To beautify the earth.[92]

Clearly by 1870 the Victorian response to flowers was an exhausted tradition. Yet opportunities were on hand in both the sacramental and the scientific way of looking at the natural world for poets to revitalise that tradition. Two phrases from an early poem ('A Nun Takes the Veil') by Gerard Manley Hopkins, 'feel-of-primrose hands' and 'the yield of plushy sward', albeit they are metaphorically – and moreover negatively – used to image pleasures the speaker is prepared to sacrifice, powerfully convey the primrosing joys that are limply expressed by lesser poets. And in his mature work, pleasures like these are not repudiated but transformed by a sense of the divine in all organic life. Hopkins's poetry, however, was not published

---

[90] Anne Pratt, *Flowers and their Associations* (1840), p. 26. The plant was a species of *Douglasia*.
[91] Quoted by Scourse, *The Victorians and their Flowers*, p. 177.
[92] *Mary Howitt's Poems: Birds and Flowers* (1872), p. 45.

until the first major war of the twentieth century had given the *coup de grâce* to poems about primroses. The worn-out tradition could likewise have been transformed by the Darwinian delight in alterity; the more so in that Darwin kept the common touch at a time when the language of science was becoming increasingly arcane. That this did not happen was in large part the result of the extraordinary hold over Victorian ways of seeing exercised by one man, John Ruskin. Despite his earlier appeal to readers to free the primrose from all sentimental associations, Ruskin was appalled by the revelation that flowers were beautiful in order that their species might survive. It was above all his revulsion against insect pollination that drove him to declare war on science in his final series of lectures at Oxford, and to substitute sentiment for scientific fact in *Proserpina*. As a result, a work he intended as a textbook of botany dissipated itself (for it was never finished) into the most wilfully anthropocentric and most elegantly written of all flower-books.[93]

In fairness to Ruskin it has to be remembered that at the time the parts of *Proserpina* were appearing, natural selection and its mechanisms did not command the universal assent Hooker had claimed for them in 1868.[94] But there were plenty of biologists to continue Darwin's work on cross-fertilisation after his death, and before long their findings began to be publicised by the new race of scientific journalists. In a rival work to *Proserpina*, John Ellor Taylor asserted that modern botany had abolished the crude view that plants were made for man, and had instead 'taught us to regard plants as *fellow creatures*'. His title, *The Sagacity and Morality of Plants* (1884) stands the didacticism of the conventional flower-book on its head, for the work is fundamentally a lively popularisation of Darwinian botany; it gives, for example, a sound account of the two forms of primrose and their function. Taylor's book was re-issued in 1904, by which time the wave of anthropocentric sentiment that in the end overwhelmed Ruskin, despite the Canute-like stand he had taken in his chapter on the pathetic fallacy, had spent its force. Even so, D. H. Lawrence, who began to write about this time, felt the after-tow. Emotionalism about flowers, of a Pre-Raphaelite cast, was a part of the atmosphere in which he grew up (it spelt refinement to working-class Edwardian women) and it colours his early poems and fiction. But the Darwinian perspective on plant life that he met

---

[93] Sabine Haass, in 'Speaking flowers and floral emblems: the Victorian language of flowers' (K. J. Höltgen (ed.), *Word and Visual Image* (1988)) and Beverley Seaton in *The Language of Flowers: a History* (1995) both stress the link between the flower-books and *Proserpina*.

[94] As late as 1902 'a Field Naturalist' [Edward Bell] could publish a whole volume, *The Primrose and Darwinism*, denying the cross-fertilisation of heterostyled plants.

in his study of botany at university nourished his innate feeling for the autonomy of the organism:

A primrose has its own peculiar primrosy identity . . . its own individuality which it opens with lovely naïveté to sky and wind and William and yokel, bee and beetle alike. It *is* itself. But its very floweriness is a kind of communion with all things: the love unison.[95]

'William' is of course Wordsworth whom Lawrence, in the journalistic piece written in 1925 from which this is taken, quite unfairly berates for not letting the primrose call its soul its own. But the passage is given a Coleridgean tinge by its closing words, which take it a vital step beyond its recall (probably unconscious) of *Modern Painters*. 'Love unison', in association with Lawrence's own *Naturphilosophie* as he struggled to express it in his essays and, much more importantly, in association with the poems about flowers that he wrote in his last decade, suggests a strengthening of the scientific vision by the sacramental which entitles him to be seen as the Poet Laureate of the plant kingdom.

In the first half of the twentieth century, as advances in genetics began to underpin the theory of natural selection in what would be known as the Darwinian synthesis, the autonomy of the organism – in other words, the primrose's right to call its soul its own – came to be a widely held assumption. Poetry, it would seem, could only gain from what appeared to be a fulfilment of Shelley's prophecy in *The Daemon of the World* that man would lose 'his desolating privilege' and stand 'an equal amidst equals' (lines 458–60). Sensibility towards other forms of life, a legacy of late eighteenth-century thought, could now be channelled into free-running sensitivity rather than stagnating into the sentimentality that marred so much nineteenth-century writing about the natural world. But given that poets no longer thought of flowers existing for God's or humanity's pleasure, the world confronting poets of the last two or three generations has been one in which man's desolating privilege has often denied them the right to exist at all.

It was not just a matter of the odd acquisitive botanist carrying off a clump of moss campion, reprehensible as that was. In the second half of the last century, an acquisitive society was directly or indirectly responsible for the decline and threatened disappearance of a host of species. Even *Primula vulgaris* appeared threatened, so that there was an outcry when, in the 1970s, a group of Devonshire paper mills was discovered to be sending

[95] Michael Herbert (ed.), *Reflections on the Death of a Porcupine and other Essays* (1988), p. 335.

boxes of primroses to favoured customers. In fact, as an investigation by academic botanists showed, picking the flowers had virtually no effect on the plants' productivity.[96] It was the human race's obsession with its own economic productivity that did the real harm: street traders could make a killing by stacking their vans with rootstocks; farmers were too busy gaining higher yields elsewhere to coppice their woodland; factories were belching out greenhouse gases with the result that, at the very end of the century, the foremost authority on English woodland had to answer his own question 'Where have the primroses gone?' with the sad disclosure that they were beginning to dry out from eastern counties.[97] And so this sketch of the ways in which people have seen primroses has to break off at a point where the possibility has to be faced that, in time, some *Primula* species will not be there to be seen. How today's poets have responded to this and related situations is a concern of my closing chapter.

---

[96] T. Hull *et al.*, 'Primrose picking in south Devon – the social, environmental and biological background', *Nature in Devon* 3 (1984), pp. 44–54.

[97] Oliver Rackham, 'The woods 30 years on: where have the primroses gone?' *Nature in Cambridgeshire* 41 (1999), pp. 73–87.

CHAPTER 2

Erasmus Darwin's feeling for the organism

I

A flower less like the primrose than the canna lily is hard to imagine. With its shield of high-held leaves and casque of huge blossoms, *Canna indica* is a piece of conspicuous expenditure in municipal gardens, suggestive of well-tended greenhouses and an army of bedders-out. Today we think of it as a typically Victorian plant; most at home, perhaps, in Mumbai or Calcutta, where ordered ranks of it form an imperial guard before the monuments of the Raj. Yet it reached Europe from the other – the West – Indies at the time of the Discoveries. It soon acclimatised in southern Europe, and sometimes shines out from the pages of a seventeenth-century florilegium. But Gerard could not coax it to produce its 'fantastic' flowers in his London garden, where he found it 'very impatient to endure the injury of our cold climate'.[1]

Cannas would have been even more impatient of the Swedish climate. Carolus Linnaeus had not seen one in flower at the time he devised his classification of plants according to what he called the sexual system: one based, that is, on the number and arrangement of stamens. Linnaeus was not the discoverer of plant sex. Gardeners had always known that, to obtain fruit from certain plants, pollen had to be transferred from individuals carrying it in their flowers to the stigmas of other individuals of which the flowers had no pollen. Then over the closing years of the seventeenth century and the first two decades of the eighteenth, it dawned upon Europe's savants that this was the same process as copulation in animals, and that bisexual or 'her-maphrodite' flowers – those with male and female parts within the same floral envelope, as in the great majority of flowering plants – also reproduced in this way. This realisation was given its greatest publicity at the opening of a new Jardin du Roi in 1717, in a lecture which Sebastien Vaillant livened up for a largely student audience by pleasantries about the joys of floral sex.

[1] *Herbal* (Thomas Johnson's 1633 edition), p. 39.

A decade later Linnaeus, still himself a student, came across Vaillant's ideas, and by the end of 1730 he had produced his first celebration of flower nuptials, in which he prefaced the Frenchman's forthright use of terms from human physiology with pious and sentimental fancies of his own:

The flowers' leaves [i.e. calyx and corolla] contribute nothing to generation, but only do service as bridal bed, which the great Creator has so gloriously arranged, adorned with such noble bed curtains and perfumed with so many soft scents that the bridegroom with his bride might there celebrate with so much the greater solemnity. When now the bed is prepared, it is time for the bridegroom to embrace his beloved bride and offer her his gifts; I mean, then one sees how the testicula open and powder [i.e. release] the pulverem genitalem, which falls upon the tubam and fertilizes the ovarium.[2]

Images of matrimony persist in the classification that Linnaeus went on to devise, although such categories as '*Decendria*: ten husbands in the same marriage' and '*Necessary polygamy*: when the married females are barren and the concubines fertile' make plain that he believed the means provided for the continuation of plant life were different from those imposed upon the human race. All the same, some example of a monogamous plant to correspond with his image of the bridal bed would have been very welcome to Linnaeus in 1731, when he published his first list of plants arranged according to his new plan. But he had to admit to never having seen one. Subsequently he did come across an instance of Monandria Monogynia in the humble pondweed *Hippuris vulgaris*, or mare's-tail; but that, being without petals, had an uncurtained bridal bed from which the bridegroom (though Linnaeus may not have known this) was frequently absent. So it is perhaps not too fanciful to imagine his satisfaction when, looking into a canna's tangle of petals at some time between 1731 and 1735, he saw that one of them had on one edge a half-anther, and was in fact a single petal-like stamen, and that another had a gleaming stigma on one edge and was in fact a single petal-like pistil.[3] Here was a spectacular genus to be inserted below *Hippuris* in the space that he had left for his first class in the plant chart of the *Systema naturae*, the work published, thanks to the generosity of patrons, within months of his arrival in Holland in 1735. Two years later,

---

[2] Translated from the *Praeludia sponsaliorum plantarum* by J. L. Lawson, *Reason and Experience: The Representation of the Natural Order in the Works of Carl von Linné* (1971), p. 53.

[3] The plant figures in *Adonis Uplandicus* (1731) as a three-stamened flower, with a reference, among others, to a catalogue of the Uppsala botanic garden published in 1685. As the garden fell into neglect in the early eighteenth century, it is probable that it could no longer offer the sight of a canna in flower, had it ever been able to do so, and that Linnaeus either misinterpreted a dried specimen or had to rely on the other printed authorities he cites.

in the *Methodus sexualis*, he was able to give *Canna* the precedence in his first class, and to add the botanical names of such trophies of the spice trade as arrowroot, galangal, turmeric and cardamom: apt representatives of the Dutch wealth that was making possible the publication of his writings. How fitting therefore that, when he returned to Sweden as an established scientist in a position to marry, verses composed for the wedding should have portrayed him as a 'monandrian lily';[4] in short, a canna.

The strange conjunction of cannas and mare's-tails brings home the oddness of Linnaeus's taxonomy. He was himself the first to acknowledge that a natural system, arising from the totality of each organism's character-istics, would be preferable to his artificial one; and by the middle of the nineteenth century, such a system was in fact generally preferred. But though Linnaeus's higher taxa were soon abandoned, he retains his title of prince of botanists by virtue of the lynx-eyed accuracy with which he distinguished what were in essence the natural groupings of the lower taxa as he set them forth in the *Genera plantarum* and then, in 1753, in the *Species plantarum*: still the starting point for the classification of any newly discovered plant, and the work in which he established the genus-plus-species nomenclature by which all organisms are now known.

Moreover Linnaeus's sexual system, however erroneous it may look to modern eyes, had the appeal of simplicity, as too did Linnaeus's two-part names by contrast with the wordy, phrasal names of earlier classifiers. It was this appeal, together perhaps with an amused wonderment at such goings-on in the garden, which gave rise to the craze for botany that possessed English polite society in the second half of the century. At first the cult was limited to the fashionable world of the Town and its country estates. Its icon was Sir Joseph Banks: leader of the *Endeavour* scientific team whose activities gave a name to Botany Bay, host in his specimen-packed London house to Europe's cognoscenti, and guardian of the royal botanists' collec-tion at Kew. As yet, working men had not taken to gathering weekly in the local pub to discuss their botanical finds. Their employers, too, were slow to take up the new craze: the group of Midland industrialists including men such as Matthew Boulton and Josiah Wedgwood who achieved the first technological revolution had strongly relevant interests in physics and chemistry (James Watt and Joseph Priestley were part of their circle, known among themselves as the Lunar Society)[5] but they left biology to the medical men. For them, of course, herbs had always been the essential

---

[4] Wilfrid Blunt, *The Compleat Naturalist: A Life of Linnaeus* (1971), pp. 134–5.
[5] Because they met at the full moon. See Jenny Uglow's collective biography, *The Lunar Men* (2002).

materia medica. Long before Linnaeus led his students home from their botanical forays 'with banners waving and horns and kettledrums playing',[6] the Apothecaries' Company of London had held simpling days for its apprentices in riverside woods and fields, whence it returned them to the city by barge with accompanying musicians.

In 1775 the Lunar Society was strengthened by the arrival of Dr William Withering, who had just completed the English flora that would one day be used and annotated by William and Dorothy Wordsworth. Withering had bought a practice in Birmingham at the suggestion of a highly successful doctor in nearby Lichfield, Erasmus Darwin. Though the two men were soon to quarrel, Withering appears to have inspired Darwin with an interest in the new Linnaean botany. In the year of Withering's arrival Darwin, who did nothing by halves, bought four acres of land near Lichfield and set about transforming them into a botanic garden. As soon as this was established, he took his friend and neighbour from the cathedral close, Anna Seward, to view it. He was then called away on a case: but Miss Seward, full of admiration of his skill in 'uniting the Linnaean science with the charm of landscape',[7] sat down on a flowery bank and wrote a poem in appreciation of the way that his landscaping and planting 'gave to beauty all the quiet scene'[8] – a good line that Darwin would later appropriate. According to her, Darwin was pleased with the poem, declaring that

it ought to form the exordium of a great work. The Linnaean system is unexplored poetic ground, and an happy subject for the muse. It affords fine scope for poetic landscape; it suggests metamorphoses of the Ovidian kind, though reversed. Ovid made men and women into flowers, plants and trees. You should make flowers, plants and trees into men and women. I . . . will write the notes which must be scientific; and you shall write the verse.[9]

Canon Seward's daughter thought the subject 'not strictly proper for a female pen', and suggested to Darwin, with a nice feeling for the *mot juste*, that it was better 'adapted to the efflorescence of his own fancy'.[10] Darwin demurred in turn: he did not want to jeopardise his reputation as a medical man by mixing hard facts about curative plants with poetic fancies. In the end, however, he wrote both the verses and the notes in *The Loves of the Plants*, a celebration of vegetable nuptials that is itself an extraordinary, and wholly fascinating, attempt to marry science and poetry.

An entry in Darwin's commonplace book dated a year or two earlier than this has been taken to suggest that he already had such a poem in

[6] Blunt, *Compleat Naturalist*, p. 169.   [7] *Memoirs of the Life of Doctor Darwin* (1804), p. 127.
[8] *Ibid.*, p. 129.   [9] *Ibid.*, pp. 130–1.   [10] *Ibid.*, p. 131.

mind. However, the words 'Linnaeus might certainly be translated into English without losing his sexual terms, or other metaphors, and yet avoiding any indecent idea',[11] more probably hint at a wish that Linnaeus's taxonomic works might be translated in a less coy manner than that of Withering, who even eschewed the use of 'stamen' and 'pistil'. This wish became deed with the publication, in 1782, of a translation of the *Systema vegetabilium*, credited on its title page to 'A Botanic Society in Lichfield' – a society of three members, including Darwin as guiding spirit.[12] There are signs that the prose translation and the poem progressed side by side. For example, a letter written in the autumn of 1781 indicates that Darwin was seeking Banks's opinion of a poem designed 'to induce ladies and other unemployed scholars to study botany, by putting many of the agreeable botanical facts into the notes'.[13] Though the letter attributes its composition to Anna Seward and a Mr Sayle, it may well have been a draft of part of *The Loves of the Plants*.

When the work, finished in 1784, was published anonymously in 1789, Darwin continued his promotion of the new botany in a preface listing all the classes of the Linnaean system, and referring the reader who wished 'to become further acquainted with this delightful field of science' to the Lichfield translations. Then, after a Proem preparing the work's more idle readers for its Ovidian fantasies, and some pleasing Popeian mock-heroics calling upon other forms of life to be attentive to the Botanic Muse –

> Ye painted moths, your gold-eyed plumage furl,
> Bow your wide horns, your spiral trunks uncurl   (canto I, 25–6)

---

[11] Quoted by Desmond King-Hele, *Erasmus Darwin: A Life of Unparalleled Achievement* (1999), p. 50. I am very much indebted in this chapter to this and other studies of Erasmus Darwin by Desmond King-Hele.

[12] From Darwin's letters to Banks it appears that the Lichfield trio intended translations of Linnaeus's *Genera plantarum* and *Species plantarum* but, on learning that a new edition of the former was expected, switched to a translation of the *Systema vegetabilium*, a posthumous edition (ed. J. A. Murray, 1774) of the plant section of the *Systema naturae*. This appeared as *A System of Vegetables* in 1783. *The Families of Plants*, translated from the *Genera*, followed in 1787. On the endpapers of Banks's copy of *A System of Vegetables* (now in the British Library) someone has transcribed an amusing poem in which Flora, summoned before Jove to explain the backwardness of the spring of 1782 (erroneously written as 1772), tells him

> Some Scholars of Litchfield that came recommended
> By the Muses who there on Miss Seward attended
> Now constitute wholly my administration
> Indeed they are men of no small reputation
> And they are compiling my Classification.

[13] Desmond King-Hele (ed.), *The Letters of Erasmus Darwin* (1981), pp. 116–17.

– Darwin begins his enumeration just where Linnaeus had begun his:

> First the tall C A N N A lifts his curled brow
> Erect to heaven, and plights his nuptial vow;
> The virtuous pair, in milder regions born,
> Dread the rude blast of autumn's icy morn;
> Round the chill fair he folds his crimson vest,
> And clasps the timorous beauty to his breast   (lines 39–44)

These lines, so curious and yet so characteristic, point up the quandary in which I now find myself. How is it possible not to begin a study of poet–botanists with Erasmus Darwin, whose three long poems comprise a poetic presentation of the Linnaean system, a scientific survey focused on the late eighteenth-century revival of plant physiology, and a celebration of life's gradual evolution on earth for which his grandson would one day offer persuasive evidence? Yet how can such prominence be accorded to a poet whose work has been declared to be 'dead eternally for the general reader',[14] and who has been the butt of other poets, from Byron ('Darwin's pompous chime, / That mighty master of unmeaning rhyme')[15] to Geoffrey Grigson, who found him 'a pompous, dabbling, self-satisfied, yet most attractive ass'?[16]

My final line of defence has to be simple enjoyment. With Coleridge, I find Darwin 'a wonderfully entertaining and instructive old man'[17] and hope my readers may too. First, however, the dismissal of Darwin's poems as literary curiosities calls for some exploration of the ways in which they are curious – bearing in mind that, at the time, the term was not pejorative. It has even been suggested that 'the curious' (or novelty, as Darwin terms it) was, for his generation, an aesthetic category alongside, though not on a par with, the sublime and the beautiful.

2

Darwin's poems are certainly curiosities in one eighteenth-century sense: the books themselves are rarities that take some hunting out. Early in the last century, the evolutionary thrust of *The Temple of Nature* earned it publication in Germany and (in translation) in Russia; the Russian translation reappeared twice in book form in Soviet times, presumably because

---

[14] J. V. Logan, *The Poetry and Aesthetics of Erasmus Darwin* (1972), p. 94.
[15] *English Bards and Scottish Reviewers* (1809), lines 893–4.
[16] 'The first of the Darwins', *The Bookman* 79 (1930), p. 109.
[17] Earl Leslie Griggs (ed.), *Collected Letters of Samuel Taylor Coleridge* (1956–9), vol. I, p. 179.

Darwin's belief that acquired adaptations could be inherited accorded well with Marxist biology. But at home neither *The Botanic Garden* (umbrella title for *The Economy of Vegetation* and *The Loves of the Plants*) nor *The Temple of Nature* was republished until the 1970s, and then in the form of facsimiles, now out of print.[18] And it would be a brave publisher who commissioned a modern scholarly edition: where could essential annotations to Darwin's own massive annotations be placed?[19] The appearance of the work on the page also creates a problem for modern readers, who find themselves inhibited from responding to the formal qualities of the verse, let alone yielding to the reverie which Darwin defines as the proper response to poetry, by having their eye repeatedly drawn to the foot of the page or the back of the book, and their mind driven into a different register of discourse.

Yet this method of presentation would have been reassuring for Darwin's contemporaries. It made plain to them the genre to which the poems belonged. A work in four cantos, each of some 500 lines liberally and learnedly annotated, was immediately recognisable as an English Georgic: a poem, that is, at once didactic and descriptive. The eighteenth century produced dozens of such works, and Linnaean taxonomy was quite as good a subject as cider-making or hairdressing or the solar system. Even in the 1780s, however, instructive verse was beginning to seem anachronistic, and the recognition that it was once hugely popular does little to dispel today's misgiving that it is a contradiction in terms.

A bigger anachronism in *The Loves of the Plants* was versification that out-Popes Pope. Since the success of *The Seasons*, many poets had abandoned the heroic couplet for blank verse, while those who kept it, such as Johnson and Goldsmith, gave it a weightier, more measured tread. Darwin in contrast gave it back the Popeian symmetry that Keats was to complain turned Pegasus into a rocking-horse: line balanced against line, half line against half line, stress against stress, all with the help of alliteration and chiasmus. In Pope's own poetry, the effect can be devastating, as in 'A fop their passion, but their prize a sot, / Alive, ridiculous, and dead, forgot'.[20] But Darwin, while he shared Pope's delight in all things small and delicate,

[18] The Scolar Press facsimile of *The Temple of Nature* has been reproduced in a very limited edition by the Erasmus Darwin Foundation, and there is a costly facsimile edition of *Collected Writings*, with an introduction by Martin Priestman (2004). Stuart Harris has edited the texts of Darwin's three major poems, without the annotations, under the title of *Cosmologia* (2002).

[19] The Internet has provided the answer. Martin Priestman's annotated edition of *The Temple of Nature* is now available on the *Romantic Circles* website, www.rc.umd.edu/editions/darwin_temple.

[20] 'Of the Characters of Women', lines 247–8.

could not respond to the underlying sadness with which the older poet contemplated their fragility. Far from having an annihilating effect, his own couplets bounce with exuberance, their rise-and-fall motion emphasised by a relentless play of epithets: there are ten in the six lines quoted above. Such a plethora of adjectives could be cloying, but Darwin manages to avoid this effect by reverting to another Popeian habit, that of starting a line with an active verb. This may have been an unconscious reaction from the task of translating 900 pages of verbless descriptive phrases; botanical Latin is mostly in the ablative case. Whatever its source, the habit gives his lines a liveliness missing from the substantive-heavy verse of some contemporaries. Anna Seward, herself a competent poet, drew attention to the force of Darwin's verbs and called the results 'spirited and energetic'.[21] But their effect, when combined with the strong antitheses of his couplets, can be near-manic and thoroughly disconcerting to the reader.

More disconcerting still, in the substance of the poem, is the manner in which Darwin presents his metamorphoses. In contrast to Ovid's step-by-step transformation of people into plants, the changes of plants into people are here *faits accomplis*. Promised visual delights – 'diverse little pictures'[22] – by the Proem, and with the brilliant botanical illustrations of the period in our mind, we begin to read *The Loves of the Plants* in the hope that *Canna indica* and the rest will appear in all their glory. After all, the work was to inspire Thornton's *The Temple of Flora*, reproductions from which are nearly as ubiquitous as Van Gogh's sunflowers. But before long we find ourselves asking: where have all the flowers gone? The dutiful student of Linnaeus soon discovers they are still there, but he or she has to work hard to transform a plant such as the canna back from its human metamorphosis. 'Erect to heaven', Darwin begins, with the *Genera* open on his desk. Linnaeus uses *erecta* three times in as many lines in his description of the canna flower; only one petal curls backwards, *reflexa*, or as Darwin puts it, like a 'lofty brow'. This first metamorphosis in the poem is by no means the most arcane. Linnaeus's *Curcuma* (turmeric), for example, has a flower in which the fragile style is supported between the two anthers of the only stamen ('*Stylus longitudine stamen*'), its stigma drooping forward towards four staminodes which are without anthers ('*quatuor* erecta, lineraria, sterilia'):[23] a configuration which Darwin translates into a four-line story of the frigid flirt:

> Wooed with long care, CURCUMA, cold and shy,
> Meets her fond husband with averted eye:

---

[21] *Memoirs*, p. 181. [22] *Loves of the Plants*, p. xvi, 1799 edition. [23] *Genera plantarum* (1754), p. 1.

> *Four* beardless youths the obdurate beauty move
> With soft attentions of Platonic love. (lines 65–8)

The *Genera plantarum* is as usual at Darwin's elbow, but the exactness suggests he has seen the flower for himself, perhaps in the greenhouse of Sir Brooke Boothby who was a keen plantsman: the lines have the air of an in-joke between two of the three members of the Lichfield Botanical Society. How on earth can we – for whom turmeric is primarily an ingredient of curry – be expected to know all this? Yet such was the enthusiasm for Linnaeus that the eighteenth-century reader apparently was expected to seize the point of even the most fantastical metamorphoses: *Cannabis* wielding her distaff (twining up a pole) as she half heeds the courtship of five swains; *Dipsaca* (teasel) accepting water in silver goblets – the rain-reserve at the base of the leaves – from four sylvan youths; five rival suitors of *Lonicera*, or honeysuckle, covetously eyeing her nectar-filled horns of plenty.

Even in the Linnaean heyday, there must have been readers who did not grasp these niceties, and for them Darwin provided the relief of extended similes. Some of these have a rococo charm, as when the opening wood anemone is presented both as the society beauty casting aside the calash protecting her elaborate coiffure and as the landau with its hood lowered so that the beaux and belles may bowl through the park in the spring sunshine. Others again introduce mythological figures of Angela Kaufmann-like elegance, as when bladderwrack, drifting with the tide, conjures up a vision of Galatea steering her dolphins over the waves. But in the end the similes only add to the roller-coaster effect. Darwin held that similes ought not to 'go upon all fours'[24] with the exactitude of a scientific analogy. His own are liable to hop wildly on one foot, as when the change from white to green in the colour of hellebores (Christmas roses) brings to his mind the fate of Nebuchadnezzar – a digression that inspired one of Blake's greatest colour-prints.[25] Time and again incongruity is used as a poetic shock-tactic. Untrue to her benign name of balsam, *Impatiens* is metamorphosed into Medea as, with the aid of an explosive form of seed dispersal, she 'hurls her infants from her frantic arms' (III, line 134), while all the agreeable associations of 'the gentle Cyclamen' (III, line 381) are

---

[24] *Loves of the Plants*, Interlude II.
[25] Blake's immediate response to *The Loves of the Plants* is shown in the frontispiece to *The Book of Thel*, a work that, in that its theme is the adolescent's discovery of the facts of life, may owe something to Darwin's poem. The 'bed of crimson joy' in *Songs of Experience* (1793) is Darwinian, and the same year a preliminary drawing of Nebuchadnezzar figured in *The Marriage of Heaven and Hell*. David V. Erdman's annotations to *The Illuminated Blake* (1975) call attention to many other visual echoes. Blake engraved six of the plates for *The Botanic Garden*.

swept aside for a grim account, based upon Defoe, of a mother burying her children in time of plague – the pretext being that the plant appears virtually to thrust its fruits (containing the seeds) into the ground.

What heightens the reader's sense of being taken for a very bumpy ride is the further insecurity engendered by Darwin's tone. There are hints from those who knew him that they were never sure quite where they were with him. Two generations of Romantics were taken for a ride by his account of the death-dealing Upas Tree, though Anna Seward always knew this to be a joke. Religious credulity is a favourite target. The alleged power of *Cocculus*, the Indian berry, to intoxicate fish offers the chance to present the fishy congregation addressed by St Anthony of Padua as the writhing congregation, 'inebriate with their zeal' (II, line 264) of a Methodist preacher, while travellers' tales (since discounted) of a salt-bearing basil in the Andes prompt a description of the emotions felt by Lot, and even more remarkably by Lot's wife, as he 'strained the briny column to his breast' (IV, line 270).

A near-parodic style, fantastic transformations, far-fetched similes, and the suspicion that the poet is having us on: all combine to disconcert today's readers of *The Loves of the Plants*. It is tempting to explain this uneasiness as the disorientation to which we are liable whenever we retreat across the time-threshold of our modern sensibility. Darwin died at the opening of the nineteenth century: at the time, that is, when poets began to take off their neckties. To step back from *Lyrical Ballads* into the poetry of the 1780s is to find ourselves in an overdressed, bewigged world; just how alien its conventions are can be brought home by the shock of recognition we feel at Reynolds's great portrait of Johnson *en déshabille*. But the realisation that, whenever we laugh at what strikes us as Darwin's man-nered ineptitude, he may already have had the first laugh, encourages us to seek another explanation. Is he in fact a Modernist before his time, exploiting the possibilities of the absurd? And were not the bright young critics of the 1920s insensitive to the irony they elsewhere valued so highly when they pilloried such a delicious line as 'Unknown to sex the pregnant oyster swells'?

The pregnant oyster, however, is from a later and more accessible poem.[26] *The Loves of the Plants* remains a bewildering experience for the reader, and I would suggest that the cause of our discomfort is not so much that Darwin is a poet behind or ahead of his time, as that he is himself discomforted at finding himself a poet at all. In his mid-fifties he had

---

[26] *The Temple of Nature* (1803), canto II, line 89.

somehow become – since there is no reason to doubt that he would have preferred to leave the versifying to Anna Seward – a poet by default. Like any educated man of his epoch, he had always been able to turn out competent occasional verse. But at heart he mistrusted poetry. This was in part the natural philosopher's mistrust of the imagination, all the more severe in Darwin's case because his own imagination was so liable to bolt, and in part a Gradgrind-like suspicion, such as he may have gained from his association with the most powerful industrialists of his time, of everything that was not hard fact. He did not breathe a word about *The Loves of the Plants* to Matthew Boulton, his closest friend in the Birmingham circle, until he could write to tell him that 'an idle book' he had written 'sells so well as to pay me'.[27] He then goes on to request facts about Boulton's minting machine for inclusion in the sequel, as if to reassure his friend that this time he will be dealing with life's realities. And in its turn this concern with fact points to another cause for the misgivings that can be sensed beneath his first major poem.

Darwin's enthusiasm for Linnaeus was beginning to erode as he realised that the so-called sexual system had virtually nothing to do with sex as the means of reproduction. 'Systematics', complains a contributor to *Nature*, 'is deeply unsexy':[28] and this was basically true even of a classificatory system founded on the number and position of the reproductive organs in flowering plants. As generations of botanists have pointed out, the number of stamens and pistils in a flower has no bearing on its ability to fertilise; a canna with half an anther is as well able to set seed as a poppy, though not as prolifically. In face of this, the process of inventing fresh dramatic situations for Tetrandria, Pentandria, Hexandria *et al.* became meaningless as well as monotonous. Furthermore, in all these classes the most common order was Monogynia, or one-styled – which created difficulties in the way of Darwin's wish to avoid 'any indecent idea'. Even if he limited his fables to drawing-room intrigues as a way of circumventing thoughts of polyandry and group sex, he was up against the convention that no nice young woman kept five or more suitors in tow.[29] It is an obstacle that he gets round, in part, by inventing scenarios in which sex has no role. Thus, in a set piece of rococo orientalism, the sunflower's disk of florets is transformed into a throng of sun-worshippers

---

[27] *Letters*, p. 193.   [28] Simon Conway Morris in *Nature* 346 (1990), p. 213.
[29] In 'Botany for gentlemen: Erasmus Darwin and *The Loves of the Plants*', *Isis* 80 (1989), pp. 593–621, Janet Browne associates Darwin's metamorphoses of various flowers with the gender relations of the time.

made up of groups of five dervishes, each group whirling around a branched style:

> GREAT HELIANTHUS guides o'er twilight plains
> In gay solemnity his dervish-trains;
> Marshalled in *fives* each gaudy band proceeds,
> Each gaudy band a plumèd lady leads;
> With zealous step he climbs the upland lawn,
> And bows in homage to the rising dawn;
> Imbibes with eagle eye the golden ray,
> And watches, as it moves, the orb of day.   (I, lines 221–8)

At the end of what struck William Cowper, even in a favourable review, as 'a long succession'[30] of forty such descriptions Darwin, in his second and third cantos, sought another kind of relief from his Linnaean task by building brief fables round aspects of plant life other than floral structure: first, the benefit to mankind of cotton, papyrus, quinine and the like, and then the threats posed by noxious plants. The former gave him the chance to enthuse, in epic-style similes, over the no less beneficial (as he saw them) technical inventions of the age, and the latter fed the appetite for exotica aroused by the plant-hunting expeditions of Linnaeus's pupils. But while Darwin is in his element celebrating the thistledown flight of the Montgolfiers' balloon or the wonders of Arkwright's spinning jenny, he is not very good at Gothic horrors, and the reader who has succumbed, in the first canto, to the odd fascination of his Linnaean descriptions is glad when he reverts to them in the last canto. Here he copes ingeniously even with the category of Icosandria Monogynia, or *twenty* males to one female. 'Refulgent Cerea', the night-blowing *Cereus*, ignores this crowd of suitors, and so does Darwin by focusing upon the great circle of golden petals which are variously her 'pencilled brows' and 'shadowy hairs' as he relates how she breathes her virgin vows to the night air (IV, 13–32): lines that inspired one of the most haunting plates in *The Temple of Flora*.

For all this resourcefulness, *The Loves of the Plants* remains a curiosity. Darwin in this first poem could surmount neither what he had begun to realise was the unsatisfactory nature of his subject, nor his own mistrust of poetry. But with botanomania now at its height, the Town loved it. One good result of this success was that Darwin, while still guarding his anonymity, stopped posing at being a poet, as he had hitherto rather self-mockingly done even in the critical prose interludes between the cantos of his first work, and began to take seriously the poet's craft and calling;

---

[30] *The Analytic Review* 4 (1789), p. 30.

seriously enough, that is, to embark on a second four-canto poem that covered, along with other scientific interests of the time, aspects of botany he found much more appealing than taxonomy. *The Economy of Vegetation*, as it was rather forbiddingly titled, is a shapely and confident work and it rightfully took precedence over *The Loves of the Plants* when both poems appeared together early in 1792 (though dated 1791) as *The Botanic Garden*.

3

That the first part of *The Botanic Garden* is a much better poem than the second is due to factors beside the self-confidence fame brought to its author. Classical mythology is handled quite differently in the two works. In *The Loves of the Plants* it is prettily decorative. Darwin assumed that readers who had had the classical education of the time would expect that sort of thing; they took sugar, so he spooned it out. But it would seem that between the completion of his first long poem and the publication of his second he discovered what was, for him, a much more meaningful approach to mythology in the pages of Bacon's *Instauratio magna* and in a recent work which was by way of being *The Golden Bough* of the period: Jacob Bryant's *New System of Mythology* (1774). Bacon and Bryant together instilled in Darwin (as he explains in a prefatory 'Apology') the belief that

The Egyptians were possessed of many discoveries in [natural] philosophy and chemistry before the invention of letters; these were then expressed in hieroglyphic paintings of men and animals; which after the discovery of the alphabet were described and animated by the poets, and became first the deities of Egypt, and afterwards of Greece and Rome. (p. xviii, 1799 edition)

A second factor, and one which helped even more to tighten Darwin's hold on reality in his second work, was his shift in interest from Linnaean taxonomy to something closer to what we would today understand as 'botany'.

The shift can be seen taking place in 1782, in the course of a correspondence with Banks. Darwin has been reading Malpighi, Grew and Hales – three pioneer investigators into plant physiology in the early days of the scientific revolution – and has been conducting experiments of his own into the transport system of plants, even if in the end he has had to return to 'perhaps more important, though less ingenious occupations'[31] – by which he means plodding a translator's path through Linnaeus's bulky

---

[31] *Letters*, p. 123.

classificatory volumes. For Linnaeus himself, there was no 'perhaps' about it: only those 'who can affix similar names to similar vegetables, and different names to different vegetables'[32] deserved the name of botanist. The rest – and he specifically names Malpighi, Grew and Hales – were only 'lovers of botany':[33] dabbling amateurs. Darwin, however, was beginning to realise that the living bodies of plants were as interesting, and almost as complex, as those of his patients, and the notes to both parts of *The Botanic Garden*, together with a very substantial book on plant physiology, *Phytologia*, published in 1800, show how completely he immersed himself in the subject. Hardly any botanical publication of the age, at home or abroad, escaped his notice. Nor was he content with reading. *Phytologia*'s sub-title, *The Philosophy of Gardening and Agriculture*, places him firmly in the practical, utilitarian tradition of the Royal Society. He assiduously observed and experimented, and though the claims of scientific break-throughs that have been made on his behalf do not always stand up to scrutiny, he nevertheless was at the cutting edge of one set of investigations which led to the time's most important discovery about plant life.

That discovery began in 1771, with a sprig of mint. Joseph Priestley, who was to become the leading light of the Lunar Society, placed the sprig in a sealed container, expecting that, like a candle flame or breathing mouse, it would 'vitiate' the air and die. Instead, it flourished and grew. He then tried the mint in air that had already been 'vitiated': ten days later the air in the container was sufficiently 'pure' to keep a mouse alive or a candle burning. When Priestley published his accounts of these and many other experiments involving gases, the President of the Royal Society, with striking percipience, seized upon the implications of the discovery that plants effect a gas exchange that is the reverse of respiration:

In this the fragrant rose and deadly nightshade cooperate: nor is the herbage, nor the woods that flourish in the most remote and unpeopled regions, unprofitable to us, nor we to them; considering how constantly the winds convey to them our vitiated air, for our relief, and their nourishment.[34]

These very modern-sounding words – they could be a plea for the rain forests – were quoted by Jan Ingenhouz in 1779 when he reported on further investigations which showed that oxygen was given off only from the green parts of plants, and only in sunlight – soon (1782) to be followed by Jean Senebier who demonstrated that this evolution of oxygen by green

---

[32] *The Families of Plants*, p. lx.

[33] Hugh Rose, *The Elements of Botany . . . being a Translation of the* Philosophia Botanica (1775), p. 16.

[34] Sir John Pringle, *A Discourse on the Different Kinds of Air* (1774), p. 27.

plants in light depended on carbon dioxide being present. Photosynthesis, as we now call it, had been identified.[35]

Darwin closely followed this development in plant physiology as well as the revolutionary changes in chemical thinking that took place mainly in France in the 1780s. When in the third canto of *The Economy of Vegetation* the Goddess of Botany speaks of the Nymphs, or spirits of water, effecting a union of 'pure air' with 'flaming gas' (line 204) a footnote translates this into Lavoisier's new terms as the formation of water from oxygen and hydrogen, and goes on to state that this recognition that water is a combination of two elements affords a basis for the theory that, 'by the assistance of light', water is split back again in the photosynthetic process. In its turn this light reaction of photosynthesis is presented in the next canto as the marriage of Cupid and Psyche:

> SYLPHS! From each sun-bright leaf, that twinkling shakes
> O'er Earth's green lap, or shoots amid her lakes,
> Your playful band with simpering lips invite,
> And wed the enamoured OXYGEN to LIGHT.
> Round their white necks with fingers interwove,
> Cling the fond pair with unabating love;
> Hand linked in hand, on buoyant step they rise,
> And soar and glisten in unclouded skies.
> Whence in bright floods the VITAL AIR expands,
> And with concentric spheres involves the lands;
> Pervades the swarming seas, and heaving earths,
> Where teeming Nature broods her myriad births;
> Fills the fine lungs of all that *breathe* or *bud*,
> Warms the new heart, and dyes the gushing blood;
> With life's first spark inspires the organic frame,
> And, as it wastes, renews the subtle flame.   (IV, lines 31–46)

Like Anna Seward we could do without the simpering sylphs, while the embracing Cupid and Psyche are lay figures: a footnote shows them to be from an illustration to Joseph Spence's *Polymetis* that is known to have been the model for one of 'Tassie's gems'. Keats's Cupid and Psyche also, of course, owe much to popular works of reference and replica *objets d'art*. But Keats was in love with the myth, Darwin with the chemical facts that he believed the myth to represent. True to his Baconian theory of legend, he has to get behind the personifications before, in the rest of the passage,

---

[35] The history of the discovery of photosynthesis is very clearly told by A. G. Morton in *History of Botanical Science* (1981), pp. 328–42.

the facts took on a vitality of rhythm and expression born of the excitement he felt as a natural philosopher.

Eloquent though they are, the last eight lines concern themselves with only half of the process of photosynthesis; with the light reaction, or splitting of water, but not with the so-called dark reaction, the production of sugar from the remaining hydrogen and from carbon dioxide. Darwin's footnotes here and elsewhere in the poem show, however, that he understands the process to be in two parts and an additional note to the next canto sums up the full significance of the Priestley–Ingenhouz–Senebier discoveries: 'it would seem that the sugar-making process carried on in vegetable vessels was the great source of life to all organised beings'.[36] There was, however, another discovery to be made. In 1797 (and so ahead of Darwin's *Phytologia*) Nicolas de Saussure published in *Annales de Chimie* his preliminary findings on photosynthesis. These showed that fixed carbon appeared in the leaf simultaneously with the disappearance of carbon *from the surrounding atmosphere* and its replacement by oxygen, and thus validated Hales's demonstration, made seventy years previously, that water and air could of themselves make a plant grow. A number of passages in *Phytologia* in which Darwin disassociates himself from this view reveal that de Saussure's conclusions were more than he could swallow. Even if leaves could take in some carbon from the atmosphere, 'carbonic gas in its fluid state, or dissolved in water, not in its aerial or gaseous state, is the principal food of plants' (175); he believed that the bulk of a plant's carbon content came as a solute in water from its root, and was ultimately derived from decaying matter in the soil.

That Darwin should have had difficulty with the photosynthetic equation is not surprising. It has taken many generations for gardeners to accept that manure and compost do not produce potatoes in the way that everything Miss T. eats turns into Miss T. But Darwin's scepticism, though too late to affect his poetry, is of interest to us here because it arises from the great underlying – and undermining – fallacy of eighteenth-century thinking about the natural world: the belief, as he repeatedly phrases it, that 'vegetables are an inferior order of animals'. He wrote *Phytologia*, he tells Banks, because he wanted to see if plant physiology could be brought to anything like science 'or be compared with that of animals' – for, he explains in his next letter, botany has not 'hitherto been under the attention of anyone perfectly acquainted with the animal economy'.[37] A plant, he

---

[36] *The Economy of Vegetation*, note xxxix (p. 470 of the 1799 edition); repeated verbatim in *The Temple of Nature*, p. 134.
[37] *Letters*, pp. 122 and 123.

believed, performed all the functions of an animal though in a more rudimentary manner as befitted its lower place on the scale of nature. It therefore had a circulatory system, in which he believed leaves acted in the role of lungs, and he must have been pleased by de Saussure's emphasis on respiration – a vital process going on at all times and in all parts of the plant, though masked in daylight by photosynthesis – as being of equal importance to animals and plants, even though he could not go all the way with him in his demonstration that plants built their food from inorganic matter. And if de Saussure's photosynthetic experiments had undermined the analogy between plants and animals, the arrival from the New World of several hitherto unknown plants was strengthening the belief that, within the limits imposed by their being rooted in the ground, plants shared to a remarkable degree another animal faculty: the power of movement.

All visible plant activity fascinated Darwin, whether it was growth-movement like the spiralling of climbers, or repeatable and reversible change such as the 'sleep' of flowers that close their petals at night. But it was 'vegetable spontaneity', sudden movement, that struck him as sure proof of plant animality. European botanists had known for 200 years about the touchiness of the sensitive plant, *Mimosa pudica*. In the previous century, Locke, Ray and a panel of the Royal Society (acting on Charles II's directive) had all explained it in mechanistic terms, although other natural philosophers such as Sir Thomas Browne and Henry Power were ready to believe that the plant had actual feelings. Darwin's first use of the sensitive plant, in *The Loves of the Plants*, shows him poised between these views. In the poem itself the shrinking of its leaves is likened, as if in accordance with Locke's phrase, 'all bare mechanism',[38] to the motions of inorganic matter – mercury in a thermometer, the steel needle of a compass:

> So sinks or rises with the changeful hour
> The liquid silver in its glassy tower.
> So turns the needle to the pole it loves,
> With fine librations quivering, as it moves.   (I, lines 311–14)

In a footnote, however, Darwin insists that *naturalists* have not yet discovered why the leaves collapse when touched. Himself a naturalist, he goes on to submit the plant to much prodding, and asks if the consequent

---

[38] Quoted by Robert M. Manquis, 'The puzzling *Mimosa*: sensitivity and plant symbolism in Romanticism', *Studies in Romanticism* 8 (1969) pp. 129–55, 137. See also Charles Webster, 'The recognition of plant sensitivity by English botanists of the seventeenth century', *Isis* 57 (1966), pp. 5–23.

reactions may not 'be owing to a numbness or paralysis consequent to too violent irritation, like the faintings of animals from pain or fatigue?' And by the time he writes the notes to *The Economy of Vegetation* he is ready to attribute all plant movements to an animal-like sensibility. 'This action of opening and closing the leaves or flowers does not appear to be produced simply by irritation on the muscles themselves, but by the connection of those muscles with a sensitive sensorium or brain existing in each individual bud or flower' (note to III, line 460).

This was a startling conclusion, though by the late eighteenth century the sensitive plant, which Darwin here goes on to instance, had rather lost its power to startle. He had found more arresting examples of observable movement in the plant world. A member of the pea family, called *Hedysarum girans* when it was first described in 1784, but to be labelled '*Desmodium girans* –Telegraph Plant' in Victorian greenhouses, has at the base of each leaf two small leaves (stipules) which rotate like semaphore arms. Modern botanists have given the plant yet another name, *Codariocalyx motorius*, but they still cannot explain its behaviour. Darwin's belief was that the plant has found a way of fanning itself in the killing dry winds that seasonally afflict the tropics. In the fable he invents for it in *The Loves of the Plants*, '*Ten* brother youths' (the flower is ten-stamened) 'with light umbrellas shade, / Or fan with busy hands the panting maid' (IV, lines 337–8). As even the fastest rotation takes about ninety seconds, this explanation will scarcely do. But then Darwin had not seen the plant for himself, in the way that he had seen and experimented upon other plants whose leaf movements are a good deal more rapid because their function is to trap insects. The native sundew, *Drosera*, was an obvious example. Yet though it shines forth from *The Loves of the Plants* as a queen of the marsh arrayed in glossy silk and diamonds, its fly-trapping powers get only a passing mention in a footnote. Erasmus Darwin's real star was a recent arrival from America: the Venus flytrap.

When, in 1770, John Ellis FRS described this newly discovered curiosity, of which each leaf was 'a miniature figure of a rat-trap', he foretold that it was 'likely to become an inhabitant of the curious gardens in this country'.[39] It was certainly in Sir Brooke Boothby's greenhouse by August 1788, when Darwin got his first chance to tease its leaves into the instantaneous movement he interpreted as 'a wonderful contrivance to prevent the depredations of insects'.[40] For all his pioneer insistence on the importance

---

[39] 'A botanical description of the *Dionaea muscipula*' appended to *Directions for Bringing Over Seeds and Plants* (1770).
[40] *Loves of the Plants*, note to canto I, line 139.

of nitrogen to plants, he failed to realise that the Venus flytrap extracted nutrients from its victims. But the mistake was understandable; only six weeks earlier and in another garden, that of his brother Robert, he had been shown an equally ferocious plant which was not a carnivore. *Apocynum androsaemifolium*, a kind of dogbane, has the unpleasant habit of seizing insects by the proboscis, so that many of them die and fall to the ground. At least Erasmus Darwin's belief that the plant was slaying its natural enemies gave him a satisfaction denied to the Victorian naturalist who wrote despairingly: 'our ignorance favours the idea of a wanton cruelty in the herb'.[41] Dogbane, like the Venus flytrap, is given the distinction of an engraved plate in *The Loves of the Plants*. What Darwin must have found particularly striking was that it trapped insects by a sudden movement, not of its leaves, but of its ring of joined anthers. Its flowers were thus among many others that were distinguished by movements of their sexual parts and which therefore had a special interest for him when he considered a third aspect of plant physiology: reproduction.

Fertilisation itself was to remain a mystery until well into the next century, and although Darwin struggles to give an account of it in *Phytologia*, his animal analogies were of little help as long as animal generation was itself the subject of wild and conflicting theories. But pollination, the beginning of the process, was open to observation. Darwin noticed, for example, that the stamens of grass-of-parnassus bend each in turn over the stigma, explaining in a footnote that 'the vegetable passion of love is agreeably seen in the flower of the parnassia, in which the males alternately approach and recede from the female'.[42] And so they do, as they are described in the standard modern work on pollination, *The Pollination of Flowers* (1973), by Michael Proctor and Peter Yeo:

the filaments are at first very short, but one soon elongates and becomes bent over the top of the ovary, so that its anther, which then dehisces, is directly in the centre of the flower; after about a day the first stamen bends outwards and another takes its place, and so on. (p. 57)

The observations, nearly two centuries apart, are the same, the conclusions completely different. For Darwin, the purpose of *Parnassia*'s slow-motion ballet is that the stamens may deposit their pollen on the stigma beneath; Proctor and Yeo, however, know it to be the flower's device for getting its

---

[41] Quoted by Paul Simmons, *The Action Plant: Movement and Nervous Behaviour in Plants* (1992), p. 42. It is now thought that the flower seeks only to detain the larger insects, for pollination, and that the fate of the smaller ones is collateral damage.

[42] *Economy of Vegetation*, note to canto IV, line 472.

pollen onto the bodies of several insects before its own stigma becomes receptive. In brief, what Darwin explains as a device for self-pollination turns out to be a method of ensuring cross-pollination. This happens again and again. What Darwin describes as the 'wonderful contrivance' of a broom flower's keel breaking open in order that the style may curl round among the stamens 'like a French horn',[43] is now known to be the explosively sudden result of a bee's landing, whereby pollen is scattered over both sides of its body but the flower's stigma is at the same time protected from self-pollination. No less wonderful to Darwin was the 'irritability' of the chicory floret: 'if the top of the floret be touched, all the filaments which support the cylindrical anther will contract themselves, and . . . by thus raising or depressing the anther the whole of the prolific dust is collected on the stigma'.[44] This is faithfully observed: but today we know that the stigma is not yet receptive, and that this squeezing out of the pollen like toothpaste from a tube occurs in response to the repeated pressure of a series of insect visitors which will transfer the pollen piecemeal to receptive stigmas on other plants.[45]

With the advantage of hindsight, the modern reader is tempted to feel that Darwin had a genius for drawing wrong conclusions.[46] In this matter of pollination he could, after all, have known better. The interdependence of plants and insects was beginning to be understood by the 1780s, when Cowper wrote his mock-Georgic account of the cultivation of cucumbers:

> These have their sexes; and when summer shines
> The bee transports the fertilising meal
> From flower to flower, and e'en the breathing air
> Wafts the rich prize to its appointed use.
> Not so when Winter scowls. Assistant Art
> Then acts in Nature's office, brings to pass
> The glad espousals, and insures the crop.[47]

Darwin too grew cucumbers and melons under glass, and he would appear to be remembering Cowper's lines when, in *Phytologia*, he breaks into verse to describe their cultivation. But for him it is the absence of wind, not of insects, that necessitates human intervention: a reasonable assumption to

---

[43] *Loves of the Plants*, note to canto I, line 57.   [44] *Ibid.*, note to canto I, line 97.

[45] Two-thirds of plants of the Asteraceae family so far tested are known to have this mechanism. Darwin learnt of it from Giambattista dal Covolo's *A Discourse concerning the Irritability of some Flowers*, translated by Benjamin Stillingfleet (c.1767).

[46] An example would be his topsy-turvy notion (*The Economy of Vegetation*, additional note xxxix) that the hydrogen isolated from water in photosynthesis turns leaves and stems green.

[47] *The Task* (1785), book III, lines 537–60.

make about single-sex plants. Yet already in his lifetime there was some awareness of the cross-pollination of bisexual flowers. The Royal Society's *Transactions*, which he read assiduously, contained an account of observations made in 1750 in Irish meadows and gardens, which convinced Arthur Dobbs that 'Providence has appointed the bee to be very instrumental in promoting the increase of vegetables'.[48] We also know from *Phytologia* that Darwin was familiar, as hardly anyone else in England seems to have been, with the publications of Josef Kohlreuter, whose day-long observations of single flowers (admired and imitated by Charles Darwin) revealed that many bisexual plants could be pollinated by insects. Some of the records of stamen movements in *The Botanic Garden* may have originated with Kohlreuter, who even noticed that anthers and stigmas could mature at different times – though he never got as far as to conclude that this was a way of ensuring cross-pollination. Darwin himself remained far from such a conclusion; so committed was he to the Linnaean concept of the flower as a marriage bed that he interpreted pistil movements away from the stamens in *Collinsonia* (the American richweed) as 'manifest adultery'.[49]

This resistance to a growing body of evidence is hardly surprising if we glance at the later fortune of what is now known as floral biology. Karl Sprengel's exquisitely illustrated, but never translated, study of pollination by insects, *Das entdeckte Geheimniss der Natur im Bau und in der Befruchtung der Blumen* (1793), appeared to those who could read it to substitute contrivances such as nectar-guide markings, which did not appear necessary let alone wonderful, for the elegant simplicity of self-pollination. Why fly in the fertilising dust by insect transport, when it lay to hand? Sprengel's book was forgotten for seventy years, until Charles Darwin rediscovered it and took it as the starting point for his own enquiries into plant fertilisation. And even Charles Darwin could not explain why there were orchids that looked exactly like insects, once his grandfather's explanation – that the flower's shape was a way to warn off insects, by deceiving them into supposing that they were forestalled – could no longer be entertained. Another lifetime had to pass before the hardly conceivable true answer could be found, namely, that the flowers were inviting male insects to attempt copulation.[50] Back in the lifetime of Erasmus Darwin, the notion that insects were necessary to the fertilisation of most flowers must have

---

[48] Quoted by Proctor and Yeo, *The Pollination of Flowers* (1973), p. 24.
[49] *Economy of Vegetation*, note to canto IV, line 472.
[50] Strangely the bee orchid, *Ophrys apifera*, is self-fertilised in Britain, although since Charles Darwin's time some evidence of its being pollinated by bees has been found in Mediterranean countries.

seemed no less fantastic. Nor could the 'mechanistic' explanation that *Parnassia*'s stamens were one by one positioned in order to facilitate insect pollination have occurred to anyone who believed that a plant was a sentient being, subject to 'a vegetable passion of love'. And there were many besides Darwin who did so believe. Wordsworth's faith that every flower enjoys the air it breathes takes on a startling literalism when placed in a contemporary context of pamphlets and scientific papers battling out the question of plant sensibility.[51]

To sum up: Erasmus Darwin's wish to see if the study of the growing plant, as distinct from the Linnaeans' dissection of the plucked flower, could be brought to 'anything like science' alerted him to the importance of the photosynthetic theory, although his belief in vegetable circulation, with the leaves in the role of lungs, kept him from a full understanding of the process. It led him to explore many plant movements, only to find in them indications that plants must have undetected nerves and muscles. And when it caused him to explore plants' means of reproduction, he found ample evidence of 'the sensation of love'. In modern eyes there is *nothing* like science in these repeated appeals to the plant–animal analogies which Philip Ritterbush has shown to be the *ignis fatuus* that led astray scores of eighteenth-century naturalists. Darwin's arguments from analogy certainly marginalise him in the history of scientific discovery, and it is easy to dismiss them as an illusion of his age. But before so doing, two qualifications have to be made. The first is that even a demoded and discredited habit of thought like the argument from analogy can – when it provides hypothesis rather than premise – lead to the discovery of new truths. As it happens, one of the best examples of this involves the Venus flytrap – and the more famous Darwin.

Charles Darwin, who was fascinated by carnivorous plants – in 1860 he told a correspondent that currently he cared more for *Drosera* 'than the origin of all the species in the world'[52] – speculated that the Venus flytrap's rapid seizure of its insect prey was due to an electrical impulse, similar to the nervous response of an animal. He asked a medical friend, Sir John Burdon-Sandison, to test this idea in the laboratory at Kew. Burdon-Sandison's equipment soon registered what we would now call an action potential, and he was able to tell Charles Darwin that 'the analogy which

---

[51] The controversy is documented by Maniquis in 'The puzzling *Mimosa*'; Philip Ritterbush, *Overtures to Biology: The Speculations of Eighteenth-century Naturalists* (1964), pp. 141–57; François Delaporte, *Le Second Règne de la nature* (1979), *passim*.

[52] *Correspondence*, vol. VIII, p. 491.

had suggested the discovery was a true one'.[53] But when he published his findings, the botanical establishment rejected them with disdain. In its eyes, animal–plant analogies could only belong to the benighted eighteenth century. This certainty that a plant, having no nervous system, could not transmit electrical impulses, was of course every bit as *a priori* a position as the previous age's conviction that a plant which was able to move like an animal must have nerves like an animal. But not until 1965 – incidentally, a year after the publication of Ritterbush's study of the presuppositions impeding eighteenth-century biology – was it conclusively shown that the trigger hairs on the leaves of the Venus flytrap respond to touch with an action potential that results in a rapid closure of the leaf. Since then, similar reactions have been found in a considerable number of species. Plants, at their own pace, *can* sometimes behave like animals.

My second defence of Darwin's notion that a plant was a failed animal is that, however erroneous it may be in itself, the reason he so readily embraces it is that it corresponds to an underlying cast of mind which is the source of his most effective poetry. The breath-taking splendours of the geocentric universe in *Paradise Lost* offer a parallel: Milton could have got his astronomy right, but his humanism directed him otherwise. Darwin's imagination too has a driving force, which can be felt in *The Botanic Garden*, even when his delight in the form of flowers is submerged in Linnaean taxonomy and his awareness of the life processes of the whole plant is trammelled by the plant–animal analogy. The nature of that force is most palpable in the poetry to which I now turn: the closing sections of *The Economy of Vegetation* and Darwin's last poem, *The Temple of Nature*.

4

Like his more famous grandson, Erasmus Darwin possessed to a high degree the way of looking at the world that I have already, appropriating a term used by Barbara McClintock, called a feeling for the organism:[54] the ability, that is, to affiliate to the individual of another species, whether plant or animal, by recognising its power, both in the form it takes and in the ways it interacts with its surroundings, to promote, sustain and transfer its life-identity. On occasion this empathy may embrace much more than individual existences. Then life is felt to delight in life in all its fecund complexity: the plenitude of a tangled bank, or of a hedge beside a tropical

---

[53] Quoted by Simmons, *The Action Plant*, p. 79.
[54] See Evelyn Fox Keller, *A Feeling for the Organism: the Life and Work of Barbara McClintock* (1983).

airport; or, for Erasmus Darwin, of the entire biosphere, as we now call the thin wrapping of Planet Earth within which life is sustainable:

> Life *buds* or *breathes* from Indus to the Poles,
> And the vast surface kindles, as it rolls!

In the final canto of *The Economy of Vegetation*, from which these lines are taken (419–20) the same biophilic fervour is to be felt in the Botanic Goddess's command to the aerial spirits to 'brood the green children of parturient spring' (line 364) with the warmth that will cause germination:

> Lo! on each seed within its slender rind
> Life's golden threads in endless circles wind;
> Maze within maze the lucid webs are rolled,
> And, as they burst, the living flame unfold.
> The pulpy acorn, ere it swells, contains
> The oak's vast branches in its milky veins;
> Each ravelled bud, fine film, and fibre-line
> Traced with nice pencil on the small design.
> The young narcissus, in its bulb compressed,
> Cradles a second nestling on its breast,
> In whose fine arms a younger embryon lies,
> Folds its thin leaves, and shuts its floret-eyes;
> Grain within grain successive harvests dwell,
> And boundless forests slumber in a shell.   (lines 393–406)

Diverted by the foreshadowing of the double helix in 'Life's golden threads in endless circles wind', we belatedly discover the passage to be riddled with the eighteenth-century fallacy of preformationism (familiar to all readers of *Tristram Shandy*) – only to realise the next instant that this makes no difference to the vigour of the verse nor to the tenderness of observation in the lines about the narcissus's 'nestling'. Darwin's empathic response to the seed as life-in-waiting, irrespective of whether that life is already minutely preformed or will be shaped anew in each generation, leads him to a close of expansive calm in a couplet, at once succinct and stately, that rivals Pope at his best. And in the next paragraph the seedling's growth, speeded up to a time-lapse effect by the run of imperatives, is nowise decelerated by the thoughts that pith is *not* a growing tissue, and that sap does *not* circulate like blood. Once again it is Darwin's empathy with the living plant that here through the green fuse drives the flower and enables us to assimilate his 'golden quintessence of day' to our superior (but still incomplete) understanding of photosynthesis:

> Teach the fine seed, instinct with life, to shoot
> On Earth's cold bosom its descending root;

With pith elastic stretch its rising stem,
Part the twin lobes, expand the throbbing gem;
Clasp in your airy arms the aspiring plume,
Fan with your balmy breath its kindling bloom,
Each widening scale and bursting film unfold,
Swell the green cup, and tint the flower with gold;
While in bright veins the silvery sap ascends,
And refluent blood in milky eddies bends;
While, spread in air, the leaves respiring play,
Or drink the golden quintessence of day.   (lines 423–34)

So, up to and even including its final tableau of George III in Hygeia's shrine at Kew, *The Economy of Vegetation* celebrates what Darwin calls 'the bliss of being'.

His last and posthumous poem, *The Temple of Nature*, goes further: it celebrates the bliss of becoming. Like the two earlier works, it employs mythological 'machinery': Darwin's Muse penetrates the temple of Nature on the site of the original Garden of Eden, where Nature's Priestess, Urania, reveals to her the true, scientific meaning of the scenic representations on the temple walls. A footnote explains these as the originals of the Eleusinian Mysteries, in which a tableau of death is followed by depictions of the marriage of Cupid and Psyche, of a torchlight procession and, finally, of a series of heroic figures from remote times. Traditionally, these scenes were made to yield the Christian message of immortality's triumph over mortality. But Darwin boldly interprets them in terms of evolutionary biology as the story of life's ascent, in the course of the long eons revealed by James Hutton's study of rocks, from the first 'microscopic ens' to man as a reasoning and, ultimately, a moral and social being: Darwin's own title for the work was *The Origin of Society*.[55] Patently there is a link with Pope's *Essay on Man* and, like that work, the poem is dominated by the idea of the *scala naturae*. But now that ladder has become an upward-moving escalator:

> Organic life beneath the shoreless waves
> Was born and nursed in Ocean's pearly caves;
> First forms minute, unseen by spheric glass,
> Move on the mud, or pierce the watery mass;

---

[55] It began as *The Progress of Society*, of which drafts survive, but Darwin appears to have changed the scope of the poem (with much resultant confusion in its first 222 lines) from human history to evolution after reading Richard Payne Knight's *The Progress of Civil Society* (1796). See King-Hele, *Erasmus Darwin* (1999), pp. 346 and 354–5, and Martin Priestman, 'The progress of society? Darwin's early drafts for *The Temple of Nature*', in C. U. M. Smith and Robert Arnott (eds.), *The Genius of Erasmus Darwin* (2005). Priestman has edited the drafts on www.rc.umd.edu/editions/darwin_temple.

These, as successive generations bloom,
New powers acquire, and larger limbs assume;
Whence countless groups of vegetation spring
And breathing realms of fin, and feet, and wing. (I, lines 294–301)

   To anyone brought up, as Linnaeus's generation had been, to accept the
fixity of species, the ladder of creation presented itself as a sequence of
distinct entities, in which the hand of God had placed the most stone-
like plant a step above the most plant-like stone, while at the next join
(for this is a ladder in sections) animal-like plants took up their appointed
place below, but irremovably distinct from, plant-like animals. Even
after life-forms were conceived as capable of ascending the *scala naturae*,
the sense of linearity lingered on; later, it would fuel the Victorian obsession with missing links and colour the popular Darwinism of the early
twentieth century. It is to the earlier Darwin's credit as a thinker that
in his last poem he was able to break free, in a way very few of his
contemporaries managed to do, from the concept of life as a chain of
being and to conceive it, as the conclusion of the lines just quoted implies,
as a growing and branching tree. In the famous chapter on evolution
in *Zoonomia*, his treatise on animal physiology published in 1794, he
speculates on whether life has evolved from a single 'filament' or from
different plant and animal originals. By the time he writes *The Temple of
Nature* he appears (as the conclusion to the lines just quoted suggests) to have
decided in favour of an early division of the two kingdoms. Early forms of
maritime life are pictured as minuscule plants as well as minuscule animals,
and when life emerges onto land, there are 'amphibious' plants whose
submerged leaves differ from their aerial ones, just as there are 'amphibious'
invertebrates such as mosquitoes whose underwater larvae transform into
airborne throngs ready to dip their 'red trunks' into human blood-vessels.

   Old habits of thought die hard however, as is evidenced even in this last
and most adventurous work by Darwin's way of looking at one particular
plant that had already figured in his two earlier poems. *Vallisneria spiralis*,
or tape-grass, is an aquatic species that most of us are never likely to meet,
even though the heavily fuelled processes initiated by Darwin's friends have
caused it to naturalise in Midland waterways. But it is a favourite of
botanists because it affords a rare instance of water-pollination. Some of
its plants bear female flowers that rise to the surface on long spiralling
stems; on others, tiny male flowers break free, drift to the surface and, with
luck, topple into the surface depression made by a female flower. In *The
Loves of the Plants*, *Vallisneria* is metamorphosed, not very aptly, into a
woman wailing for her errant lover, but a footnote likens its pollination,

much more aptly, to the nuptial flight of ants and other insects. This is one of the happier of Darwin's plant–animal analogies, and he repeats it in *Phytologia*. But when *Vallisneria* crops up again, in an additional note to *The Economy of Vegetation*, it is to illustrate a theory so startling that Darwin has to attribute it to an unnamed *philosophe*:

It is not impossible that the first insects were the anthers and stigmas of flowers; which had by some means loosened themselves from their parent plant, like the male flowers of Vallisneria; and that many other insects in process of time had been formed from these; some acquiring wings, others fins, and others claws, from their ceaseless efforts to procure their food or to secure themselves from injury. (Note xxxix, pp. 465–6 of 1799 edition)

Although Darwin is content, when he reverts to *Vallisneria* in *The Temple of Nature*, to repeat his simple plant–insect analogy in a footnote, a page later he is quoting word for word the theory of his naturalist-friend (who probably is his own invention). Clearly the idea of a linear chain of being retained its appeal, especially when it was possible to reconcile it with evolutionary thought. Here, it seemed, was a real link, or intermediate form: not just a plant with features that resembled those of animals, as was the case with carnivorous or sensitive plants, but a plant actually on its way to *becoming* an animal.

When *Vallisneria* reappears in *The Temple of Nature*, it is no longer as an abandoned beauty, for in the second canto Darwin's theme is 'Reproduction of Life', presented as Nature's answer to the decay and death of the individual organism. At first this is asexual, as in the 'lone truffle' and 'pregnant oyster', until plants and animals find a way – and here Darwin is a Lamarckian *avant la lettre* – to escape the resultant degeneration:

> So tulip bulbs emerging from the seed,
> Year after year unknown to sex proceed;
> Erewhile the stamens and the styles display
> Their petal-curtains, and adorn the day;
> The beaux and beauties in each blossom glow
> With wedded joy, or amatorial woe.
> Unmarried aphides prolific prove
> For nine successions uninformed of love;
> New sexes next with softer passions spring,
> Breathe the fond vow, and woo with quivering wing
>
> (canto II, lines 125–34).

This transition from one form of reproduction to another has, as befits an Eleusinian mystery, its mythic counterpart: the extraction of Eve from

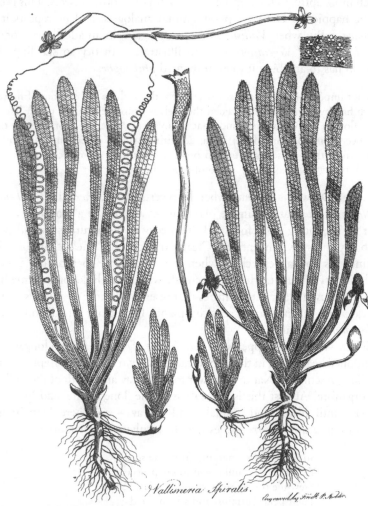

Vallisneria Spiralis.

3 Female (left) and male (right) plants of tape-grass, *Vallisneria spiralis*, as depicted in an engraving from Erasmus Darwin's *The Loves of the Plants* (1789). The sketch on the right (Proctor and Yeo 1973, after Kausik 1939 and Sculthorpe 1967) shows male flowers that have broken free and risen to the surface of the water, where the pollination of the female flowers occurs.

Adam's rib and their subsequent courtship. Outrageous to the poem's first readers, the analogy is a typical Darwinian embellishment, tossed in for those who expected Miltonic similes. His own sense of the miraculous has nourishment enough in the life histories of tulips and greenflies (especially as he believes the latter, which are actually parthenogenetic and so female, to be 'parturient sires'), whereas the Mother of Mankind, despite lavish capitalisation, the appropriation of a whole line from Milton and the help of Fuseli's impressive design on a facing page, is scarcely distinguishable from Darwin's other provocative nymphs.

Nor does classical mythology fare much better. Though given a new role as 'the deities of sexual love', Cupid and Psyche once again resemble artists' models decked out in studio props. Darwin seems impatient to get back to what he calls Nature's *chef-d'œuvre*, sex, as it operates in the real world, beginning with the loves of the plants, whether their flowers are bisexual –

> The wakeful anther in his silken bed
> O'er the pleased stigma bows his waxen head   (lines 265–6)

– or single-sex:

> Or buoyed in air the plumy lover springs,
> And seeks his panting bride on Hymen-wings.   (lines 269–70)

As for the process of fertilisation itself, Darwin has, it appears, abandoned preformationism in favour of epigenesis from a union of male and female 'particles':

> These in the pericarp erewhile arrive,
> Rush to each other, and embrace alive   (lines 275–6)

– an image which causes hordes of minute ribbon-grass flowers to swim into his imagination; no longer suffering 'amatorial woe', but embodying 'wedded joy':

> So in fond swarms the living anthers shine
> Of bright Vallisner on the wavy Rhine;
> Break from their stems, and on the liquid glass
> Surround the admiring stigmas as they pass.
> The love-sick beauties lift their essenced brows,
> Sigh to the Cyprian queen their secret vows,
> Like watchful Hero feel their soft alarms,
> And clasp their floating lovers in their arms.   (lines 279–86)

This account of *Vallisneria* is cunningly placed. It links the sex drive in plants with that of the lower animals in a way that makes the notion of the transformation of species palatable to those for whom a linear chain of being was still a living concept. At the same time it offers those who have accepted an early division of the kingdoms an instance of parallel development. Just as bisexual flowers have their counterparts in such hermaphrodite creatures as snails whose 'two-fold love unites the double sex', so the dioecious ribbon-grass with its detachable male flowers has its counterpart in the silkworm that is 'uninformed of love' when it spins its cocoon, but then

> Wakes from his trance, alarmed with young desire,
> Finds his new sex, and feels ecstatic fire.
> From flower to flower with honeyed lip he springs
> And seeks his velvet love on silver wings.   (lines 303–6)

In the rest of the canto this ecstatic fire spreads through the animal kingdom, until everything that has breath swells the triumph of Cupid and Psyche: alongside their chariot drawn by all the beasts of the field, the fish in their own element 'Move on quick fin with undulating train' (line 373), paired birds throng the air, emerging insects rise in dark clouds, and fauns and tritons (standing in, perhaps, for intermediate species between beast and man) complete the effect of a lavish Renaissance painting. Plants, however, cannot of themselves move in procession, so the poet resourcefully calls up Flora who 'Bursts her green gems and opens all their flowers' (line 394) in order to decorate every part of the bridal chariot:

> Slow roll the silver wheels with snowdrops decked,
> And primrose bands the cedar spokes connect;
> Round the fine pole the twisting woodbine clings
> And knots of jasmine clasp the bending springs.   (lines 397–400)

The Triumph of Sexual Love is Darwin's apogee as a poet, the part of his work in which he comes closest to finding the right mode of expression for his organic vision. It is, however, heady stuff for the poem's crowd of attendant nymphs. So Urania, after warning them to be careful, sends them off to gather the no longer forbidden fruit of the tree of knowledge for a repast over which, in a gentle parody of *Paradise Lost*, she and the Muse make intellectual conversation. Darwin was a strong champion of women's education, and the opening of the next canto finds the whole throng busy on physical and chemical experiments as prelude to Urania's revelation of the Progress of the Mind towards its highest power: the ability to enter into the feelings of another, which for Darwin is the basis of civilised society.

But in the final canto this power of sympathy comes up against the cruelties of the natural world. Like Charles Darwin, whose early belief in a benevolent God was deeply shaken by the sight of the ichneumon fly laying its eggs along the length of a living caterpillar, Erasmus Darwin records with horror the way that 'the cruel larva . . . tears the vitals of its fostering nurse' (lines 35–6). Nor are things any better in the plant kingdom. Flora, a benevolent presence at the second canto's triumph of life, now reappears as Boudicca:

> Yes! Smiling Flora drives her armèd car
> Through the thick ranks of vegetable war;
> Herb, shrub, and tree, with strong emotions rise
> For light and air, and battle in the skies;
> Whose roots diverging with opposing toil
> Contend below for moisture and for soil;
> Round the tall elm, the flattering ivies bend,
> And strangle, as they clasp, their struggling friend;
> Envenomed dews from Mancinella flow,
> And scald with caustic touch the tribes below.   (lines 41–50)

To this picture of the natural world as 'one great slaughterhouse' the Muse next adds a catalogue of human miseries. Urania counters this in a second section with what we would now call positive thinking about human achievements and the happiness they bring. But the fact of the individual organism's vulnerability will not go away for Darwin any more than it would do for Tennyson, and in the third section he has Urania return to the universal struggle for existence. This time however it is explained and even justified as Nature's defence mechanism against over-fecundity, the mechanism that Malthus's *Essay on the Principle of Population* had demonstrated as recently as 1798:

> So human progenies, if unrestrained,
> By climate friended, and by food sustained,
> O'er seas and soils, prolific hordes! would spread
> Erelong, and deluge their terraqueous bed;
> But war, and pestilence, disease, and dearth,
> Sweep the superfluous myriads from the earth.   (lines 369–74)

Malthus, of course, was a powerful influence on the way Charles Darwin would present the struggle for existence in the third chapter of *The Origin of Species*, and the final sentence of that chapter is worth recalling at this point:

When we reflect on this struggle, we may console ourselves with the full belief, that the war of nature is not incessant, that no fear is felt, that death is generally prompt, and that the vigorous, the healthy, and the happy survive and multiply.

The last words of this measured consolation are meant to prepare us for the next, and vital, step in Charles Darwin's argument for evolution: natural selection. Erasmus Darwin's survey of the struggle for existence in *The Temple of Nature* is also the prelude to a theory, and one with a quasi-scientific basis, though its application is philosophical rather than scientific.

According to Erasmus Darwin, 'when a monarch or a mushroom dies', a process begins whereby 'Alchemic powers the changing mass dissolve' (lines 383, 386) so that, ultimately, 'Emerging matter from the grave returns' (line 399). The modern reader is tempted to think that here is an early understanding of the ecological cycles whereby organisms decompose into elements that may in time help to compose fresh organisms. Actually Darwin, though he has a strong awareness of the indestructibility of matter, is stating the 'fact' – for so it was to most naturalists until disabused by Pasteur – that minute organisms spontaneously generate from decayed matter. But either way the result is the same: new life from old. And given the drive to self-betterment which for Darwin underlies the transformation of species, that new life must in the course of generations become more abundant in both quantity and quality – always provided humanity allows this to happen. Towards the end of *Phytologia*, an anecdote is attributed to another probably non-existent 'philosopher':

I well remember to have heard an ingenious agricultor boast, that he had drained two hundred acres of morassy land, on which he now was able to feed an hundred oxen; and added, 'is that not a meritorious thing?' 'True,' replied one of the company, 'but you forget, that you have destroyed a thousand free republics of ants, and ten thousand rational frogs, besides innumerable aquatic insects and aquatic vegetables.' (p. 507)

Biodiversity had found its first champion.

Life, then, was to expand in its diversity and in its numbers (animal sustenance, Darwin elsewhere speculates, might one day be provided by artificial photosynthesis), and above all in its quality. When Charles Darwin spoke of 'the vigorous, the healthy and the *happy*' surviving he may have been unconsciously echoing his grandfather. The idea of organic happiness has no place in a strictly scientific demonstration that life has evolved from simpler to more complex forms But for Erasmus Darwin, in *The Temple of Nature*, evolution could only bring an increase of terrestrial happiness. The very rocks bear witness to that bliss of being, for mountains, thrust up from the deposited remains of countless minute creatures, are 'MIGHTY MONUMENTS OF PAST DELIGHT' (IV, line 450 – Darwin's capitals). So the hills can be joyful together, as they

> Shout round the globe, how reproduction strives
> With vanquished death – and happiness survives;
> How Life increasing peoples every clime,
> And young renascent Nature conquers Time. (lines 451–4)

Such unrestrained delight in the best possible of worlds can jar and even appal; on occasion Darwin makes us feel we are being taken on a lightning tour of the Natural History Museum by Dr Pangloss. It is hardly surprising that his fellow-townsman Samuel Johnson disliked him, and he would have liked him still less had he lived to read *The Temple of Nature*. Johnson's comments on the enlivening thought that our dead tissues furnish the 'renascent joys' of innumerable microscopic animals can well be imagined. It would be easy, too, to dismiss Darwin's poetry as just the celebration of procreation and progress we might expect from a man who made money, married money, and fathered fourteen children. But it would be unjust. Darwin experienced shocking bereavements, and his work as a physician exposed him to suffering that he was powerless to alleviate. Confronted with an entire family ravaged by the measles, which was causing 'nine innocent little animals to cough their hearts up', he demanded, much in the tone of Johnson's exasperation with the optimism of Soames Jenyns, 'if this partial evil contributes to any public good? – if this pain is necessary to establish the subordination of different links in the chain of animation?'[56] In substituting the ruthlessness of a cosmic Whiggery for the complacency of cosmic Toryism he himself, of course, was to get no nearer to solving the problem of pain. But no reader should grudge Darwin his certainty that it is good to be alive, even when it issues in overconfident speculations and over-exuberant verse. Far from being self-satisfaction, it is a satisfaction in the wonderful otherness, within a shared vitality, of 'all that buds or breathes'.

---

[56] *Letters*, p. 104.

CHAPTER 3

Crabbe's slimy mallows and suffocated clover

For a natural philosopher of the eighteenth century, botany could be an exotic and exciting pursuit. There was often the thrill of knowing that the seeds he propagated in his hothouse had been brought from the other side of the world, and the plants they grew into might prove spectacular in a number of ways. Or he might find himself nursing the inflorescence of a male palm throughout a nine-day journey from Leipzig to Berlin, in order to pollinate a female palm that had languished unfertilised for eighty years. But for the general run of English botanists at the beginning of the next century, many of them clergymen on modest stipends, the science was an altogether tamer business of distinguishing, identifying and recording the species and subspecies native to a small locality. The only excitement such a field naturalist could hope for was that, as he went about his parish duties, his eye might light upon some hitherto unrecorded grass or moss.

George Crabbe, like Erasmus Darwin a botanist and a poet, at first sight appears to conform to this more homely model. In fact, he is no more to be stereotyped as a botanist than, as poet, he is to be fitted into any of the traditional categories of literary history. Although younger than Darwin by a generation, Crabbe began to publish verse before the elder poet did, winning Dr Johnson's approbation for *The Village* as early as 1783. Shortly afterwards he fell silent for twenty-two years: an interval during which Darwin's major poems appeared and gained, but soon after his death in 1801 lost, high public regard. In 1807 Crabbe republished most of his early poetry, with the addition of *The Parish Register*. A review by Francis Jeffrey, comparing his work favourably with that of the Lake poets, brought renewed if controversial fame that prepared the way for *The Borough*, a sequel to *The Village* but with greater narrative content, that in its turn led on, in 1812 and 1819, to two collections of verse *Tales*. His reputation as moralist, satirist and storyteller was still high at the time of his death in 1832. But this was also the date that, in retrospect, came to be seen as the close of the Romantic age in literature; and when the Victorians sought to define the spirit of that age they tended to regard Crabbe – if they considered him at all – as an anachronism: a relic, in an age of profound poetic sensibility and lyric intensity, of sound but soulless Augustan common sense expressed in heroic couplets that, with Dryden's, were 'fittest for discourse and nearest prose'.

This disparagement even extended to Crabbe the naturalist. 'What he called botany was gathering plants and knowing their names', W. C. Roscoe wrote dismissively in 1859.[1] I hope in this chapter to show not only that Crabbe's plant hunting was far from being a trivial pursuit but that in other ways he was what Christopher Ricks has called him, 'a remarkable botanist';[2] and that his highly individual experience of the plant kingdom inspired some of his most memorable poetry.

I

Crabbe was a herbalist before he became a botanist. Apprenticeship to an apothecary-surgeon in the 1770s meant that his first close acquaintance with plants was with their real or supposed curative properties. In a very 'Gothick' juvenile poem the walls of a ruined church are decked, not with the expected ivy, but with pellitory.[3] The name must have mystified readers of *The Lady's Magazine*, but apothecaries, not yet quite free from the doctrine of signatures, valued pellitory-of-the-wall as a treatment for kidney stone. When, after a few months of skimpy surgical training in London, Crabbe began to practise as an apothecary-surgeon in his native Aldeburgh, he congratulated himself (in verse) on the fact that 'I make myself the med'cines I prescribe.'[4] Unfortunately the skill proved counterproductive: his patients refused to pay him, or so the story went, on the grounds that he got their medication out of ditches.

The bunches of herbs that he was seen carrying back from the Suffolk countryside were however from botanical rather than medicinal forays. Crabbe had developed what his eldest son, namesake and biographer (whom, following E. M. Forster, I shall simply call George) rightly spoke of as a passion for botany;[5] a passion that was given direction by a

[1] Arthur Pollard (ed.), *Crabbe: the Critical Heritage* (1972), p. 408.
[2] *Essays in Appreciation* (1996), p. 73.
[3] 'Solitude'. My quotations from Crabbe's poetry are taken from the edition by Norma Dalrymple-Champneys and Arthur Pollard, *George Crabbe: the Complete Poetical Works* (1988).
[4] 'Fragment Written at Midnight'.
[5] *The Life of George Crabbe by his Son, with an Introduction by E. M. Forster* (1932), p. 33. The *Life* was originally published in 1834, as the first volume of a posthumous edition of Crabbe's works.

benefactor's gift of William Hudson's *Flora Anglica*. This was not a work that Crabbe could have bought for himself, since at this period of his life he was sometimes poor to the point of hunger. An alcoholic father, with whom his relationship was painfully convoluted, had forced him to become a doctor without being able to make proper provision for his training, and though small-town chicanery could be blamed for some of his failure, the hard fact as candidly stated by George was that Crabbe was not up to the job: he was 'incompetent to his duties, both in talent and knowledge; and he felt that the opinion of the public, in this respect, was but too just'.[6] Financial considerations apart, this general disregard, amounting in his mind to rejection, must have cast Crabbe into a state of continual and painful self-doubt. It was an insecurity deepened by the sense of the precarious shared by all who struggled for a living on a vulnerable and eroded coast. The sea not only took the lives of local fishermen and those who 'went to sea' and never returned (the fate of two of Crabbe's brothers); it also took livelihoods, sweeping away dwellings and workshops or overflowing land that would then remain unproductive for years.

Yet the landward half of Crabbe's horizon offered him both refuge and escape from this insecurity. In the wide and often desolate expanses of saltings and low sandy heath that make up the Suffolk coastal landscape, he was blessedly free from despising presences. At the same time he was aware, thanks to his growing fascination with plant life, of smaller areas within these expanses where a sheltering dune or the wetness of a heathland bog allowed a small community of organisms to thrive, seemingly in enviable harmony. Years later, in describing the country round the seaport that forms the subject of *The Borough*, his memory lights on one such refuge: the quarries from which the town's building stone was once extracted.

> Here pits of crag, with spongy, plashy base,
> To some enrich th'uncultivated space:
> For there are blossoms rare, and curious rush,
> The gale's rich balm, and sundew's crimson blush,
> Whose velvet leaf with radiant beauty dressed
> Forms a gay pillow for the plover's breast.   (Letter I, lines 147–52)

In a second edition, Crabbe made changes to render the first three of these lines less idiosyncratic. He gets rid of the quasi-personal 'some' (i.e. 'people like myself') and also of the geologically exact 'crag' – an East Anglian

---

[6] *Ibid.*, p. 44.

deposit of which Aldeburgh's special limey variety, coralline crag, produces a miniflora that can indeed include species that, in Suffolk at least, are 'rare' and 'curious'. The third line now reads more generally 'There are the feathery grass, the flowery rush', and so adds other pleasures of touch and sight ('this beautiful plant' he elsewhere calls the flowering-rush, *Butomus umbellatus*) to the pleasures of sweet gale's fragrance, and the brilliant colour and glitter of sundew: none of them rarities at that time, but all of them distinctive enough to constitute a private pleasance, a *hortus conclusus* within an otherwise bleak landscape.

The sensuous final lines hint at the presence of an Eve within this paradise; and in fact Crabbe's long-standing engagement to a young woman of yeoman stock called Sara Elmy imparted, as George phrased it, 'a buoyancy to his spirits in the very midst of his troubles'.[7] The two were in no position to marry, but meanwhile the loyalty of 'Mira' extended even to learning the Linnaean classification as set forth in Hudson's *Flora Anglica*:

> . . . we plucked the wild blossoms that blushed in the grass
> And I taught my dear maid of their order and class;
> For Conway, the friend of mankind, had decreed
> That Hudson should show us the wealth of the mead.[8]

These lines remind us of the further passion that kept Crabbe going at this time: versifying. And among these early and for the most part less-than-promising poems, there occurs a sudden, unexpected revelation of the way that he would in the end find his niche as unerringly as had any of the plants he hunted along dykes and across shingle banks.

Crabbe, it would seem, wanted to try his skill at the fashionable loco-descriptive Prospect poem. To find, on the Suffolk coast, anything approaching a conventional notion of the picturesque, he had to tramp some dozen miles north to Dunwich, once England's greatest port but by then disappearing fast under the North Sea. There, according to a poem that got published but remained totally unsold, we find him dodging about to construct a Claude-like prospect complete with a foreground closed in by the side-screens of withered oaks, a middle ground featuring the obligatory ruined tower (since submerged), and a distance aglow with sunrise. But then the real splendour of the scene, the way its early morning scents and sounds fed into that lifting of the spirit that comes at the sight of a calm sea, takes possession of him, much as a similar dawn scene in which

---

[7] *Ibid.*, p. 34.   [8] *Ibid.*, p. 34.

'the sea lay laughing at a distance' would take possession of Wordsworth
and make him also 'a dedicated spirit':[9]

> Here at a pine-pressed hill's embroidered base
> I stood, and hailed the Genius of the place;
> Then was it doomed by Fate my idle heart
> Softened by Nature, gave access to Art;
> The Muse approached, her siren song I heard,
> Her magic felt, and all her charms revered:
> E'er since she rules in absolute control,
> And only Mira dearer to my soul.[10]

There could be only one outcome. In 1780, Crabbe gave up medicine
for literature. Or to put it less grandly, he exchanged semi-starvation
in Aldeburgh for semi-starvation in London's Grub Street. There, as a
last resort, he appealed out of the very depth of destitution to Edmund
Burke who, to his everlasting credit, responded with patronage on a grand
eighteenth-century scale. For Crabbe, this changed everything: it gave him
the chance to have his poetry published by Dodsley, the right of entry into
London's literary establishment and the opportunity to take holy orders.
Of the two poems that struck Burke as promising, *The Library* was well
received when it appeared anonymously in 1781; and *The Village*, published
in its final form in 1783, did even better, often reappearing in anthologised
extracts.

After 1785, however, Crabbe dropped out of the literary scene for a long
time. Ordained and married, he had settled, after an unhappy period as
chaplain to the Duke of Rutland, into what George calls his village
existence, first in the East Midlands and later in his home county. We
know he went on writing poetry, but all he published during these years
were botanical and entomological records. When he first held the living of
Muston, near Grantham, he wrote a 'natural history' – basically no more
than a set of species lists – of the Vale of Belvoir for inclusion in John
Nichols's *History and Antiquities of Leicestershire*.[11] Sara's inheritance of an
uncle's house in Suffolk took him and his family back in 1792 to Parham,
some dozen miles inland from Aldeburgh, and here – pluralism being the
order of the day – he soon picked up a couple of curacies. He also resumed
his study of the Suffolk flora. In 1798 he contributed to a history of the

---

[9] *The Prelude*, Book IV, lines 326 and 337 (1850 text).   [10] *The Candidate*, lines 290–7.
[11] Though the relevant volume of this was not published till 1811, Nichols included Crabbe's lists in the
seventh volume of his *Biblioteca topographica Britannica* (1800). Crabbe also made many smaller
contributions, some of them botanical, to other parts of the *History*: see Thomas C. Faulkner and
Rhonda L. Blair (eds.), *Selected Letters and Journals of George Crabbe* (1985), pp. 34–6.

nearby small town of Framlingham a list of the plants to be found within its parish boundaries. Some of these records recur in *The Botanist's Guide through England and Wales* (1805), compiled by Dawson Turner and Lewis Dillwyn; but Crabbe's chief contribution to the Suffolk section of this work consists in numerous entries about marsh and shore plants native to the coast north and south of Aldeburgh.

Crabbe locates his finds with precision both in the Framlingham list and in the *Guide*. 'In the old road to Parham, after you pass the run of water before the first houses on the right hand'[12] is a typical entry. But even in the few places where landmarks have survived, changed agricultural practices have seen off many of the plants. Today's flower-seeker would look in vain in the woods, fields and ponds round Framlingham for starfruit, dwarf mouse-ear chickweed, woolly thistle, small fleabane, fly orchid, frog orchid or fragrant orchid – let alone weeds such as corncockle, which Crabbe considered too common to be worth recording – and would be left exclaiming, as George once did to Edward Fitzgerald, 'How *scan*dalously they misuse the globe!'[13]

Whatever their interest for the student of Britain's changing flora, Crabbe's published botanical records convey little to the reader of his poetry. A much clearer light on what his plant-hunting really meant to him is cast by letters that he wrote during the 1790s to Edmund Cartwright, a young army officer who was the son of a clerical friend and also godfather to Crabbe's son Edmund. Cartwright was interested in botany and had the advantage of knowing Sir Joseph Banks. But he was a less practised finder-and-namer than Crabbe, and after a visit in 1792 to salt marshes near the Wash he sent the other a specimen that he could not identify. Crabbe thought he recognised it as *Bupleurum tenuissimum* (more aptly, slender hare's ear), but wanted to grow it in his Muston garden, presumably so that he might be able to decide from studying a number of individuals whether or not Cartwright had lit upon a hitherto unrecorded species. So could Cartwright send seeds or a root? There is no mistaking the eagerness in this and the two following letters. Elaborate instructions for dispatch are given – 'This is really taking too much of your time, but a new inhabitant for a botanical garden is too great a prize to be sacrificed'[14] – and the seeds when they arrive are 'treasures which money cannot purchase'.[15]

---

[12] Robert Hawes, *History of Framlingham* (1798), p. 449.
[13] Quoted by E. M. Forster in his introduction to *The Life of George Crabbe*, p. x.
[14] *Selected Letters*, p. 47.   [15] *Ibid.*, p. 51.

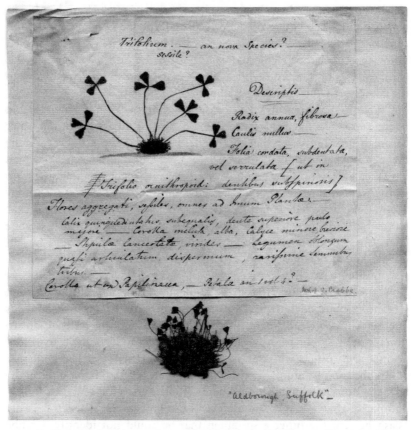

4　Crabbe's dried specimen of an unidentified clover (*Trifolium suffocatum*), with sketch and description attached, as he sent them to Sir Joseph Banks. (Banks Herbarium, Natural History Museum.)

'I had laid by three or four speciments to transmit to you and Sir Joseph but unluckily your godson, or some little mischievous creature like him, has ruined my plants and I have only one left and that discoloured and ill preserved; yet as it is the whole plant I believe Sir Joseph will be able to pronounce on its claim to a discovery.'

(Crabbe to Edmund Cartwright Jnr, 22 July 1794)

The interest he evinces in Cartwright's find is however nothing to Crabbe's excitement, two years later, at the thought that he may himself have discovered 'a new species of British plant, or rather a new species speaking more generally, for I can neither find it in the Flora of these kingdoms nor the *Species Plantarum* [of Linnaeus] of the last and enlarged editions'.[16] By then he was back in Suffolk and able to resume plant hunting at Aldeburgh. He had, he told Cartwright, been observing the return of vegetation to a stretch of shore, above the normal level of spring tides, which had been submerged a few years previously. There were yellow horned poppies, sea thrift and – still a colourful feature of the area today – the sea-pea, together with 'other hardy and frugal plants which live on little and thrust their roots far in the soil in search of food'. These included several clovers and their close relations; in all Crabbe counted a dozen species. One of these he could not identify, so he asked Cartwright to find a way of ensuring that his remaining, rather dishevelled specimen (four-year-old Edmund having wrecked the others) got to Banks. If the great man pronounced it a new species, then Crabbe intended to publish 'an account of my plant, with a plate of it and a narration of the progressive vegetation of the spot it grows on, etc etc etc'.

What was there about this minute plant to justify the exuberance that breaks out in all these et ceteras – or even the interest Crabbe had shown earlier in the identification of a thin-leaved little umbellifer, difficult to distinguish in long grass? The question has of course no meaning for the devoted field botanist, as anyone knows who has been dragged up a mountain to view a unique but unprepossessing rarity. It is, after all, in the nature of an unfamiliar species to be inconspicuous; its small but distinct characteristics are what make it a putative addition to the world's flora. But there is more to Crabbe's exhilaration than the triumph of discovery. The spot where he found his clover[17] had powerful associations for him because it was close to the quay where he had once spent an unhappy time labouring for his warehouseman father. The sea's incursion is likely to have happened in the storms that accompanied the spring tide of January 1779. Now, fifteen years later, the first 'hardy and frugal' plants were fighting to get a hold in the arid and still saline ground. No wonder Crabbe wanted to record all the stages of such plants' struggle to establish themselves in what he calls 'a remarkably sterile place'.[18] A dread of going under beneath overwhelming hostility; the defiant act of making a new start against all the odds: these were the shaping experiences of Crabbe's

---

[16] This and the two quotations that follow are taken from the extract from Crabbe's letter of 22 July 1794 that, according to James Groves ('Crabbe as a botanist', *Proceedings of the Suffolk Institute of Archaeology and Natural History*, vol. XII (1906), pp. 223–32) Cartwright sent Banks, together with a further extract from a letter of 4 August 1794 in which Crabbe spoke of his intention to publish a monograph on 'all the Trifolia which I have cultivated with so much care for three or four years past'.

[17] 'Aldeburgh, between the town and Slaughden, in the marsh', *The Botanist's Guide through England and Wales* (1805), p. 550.

[18] Quoted from Crabbe's letter of 4 August 1794: Groves, 'Crabbe as a botanist', p. 227.

late twenties, and they can have contributed more than any observation of floral details to the significance that his find carried for him.

The same is true, and to a scarcely lesser degree, of another plant evocative for Crabbe of its salt marsh habitat, Cartwright's *Bupleurum*. Crabbe, in his earlier letter, sounds fairly confident of its being *B. tenuissimum*, a plant that, as he recorded for Turner and Dillwyn, grew plentifully near Aldeburgh.[19] And here perhaps lies the true reason why he was so eager to propagate it in his Midland garden. Stranded in an intensively farmed shire, he was homesick for the wild places of his early years: just how homesick is revealed in his letter acknowledging the arrival of the seeds:

I envied your wet journey to the boggy ground of Friskney and will remember it, as one of the places I purpose to visit. People speak with raptures of fine prospects, clear skies, lawns, parks and the blended beauties of Art and Nature, but give me a wild, wide fen, in a foggy day; with quaking boggy ground and trembling hillocks in a putrid soil: shut in by the closeness of the atmosphere, all about is like a new Creation and every botanist an Adam who explores and names the creatures he meets with.[20]

'This Paradise' Crabbe goes on to call such a landscape, and there could be no clearer confirmation that his early botanising round Aldeburgh had indeed felt to him like an escape to Eden: a blessed place where he was liberated from his sense of inadequacy and sheltered from the contempt of others. Crabbe's sense of a habitat, as strong as Clare's awareness of birds' nesting places, ensured that the pleasure of plant hunting did not end with the act of naming but expanded into a true empathy with each of his finds.

2

Crabbe's clover, together with his drawing and description, is still in Banks's herbarium in the Natural History Museum. But even before he heard from Sir Joseph, he had discovered that the plant already figured in the 1771 supplement (*Mantissa*) to Linnaeus's *Species plantarum*, where it had been given the name of *Trifolium suffocatum* on account of the crowded appearance of its flower heads. Banks may also have known, from the records of the Linnean Society,[21] that the plant had already been found in Britain, at Yarmouth, by a 'Mr Lilly Wigg', who was presumably the 'Mr Wigg' who contributed many findings from that locality to *The Botanist's Guide*.

[19] *The Botanist's Guide*, p. 544.   [20] *Selected Letters*, pp. 51–2.
[21] Groves, 'Crabbe as a botanist', p. 228.

Crabbe however was not cast down, because, as he told Cartwright, 'I do not lay aside my purpose but I should be glad if you could obtain for me some information of what would be expected of him who wrote the history of incipient vegetation, etc etc'.[22] And despite the tinge of absurdity over this episode of the suffocated clover these words represent, as clearly as the flow of the tide into a Suffolk estuary, the confluence of two movements in the history of botany. Crabbe's initial excitement over his find is typical of those heady days when a shingle bank in East Anglia seemed no less likely than a stretch of the karroo or the outback to yield up a species not yet in Linnaeus's world flora. But in resigning with a good grace his dream of *Trifolium crabbei*, he is fired by a fresh botanical interest quite different from finding and naming. That interest was in what, a few years later, would come to be called *succession*: the sequence over time of plant associations in an area that has been subjected to disturbance.

The concept was not wholly new. Crabbe had read *The Economy of Nature*, which formed part of the *Miscellaneous Tracts* that, published in 1759, were the first introduction of Linnaeus's work to the British public.[23] In the course of arguing in the *Economy* for a divinely appointed balance of nature, Linnaeus briefly considers the increasing complexity and bulk of plant cover on what had once been bare stone; an account Crabbe builds upon when, in *The Borough*, he ponders the replacement of the lichens on the walls of an ancient church with, in turn, liverworts, then mosses – 'coat above coat, the living on the dead'[24] – then ferns, and finally flowering plants. Similar changes in vegetation, over space instead of time, were soon to be the interest of Alexander von Humboldt and other bio-geographers. But it would be many years before the relationships between organisms and their changing environments would constitute a distinct field of study, and when this happened one of its first concerns would be with the succession of plant cover, up to a climax of diversity, in each of the major plant biomes. If only Crabbe, gifted as he was with an instinctive understanding of the smallest plant's adaptation to its habitat, had written his 'history of incipient vegetation', he might have speeded up the growth of ecological thought and been honoured today as a pioneer ecologist.

---

[22] *Selected Letters*, p. 62.
[23] It was a translation by Bernard Stillingfleet of a number of degree dissertations of the University of Uppsala originally published as *Amoenitates academicae*. The real author in each case was, however, Linnaeus himself, the candidate having been awarded the degree for the fluency and cogency with which he defended (in Latin) his supervisor's reasoning.
[24] Letter II, line 78.

Even though Crabbe failed to step ahead of the botanical thinking of his time, he was no docile Linnaean, but kept abreast of post-Linnaean developments. One of the most important of these was a growing interest in non-flowering plants such as seaweeds, lichens, mosses and ferns, together with the fungi that were still considered a part of the plant kingdom. These held little appeal for Linnaeus himself who relegated all of them to a twenty-fourth class that he called *Cryptogamia*, or Clandestine Marriages, making use of the legal term for a practice that, in England at least, ceased in the middle of the eighteenth century. Curiously, botanists still use the word 'cryptogam', although the reproductive processes of these plants are no longer a mystery. Those of mosses, in fact, were observed, understood and described only a few years after Linnaeus's death, and this investigation and others decided Withering to add to the second edition of his *Arrangement* a whole volume (published in 1792) devoted to non-flowering plants. In the course of a letter to Cartwright[25] (in Yorkshire at the time and getting interested in marine algae), Crabbe, who in childhood must have been as familiar with seaweeds as with land plants, refers to Withering's volume and to other authorities in this field in a way that shows he was amassing an up-to-date collection of botanical works. For his part, he was fascinated by lichens, a very large group of plants[26] that Linnaeus had lumped together as a single genus. Linnaeus speaks of them as despised; but Crabbe, drawn as his son pointed out to plants 'usually considered the least inviting',[27] marvelled at the number of disparate forms to be found in a close scrutiny of what, to the casual observer, were simply areas of discoloration of a building's fabric:

> There Science loves to trace her tribes minute,
> The juiceless foliage, and the tasteless fruit;
> There she perceives them round the surface creep,
> And while they meet, their due distinctions keep;
> Mixed but not blended, each its name retains,
> And these are Nature's ever-during stains.[28]

These lines introduce the passage on succession already alluded to, and so recall Crabbe's projected study of what he terms the progress of vegetation. But he had not been able to give his mind to this, because the mid-1790s were deeply unhappy years, clouded by family disputes and, more seriously, by Sara's increasing mental instability: a bipolar disorder which in all

---

[25] A. M. Broadley's grangerised *Life of Crabbe* in the Brotherton Library, University of Leeds, vol. II, p. 129.
[26] Or half-plants. Each is an alga in symbiosis with a fungus.
[27] *Life*, p. 157.   [28] *The Borough*, letter II, lines 47–52.

probability originated with the loss of four of her seven children in their infancy, and was very much worsened by the death of six-year-old Edmund. Later on, in a narrative section of *The Borough*, Crabbe would find an indirect way to give expression to some of the unhappiness his wife's breakdown caused them both:

> Then came the woeful years:
> The husband's terrors, and the father's tears;
> A wife grown feeble, mourning, pining, vexed
> With wants and woes – by daily cares perplexed;
> No more an help, a smiling soothing aid,
> But boding, drooping, sickly and afraid.   (letter III, lines 214–19)

In his letter breaking the news of Edmund's death to the child's godfather, Crabbe, mindful that Cartwright has recently lost his young wife, does not dwell long on his own troubles. Instead he tells him about a new botanical project with which he is trying to distract his thoughts. This is nothing less than 'an English herbal divested of all the scientific terms' –

in fact a Ray's *Synopsis* in plain English was at first all my idea, but as I must introduce the leading features of the present system [i.e. Linnaeus's], I have between both, with Tournefort, Boerhaave etc etc, formed I think a very easy arrangement and I mean, if I can find time and peace, to publish it.[29]

According to George, this project reached the stage at which Crabbe felt able to approach a publisher. Unfortunately he also showed the manuscript to an eminent Cambridge don who 'could not stomach the notion of degrading such a science by treating of it in a modern language'.[30] This was tiresome pedantry, particularly in view of the success of Withering's *Arrangement*. But according to George it caused Crabbe to put the manuscript on his garden bonfire, in one of what his son terms the 'grand incremations' that had already devoured three novels which Sara thought less good than his poetry, together with much poetry that a close friend just thought not good enough.

The loss may not be total. Among Crabbe's notebooks preserved at Cambridge[31] is one containing an arrangement of plants that in all probability was to be the basis for his English Herbal. Unlike the classifications that he made use of for the rather smaller volumes that appear to have served as his field notebooks, it does not (as far as I can discover) correspond to any of the main systems that were in print at that time. It

---

[29] *Selected Letters*, pp. 65–6.   [30] *Life*, p. 128.
[31] Cambridge University Library has seven, of which three are devoted to scientific material, including the one discussed here, UC Add. 4194. The library of Trinity College, Cambridge, has another notebook, concerned with fungi.

therefore seems reasonable to assume that it represents a system of Crabbe's own devising.[32] An unexpected feature is that the names given to what we would now call families are derived from Greek. Crabbe's formal schooling ended when he was twelve and did not include classical Greek. Burke, however, spoke of his having acquired 'some smattering of Greek'[33] by the time of their first meeting, and since he would have had to teach himself further Greek in order to qualify for the priesthood, he may well have relished a chance to make use of this hard-won knowledge. The most significant thing about the groupings in the notebook is that they are natural: that is, they are based, in imitation of the 'New Method' adopted by Ray in his last major work, *Synopsis methodica stirpium britannicarum* (1690), not on numbers and arrangements of the sexual parts of the flower, but on an assemblage of characters – hairy leaves, say, or seeds in a pod, or flowers in whorls – in the plant as a whole. The classification set out in the notebook, if I am right in thinking it Crabbe's own, thus belongs, as do a number of satirical passages in his poetry, to the anti-Linnaean backlash that was beginning to gather force at the turn of the century.

Names of taxa apart, Crabbe's English Herbal was to be in 'plain English'. From this it can be inferred that he would not have employed Latinate coinages such as Erasmus Darwin and his colleagues use in their translations from Linnaeus, and such as the Preceptor Husband, in the story of that title among *Tales of the Hall*, inflicts upon his bewildered young wife:

> He showed the various foliage plants produce:
> Lunate and lyrate, runcinate, retuse.
> Long were the learned words and urged with force:
> Panduriform, pinnatifid, premorse,
> Latent, and patent, papulous, and plane –
> 'Oh!' said the pupil, 'it will turn my brain'   (284–9)

The similar affectation of parading Linnaean names for common plants prompts one of the liveliest portraits in *The Parish Register*. Peter Pratt the gardener, not content with insisting that his children be baptised Hyacinthus and Lonicera, airs his mastery of Latin names among his peers by calling onions and leeks, *Allium* and dandelions, *Leontodon*. But Crabbe insists there is more to botany than name-dropping:

> ... names are good, for how, without their aid
> Is knowledge, gained by man, to man conveyed?

[32] Dr James Cullen, an authority on systematics, concurs in this view.
[33] Quoted by René Huchon, *George Crabbe and his Times, 1754–1832* (1907), p. 128.

> But from that source shall all our pleasure flow?
> Shall all our knowledge be those names to know?
> Then he with memory blessed shall bear away
> The palm from Grew and Middleton[34] and Ray.
> No! let us rather seek, in grove and field,
> What food for wonder, what for use they yield;
> Some just remark from Nature's people bring,
> And some new source of homage for her King
>
>   (part I, lines 664–73)

The choice of names here suggests that Crabbe, beside wanting to remind his readers that plant science was well established in England before Linnaeus was born, was nostalgic for an earlier phase of the Enlightenment, in which botany was studied for better reasons than any Peter Pratt could provide. 'Nature's people' in this context associates English villagers' traditional knowledge of simples with the pursuit of beneficial knowledge – 'remark' carrying in eighteenth-century English almost the force of 'discovery' – that characterised the early researches of the Royal Society.

Beneficial knowledge and what Ray in the title of his most famous work called 'The Wisdom of God manifested in the Works of the Creation' were seldom in the thoughts of those who embraced Linnaean botany because it was fashionable and sexy. Thus Peter Pratt, in his nudge-and-wink account of pollination, enjoys showing off his knowledge of all that goes on within 'That bridal bed the vulgar term a flower' ('How rise the stamens as the pistils swell, / How bend and curl the moist-top to the spouse'), before expounding, with Pandarus-like relish, the artificial fertilisation of cucumbers (part I, lines 633–56). Here Crabbe's target is not so much Linnaeus as Erasmus Darwin, specifically named in the passage as the bard of 'floral courtship'. He was especially anxious to dissociate himself from Darwin, because twenty-six years earlier he too had played with human analogies such as the elder poet would use to create *The Loves of the Plants*. *The Library* (1781) had explored an imaginary book collection in which, as the footnotes made clear, natural philosophy was represented by Linnaeus's *Systema naturae*:

> There*, with the husband-slaves, in royal pride,
> Queens, like the Amazons of old, reside;
> There, like the Turk, the lordly husband lives,
>
> *Alluding to the Sexual System of Linnaeus

---

[34] Himself not wholly 'with memory blessed', Crabbe wrote 'Middleton' for 'Millington' – i.e. Sir Thomas Millington (1628–1704), to whom the discovery of plant sex was generally attributed.

And joy to all the gay seraglio gives;
There[†], in the secret chambers, veiled from sight,
A bashful tribe in hidden flames delight;
There[‡], in the open day, and gaily decked
The bolder brides their distant lords expect;
Who with the wings of love instinctive rise
And on prolific winds each ardent bridegroom flies.   (lines 173–82)

†The Class Cryptogamia
‡The Class Dioecia

But when, in 1807, *The Library* reappeared as one of the *Poems by the Rev. George Crabbe*, Turks and Amazons, hidden flames and ardent bride-grooms had all made way for 'silent loves':

Loves, where no grief, nor joy, nor bliss, nor pain
Warm the glad heart or vex the labouring brain;
But as the green blood moves along the blade,
The bed of Flora on the branch is made;
Where, without passion, love instinctive lives,
And gives new life, unconscious that it gives.   (lines 313–18)

In dissociating himself from Darwin, whose fantasies about the sexual system he had anticipated in 1781, Crabbe's motives were in all likelihood mixed. Never prudish himself, he had to accept that times had changed since the outspoken days of his youth. The new botany appealed to those who taught young girls because it was fashionable, required no expenditure and did not involve killing things. But at a time when, to all but a few rare spirits such as Blake, innocence was equated with sexual ignorance, Linnaeus's system posed a problem for educationalists. When one of these, Frances Rowden, attempted to make a selection from *The Loves of the Plants* for her charges, she soon discovered Darwin's language to be 'too luxuriant for the simplicity of female education'.[35] In the end she used his poem merely as the model for her *Poetical Introduction to the Study of Botany* (1801), in which brothers and sisters were substituted for husbands and wives, and all the extended similes, instead of being taken from the liaisons of classical deities, were relentlessly uplifting. This at least solved her practical problem. There had been no such excuse, a few years earlier, for the outrage expressed by the Reverend Richard Polwhele – an admirer, incidentally of *The Botanic Garden* – at the thought of girls being exposed to the sexual system. 'I have several times seen boys and girls botanising

---

[35] Advertisement to *Poetical Introduction to the Study of Botany*.

together'[36] he shudderingly records in a footnote that is part of his pre-
liminaries to an attack, in verse, on Mary Wollstonecraft who, having
recently died in childbirth, was beyond replying. Start with studying
amorous vegetables, Polwhele implies, and you end up with free love,
atheism and sedition – in short, as one of the *Unsexed Females* of his title.

It has been suggested that Crabbe's alteration of the passage in *The
Library* and his creation of Peter Pratt result as much from an ideological as
from a moral reaction against the once popular Erasmus Darwin.[37] Some
fierce reviews of *The Temple of Nature* on its appearance in 1802, together
with the work's poor sales, suggest that such a reaction did occur. But deep
as was Crabbe's detestation of freethinkers, his motive in his references to
Darwin would seem to have been something far simpler. As one of
Nature's people, he deplored the artifice and affectation both of
Linnaeus's human analogies and of the fables that Darwin erected upon
them. In the tale called 'Tracy', an old man teaches his grandchild to
distinguish the Linnaean classes and orders, but with a difference:

> With care paternal he the learned Swede
> From all his folly and illusion freed;
> And when they spoke of stamina and threads
> Nor wives nor husbands floated in their heads,
> And flowers were flowers alone, and were not bridal beds.[38]

If the classification in the notebook at Cambridge is indeed Crabbe's own,
this was exactly what he hoped to do in his English Herbal, where, for
example, Linnaeus's 'superfluous polygamy' of a daisy disk surrounded by
'concubine' ray florets is replaced by 'ray-plants' (*Actinophytum*) as distinct
from the other groups of what we now call the Asteraceae, 'tongue-plants'
(*Glossariphytum*) such as dandelions, and 'tube-plants' (*Siphoniphytum*)
such as thistles.

Folly and illusion could also, to Crabbe's way of thinking, be laid to the
charge of all those eighteenth-century naturalists who carried the animal–
plant analogy to the point of crediting plants with feelings. The controversy about plant sensibilities, aroused by the culture of sensitive plants and
kindled anew by the discovery of the Venus flytrap, did not die down with
the new century. As late as 1811 a book dedicated to the President of the
Linnaean Society debated and in the end left open the question whether or

---

[36] *The Unsexed Females* (1798), p. 9.
[37] R. L. Chamberlain, 'George Crabbe and Darwin's amorous plants', *Journal of English and Germanic
Philology* 61 (1962), pp. 833–52.
[38] *Complete Poetical Works*, vol. II, p. 827.

not plant movements were 'volitional'.[39] The changes Crabbe made in the
Turks-and-Amazons passage of *The Library* when he republished it in 1807
were not just aimed at getting rid of its Darwin-like fancies. They are also
an assertion that, contrary to the belief of many natural philosophers,
plants do not feel. In flowers, 'Love instinctive lives' without passion.

But life is there. When the Preceptor Husband asks his wife to show him
the stigmas of a flower, the poor girl, intellectually much challenged (she
picks on the anthers), declares, in one manuscript version

> You call them wives and husbands, but you know
> 'Tis all a joke, a husband cannot grow.
> 'The Loves of Plants' I in a poem read –
> Loves! What a folly! Why, the things are dead.[40]

To Crabbe, however, the struggling, shifting flora of an ever-changing
shoreline and a countryside being altered by the Enclosures was intensely
alive, and he respected its life too strongly not to protest at its being
transformed into Darwin's beaux and belles, just as he respected Suffolk
villagers too much to stand for their transformation into dwellers in
Arcadia. A dogged honesty demanded that he paint both 'the cot' and
the vegetation around it 'As truth will paint it – and as bards will not'.[41]

Crabbe's passion for botany carried him beyond simple plant hunting,
though it does not merit him a place in the history of science. When he
plucked a grass in flower – grasses being, George tells us, his special interest –
he failed, as his classificatory scheme shows, to recognise that what he
held in his hand was a plant wholly distinct from most other groups of
flowering plants. Yet his idol Ray had grasped the fundamental division
of monocots and dicots, and in 1789 Antoine Jussieu had made it the basis
of a 'natural' classification that within Crabbe's lifetime would replace
Linnaeus's sexual system. And for all his insistence on his father's scientific
cast of mind George, in the passage in question, hints at his involvement
with the neglected and the insignificant being primarily emotional.
Crabbe's instinct was to exalt the humble and meek. Hence the fascination
that cryptogams held for him; hence his empathic response to pioneer
species fighting for survival in a harsh environment. Confirmation of this
emotional involvement comes from an unexpected source.[42] Wordsworth
had no high opinion of Crabbe's poetry, and expected to find him a dull
dog when they met, in the elder poet's seventy-fifth year. But their ramble

---

[39] James Perchard Tupper, *An Essay on the Probability of Sensation in Vegetables*.
[40] *Complete Poetical Works*, vol. II, p. 913.   [41] *The Village*, book I, line 54.
[42] See Jared Curtis (ed.), *The Fenwick Notebooks of William Wordsworth* (1993), p. 59.

together on Hampstead Heath proved anything but dull. Wordsworth realised the strength of Crabbe's passion for other forms of life and saw in it both a consolation for much past and present unhappiness, and an enduring compensation for what man had made of man.

3

'Nature's sternest painter – yet the best': in the first decades of the last century, Byron's tribute to Crabbe's insight into human failings was widely misunderstood to mean that he was what Edwardian and Georgian taste most admired, a depicter of the natural scene. In 1903 A. C. Ainger praised his 'distinctness in painting the common growth of field and hedgerow'[43] and before long this was further defined as 'the detailed fidelity of a Birket Foster', 'the gift of seeing into plant life', and 'an amazing betrothal of art and science' that transformed Flora into flora. What was becoming a fixed idea then drew fresh strength from the republication of the *Life*, in which Crabbe's activities as naturalist get rather more attention than his poetry – which Fitzgerald indeed claimed that George never read. By 1936 F. R. Leavis, hardly a critic to toe the line, can be found making for Crabbe the sweeping claim 'that in the use of description, of nature and the environment generally, for emotional purposes, he surpasses any Romantic'.[44] The truth of the matter, however, is that flower passages and the like are few and far between in Crabbe's work, as was pointed out by a critic of the next generation, who sensibly attributed 'the fact that Crabbe, who wrote nature poetry very well, wrote so little of it'[45] to his central concern with human life. In this respect, the poet remained whole-heartedly an Augustan who believed that the proper study of mankind was man. But though passages with a botanical content are not numerous in Crabbe's poetry, the emotional involvement that I have been exploring ensured that such passages are, to an extraordinary degree, 'original and powerful' – to make use of the terms by which Jeffrey first distinguished Crabbe's poetry.

One of the most memorable occurs in *The Village*. The first sixty lines or so of the poem promise us a 'real picture of the poor' in place of poetic idealisations. We brace ourselves for misery and squalor, and there will be

---

[43] *Crabbe*, in the English Men of Letters series (1903), p. 14. The succeeding phrases are taken from critics writing between 1912 and 1923.

[44] *Revaluations* (1936), p. 128.

[45] Oliver F. Sigworth, *Nature's Sternest Painter: Four Essays on the Poetry of George Crabbe* (1965), p. 111.

plenty of both. But what we get initially is a supremely ironic use of that staple of the conventional pastoral, the flower passage:

> Lo! where the heath, with withering brake grown o'er,
> Lends the light turf that warms the neighbouring poor;
> From thence a length of burning sand appears,
> Where the thin harvest waves its withered ears;
> Rank weeds, that every art and care defy,
> Reign o'er the land and rob the blighted rye:
> There thistles stretch their prickly arms afar,
> And to the ragged infant threaten war;
> There poppies nodding, mock the hope of toil,
> There the blue bugloss paints the sterile soil;
> Hardy and high, above the slender sheaf,
> The slimy mallow waves her silky leaf;
> O'er the young shoot the charlock throws a shade,
> And clasping tares cling round the sickly blade;
> With mingled tints the rocky coasts abound,
> And a sad splendour vainly shines around.   (I, lines 63–78)

Anyone quoting this much-quoted passage must feel the temptation I have just experienced to leave out the last couplet. Its generality seems to let us down badly after the glowing particularity of all that has gone before. But by this final faint indication of a shoreline in the middle distance and a sombre midsummer haze beyond, Crabbe is marking his departure from another poetic convention, the picturesque Prospect. Foreground vegetation, no longer the vaguely 'embroidered' turf that it was in his description of Dunwich's scenery, now dominates the scene, as it will come to do in landscape painting of the next half century, from the docks and thistles lovingly depicted by Crome and De Wint to the botanic extravaganzas of the Pre-Raphaelites. And one suspects that in both arts this foregrounding has quite a lot to do with the close-up scrutiny demanded of the field botanist.

Looking with a countryman's as well as a botanist's eye, Crabbe sees that the miserable rye he describes has become an easy victim of blight because in that sandy soil it is starved of nutrients and parched with drought. The real power of the description however, and its advantage over any other way he might have portrayed indigence, are that he makes us see the weed-ridden field through the eyes of those who have ploughed and sown it: people so poor that they rely for cooking and warmth on turf that they know from its admixture of bracken to be scarcely burnable, and who have been driven to plant, as squatters, their own food crop on land which the owner must have abandoned after the sea's last incursion.[46] Unfortunately, they are not the only beings ready to grasp an opportunity. Weeds of cultivation, better adapted than the rye to salinity, offer fierce resistance to the efforts of the squatters' ragged children to grub them out. 'Slimy' suggests this hands-on approach to the mucilaginous leaves and stems of the bulky common mallow, which sea air could encourage to grow to a metre and a half in both height and width. Crabbe must often have got his own hands on it in his apothecary days, for the root was much used in poultices.

All these opportunist invaders of arable land are described as *rank*, a word that serves subliminally to link the invading, colonising plants with the powerful of the world in their pride of dress: mallows and poppies flaunt their silken brilliance (the mallow's 'leaves' are not foliage but its shimmering petals) and maybe there is the hint of a further pun in 'bug*loss*'. Crabbe, at the time *The Village* was published, was a ducal chaplain in the glossy setting of Belvoir Castle, a position in which it was difficult for him to lay any blame for the plight of the poor directly upon the rich and influential; in the poem as we have it (no drafts survive) he has to content himself with some telling exposure of middle-class callousness, and could only hint in these lines at the existence of oppressive weeds in the garden politic – a hint easily picked up, however, by those familiar with *Richard II*. He may even have been paying off some scores of his own, for his state of dependency at the Castle exposed him to personal slights. The best that could be said for the appointment was that it had freed him from the clutches of other servants of the rich and powerful: in his description, tares – the resonant biblical name of that world-wide pest, *Vicia hirsuta* – strangle the stalks of the crop with a debt-collector's persistence. Not that Crabbe makes his plants into symbols, far less that he personifies them. But as always in his poetry, the human aspect dominates. Its supremacy is assured here by skilled interplay between, on the one hand, weeds and crop as the exploiters and exploited that they literally are, and on the other, the direct factual link of the plants with toil and poverty.

Twenty-five years later, in the eighteenth letter of *The Borough*, Crabbe creates another flower passage that, like the one in *The Village*, momentarily strikes the reader as an inconsequential inset, but soon shows itself to be powerfully relevant to the letter's subject, 'The Poor and their

---

[46] Dr John Jamieson of the Aldeburgh and District Local History Society tells me that in Crabbe's lifetime the major incursions of the sea were to the north of Aldeburgh, where there was no common land.

Dwellings'. The poet is describing an area of impermanent shacks and decayed cottages that the authorities choose to ignore:

> Here our reformers come not; none object
> To paths polluted, or upbraid neglect.
> None care that ashy heaps at doors are cast,
> That coal dust flies along the blinding blast:
> None heed the stagnant pools on either side,
> Where new-launched ships of infant sailors ride:
> Rodneys in rags here British valour boast,
> And lisping Nelsons fright the Gallic coast.   (lines 274–81)

The shift of tone and perspective in the two last lines leads on to a description of real charm, as Crabbe abandons his voice of public-spirited indignation in order to enter imaginatively into the children's game with their toy boats. The gloom complained of by Crabbe's early readers has been lifted, and the flower passage that follows lulls us – at least at first – into the expectation of further relief:

> There, fed by food they love, to rankest size
> Around the dwellings docks and wormwood rise;
> Here the strong mallow strikes her slimy root,
> Here the dull nightshade hangs her deadly fruit;
> On hills of dust the henbane's faded green
> And pencilled flower of sickly scent is seen;
> At the wall's base the fiery nettle springs,
> With fruit globose and fierce with poisoned stings;
> Above (the growth of many a year) is spread
> The yellow level of the stonecrop's bed;
> In every chink delights the fern to grow,
> With glossy leaf, and tawny bloom below:
> These, with our seaweeds rolling up and down,
> Form the contracted flora of the town.   (lines 290–303)

The mallow's reappearance prompts an apologetic footnote: yes, this vegetation does resemble that of *The Village*, 'but that also was a maritime country' and the poet has varied the two descriptions 'as much as I could, consistently with my wish to be accurate'. Crabbe knew he was not alone in this thirst for accuracy. In this heyday of natural history, a reading public was forming which, like the man in *Cranford* who is grateful to Tennyson for telling him that ash buds are black in March, delighted in such exactitude.

True to his word, Crabbe is describing an authentic plant association. It is not a wholly maritime one, although henbane, stonecrop and the common mallow all do well near the sea. John Clare was to describe an almost identical association inland, in which plants 'driven like rebels from the cultured soil' thrive in the waste ground round dwellings. His mallows however are seen in quite a different light from Crabbe's. 'Contented with their station', they 'lift their flowers / In blushing smiles'[47] on dunghills and their fruit provides children with playthings. But Crabbe's mallow, which in *The Village* had triumphantly lorded it over the blighted rye, in this context plunges a dagger root into the soil. Menace has taken the place of the oppression and ostentation implicit in the earlier passage. And the plants with which the mallow consorts are the most menacing that were to be found in Suffolk. A twentieth-century flower-seeker, Jocelyn Brooke, writing at a time when deadly nightshade was becoming rare, doubted that the next line could refer to anything worse than black nightshade, or even the colourful bittersweet.[48] But Crabbe, always precise, could not have described either as 'dull', whereas that is the right word for the purple-brown corollas (Thomas Hardy's 'doleful-bells'[49]) inside which form the deadly berries of *Atropa belladonna*. Henbane, source of the poison used by Dr Crippen, is scarcely less lethal. And the Roman nettle, first recorded at Aldeburgh by John Ray and identified in this passage by its round fruits, has a sting ferocious enough to have ensured its virtual extermination throughout Britain by the middle of the nineteenth century.[50]

Modern readers with an interest in the history of herbalism may at this point be distracted from the venom of this unpleasant trio by the thought that they could be the relics of a collection of herbs grown for their medicinal properties, and that such a collection might be of very great antiquity. *Urtica pilulifera* was brought to Britain by the Romans, and the deadly nightshade is conceivably the introduced variety that still survives today further south on the Suffolk coast, where there was once a Roman garrison. Crabbe's concern, however, is with 'The Poor and their Dwellings' in the here and now, and he makes sure that the note of alarm sounded in 'strikes' rings out loud and clear. Henbane is described in terms with which one might warn a child – 'If it's got light green leaves and speckled flowers and smells horrid, *leave it alone.*' For children are already present in the poem, and the toxicity of such plants serves as a pointer to the less avoidable dangers that surround them. The very

---

[47] 'Spring' in *The Midsummer Cushion*, lines 253–60.   [48] *The Military Orchid* (1948), p. 83.
[49] *Far from the Madding Crowd*, chapter 22.
[50] Francis Simpson in *Simpson's Flora of Suffolk* (1982) gives, however, a post-1950 record from Iken, near Aldeburgh.

whimsicality with which their games are described brings ironically home to us that the puddles on which they sail their boats are not the Round Pond. 'Dreadless' Crabbe calls the child-admirals, in the bitter knowledge that they have everything to fear from the diseases – now known to be water-borne – that threaten to destroy their dreams of sea adventures. Child mortality had been very real to him ever since he had been appointed, in his early twenties, to provide attendance and medicine to the inmates, many among them 'parents who know no children's love',[51] of Aldeburgh's grim poor-house. A passage that we might otherwise read as a bit of botanic self-indulgence has forced us to share this awareness; and Crabbe strengthens its effect by following it up with another glimpse of slum conditions. In 'the warm alley and the long close lane' where 'we fear to breathe the putrefying mass' and the decaying seaweed adds its stench to the 'stifling fervour of the day'[52] other children are happily rolling in the dust. Even this failed physician knew the danger they were in, although he could not know its precise source: in his pre-Pasteur world, 'bad air' was of itself held to be the cause of many diseases.

In the cornfield weeds of *The Village* and the brown-field weeds of *The Borough* Crabbe puts his familiarity with the Aldeburgh flora to moral and satirical use. But both passages are driven by something beside the poet's pity and indignation on behalf of endangered slum children and of those who struggle to make a living from the soil. That something is the poet's enjoyment of the vitality, variety and – *pace* George who thought his father had no aesthetic sense – beauty of the plants he describes. Of course poverty and neglect are responsible for the thatch of the slum cottages being covered with stonecrop and for ferns thrusting through cracks in the walls. We take the point: but we recognise too that Crabbe rejoices at the expanse of yellow blossoms and that, for all his misgivings about the sentience of plants, he has transferred to the ferns his own delight in their glossy existence. Cheerfulness has broken in.

Crabbe for his part was well aware of the conflicting emotions that caused him to see the environs of his birthplace as at one moment a Godforsaken waste and at another an earthly paradise. This attraction and repulsion made, as Forster said, for an uncomfortable mind;[53] but an uncomfortable mind can be the source of vigorous poetry, as is shown, in Crabbe's case, by one of the liveliest of his stories in verse, and one inspired from start to finish by the fascination that Suffolk plant life always held for him.

---

[51] *The Village*, book I, line 233.   [52] *The Borough*, letter XVIII, lines 304–9.
[53] E. M. Forster, *Two Cheers for Democracy* (1951), p. 181.

'The Lover's Journey' opens with the poet pondering what we would now call the pathetic fallacy:

> It is the soul that sees; the outward eyes
> Present the object, but the mind descries;
> And thence delight, disgust, or cool indiff'rence rise.
>
>   . . .
>
> Our feelings still upon our views attend,
> And their own natures to the objects lend.   (lines 1–3, 10–11)

The feelings explored in the tale are those of a lover whose mood of happy expectancy, as he rides northwards along the coast towards his sweetheart's home, transforms a series of dull landscapes into idyllic scenery; but whose disappointment and jealousy when he learns she has gone to see a friend ('means she to a female friend?') render detestable the pleasant landscape through which he passes on his extended ride to join her. Once the two are reunited, however, all resentment vanishes, and on the return journey together neither pays the slightest heed to, nor is even aware of, their surroundings.

The story is autobiographical and based on an episode in Crabbe's courtship of Sara Elmy, then living at Beccles. 'It was in his walks between Aldeburgh and Beccles', his son tells us, 'that Mr Crabbe passed through the very scenery described in the first part of "The Lover's Journey"; while near Beccles, in another direction, he found the contrast of rich vegetation introduced in the latter part of that tale.'[54] From Aldeburgh to Beccles is twenty-three miles. Crabbe's generation were great pedestrians, so probably George is right and his father, at a time when he scarcely had enough money to feed himself, let alone a horse, did walk all the way, and on one occasion was understandably downcast to find he had to plod several miles further inland. Only in the fiction can Orlando – for so Laura, baptised Susan, likes to call her inamorato – be mounted, as befits a hero of chivalric romance. But there is a more structural reason for the change. Crabbe needs an objective view of the various landscapes to contrast with the lover's highly subjective one. Yet the whole point of the story is that there is no such thing as an objective view. Crabbe's way out of this difficulty is covertly to split his observer into two, so that we are aware by turns of a younger self whose experience is that of the foot traveller and of an older self on horseback. The latter takes a Cobbett-like view of the countryside's productivity – or rather, since Cobbett had yet to begin his

---

[54] *Life*, p. 35.

rural rides, a view such as would have been taken by Sara's uncles and
cousins, yeoman farmers whose consent was needed if ever the lovers were
to marry. At the time the story was written this was also a state of mind that
Crabbe, as middle-aged country rector, property-owner and magistrate,
was able to understand.

For such a character a word sums up the first stage of the journey: a
'barren' heath has to be cantered over as quickly as possible. But traversed
at a footpace and closer to the ground, the heath offers 'joy' to the lover of
Laura – and of other plants:

> 'This neat low gorse,' said he, 'with golden bloom,
> Delights each sense, is beauty, is perfume;
> And this gay ling, with all its purple flowers,
> A man at leisure might admire for hours;
> This green-fringed cup-moss has a scarlet tip
> That yields to nothing but my Laura's lip;
> And then how fine this herbage!'   (lines 36–42)

Soon heath gives place to wretchedly poor and parched agricultural land
'where the dark poppy flourished on the dry / And sterile soil' (50–1).
'Dark' seems a perverse epithet for so luminous a flower, and it is meant to
be: to the farmer, poppies are blots on the landscape. At the same time, the
adjective is diagnostic: the young botanist on foot recognises *Papaver rhoeas*
by its black centre and a colour deeper than that of the long-headed poppy.
This is hardly a distinction that would be made by the grower of the crop,
to whom all weeds would be pernicious. But the traveller who is imagined –
or remembered – tramping through the sandy lanes is less aware of the
future harvest such as might be foreseen from the saddle than he is of the
colourful weeds that, at a footpace, he is able to identify in the corn; and
these, together with the wild roses and honeysuckles at eye and nose level in
the hedgerows on either side, cause him to exclaim (in words charged with
irony for readers who remember a similar context in *The Village*), 'With
what delight is labouring man repaid!' (line 53). And because the lover's
anticipation is compounded of joy and hope, it is fitting that his eye is
caught – as the young apothecary's would have been – by 'wholesome
wormwood', which adds thoughts of cures to the pleasures of smell and
sight that flank his passage.

There are no flowers to reflect on in the next stage of the journey, across
pasture grazed by evidently unimproved sheep that must afford a scant
income to the inhabitants of the hovels scattered near by. But the lover, still
in his mood of pastoral exuberance, attributes 'ease, peace, pleasure' to
these, even as his mature *alter ego* is taking a more Cobbett-like impression

from the piles of miserable-looking turf by each dwelling and from the 'meagre herbage'. 'Herbage' is a favourite word with Cobbett when he is summing up the quality of pasture. It was not, however, of grazing that the lover had been thinking when he reflected on the heath's 'fine herbage', but of the range of delicate grass and sedge flowers above foliage that livestock might well find unpalatably tough.

A sunken boat is the only sign of human life in the desolate salt marsh across which the lover rides next. It could have once belonged to Peter Grimes, for in this descriptive set piece Crabbe evokes, as tellingly as he had done in that narrative, the smells, sounds and currents of a tidal estuary. From the causeway, the rider commands 'a prospect wild and wide' of what is today the great nature reserve of Minsmere. For a foot-traveller, however, the vegetation would have been nearer to eye level, and it is from this perspective that Crabbe lists the wetland plants, in a set flower piece that he frames between two verse triplets:

> The rushes sharp that on the borders grow
> Bend their brown flowerets to the stream below,
> Impure in all its course, in all its progress slow:
> Here a grave flora scarcely deigns to bloom,
> Nor wears a rosy blush, nor sheds perfume.
> The few dull flowers that o'er the place are spread,
> Partake the nature of their fenny bed:
> Here on its wiry stem, in rigid bloom,
> Grows the salt lavender that lacks perfume;
> Here the dwarf sallows creep, the septfoil harsh,
> And the soft slimy mallow of the marsh.
> Low on the ear the distant billows sound,
> And just in view appears their stony bound.
> No hedge nor tree conceals the glowing sun,
> Birds, save a watery tribe, the district shun,
> Nor chirp among the reeds where bitter waters run.   (lines 113–28)

Dreariness is what Crabbe is aiming at in this description of the fen's 'few dull flowers'. But the passage does not work that way. In the first place, the four species he names are either pleasing to the eye or of interest to the botanist-cum-herbalist. Though only a few plants of the admittedly scentless sea lavender would be in bloom in June (the month in which the story is set), the lover's mood of joyous anticipation could well conjure up the sheet of colour that even a sober botanical writer has called 'the most lovely sight that a salt marsh can offer'.[55] And though the flowering time of

---

[55] Ian Hepburn, *Flowers of the Coast* (1952), p. 74.

willows is past, there would be a pleasure of recognition for Crabbe the plant-seeker in identifying the *Salix repens* var. *fusca* that is special to certain East Anglian fens.[56] The cheerful yellow stars of tormentil (Crabbe's 'sept-foil') could strew the drier ground in June, and the epithet 'harsh' is a reminder of his concern with the medical uses of plants; the hard, astringent root of tormentil provided a medicine for colic – as also did the sea lavender's seeds. All the same, tormentil seems out of place in a salt marsh, and one wonders if Crabbe is using 'septfoil' for the marsh cinquefoil, (common at that time) which has suitably sombre purple flowers, astringent properties, and leaves with (frequently) *seven* leaflets as against the tormentil's three. There is no such problem of identification with 'the soft slimy mallow of the marsh': Crabbe must countless times have grasped the velvety leaves of the marsh mallow when digging up its mucilaginous and medically valuable tap root. But 'Dull' is surely the last word to describe the thick-set pink flowers of this striking columnar plant, which has been described as 'an exquisite surprise in muddy, salty, desolate, smelly surroundings'.[57]

Delight and fascination have broken into Crabbe's sombre scene. Realising that the plant-association he has described is just not dismal enough, he tries again in a long footnote to present the vegetation of a salt marsh as unattractively as possible. In the ditches are to be found 'a coarse and stained' seaweed, horsetails, 'a fat-leaved pale-flowering scurvy-grass', and 'the razor-edged bull-rush' (that is, fen sedge); the fen itself has 'a dark and saline herbage' that includes rushes, arrowgrass and saltwort. There are sea-asters and sea thrift too, but the reader who thinks of both as even more colourful than sea lavender is quickly put right. This sea-aster is 'the dullest of that genus', meaning (if I may hazard a guess) the dismal-looking East Anglian species that has no purple ray florets, and the thrift is a local blue-ish variety, 'withering, and remaining withered till the winter scatters it'. And Crabbe concludes the note in a tone that mocks the pleasure that has crept into the verse description. The marsh's smell, 'half-saline, half-putrid' would repel most people, 'but there are others to whom singularity of taste or association of ideas has rendered it agreeable and pleasant'. By now, of course, he has completely defeated his other purpose – to show the marsh flora as not only dull but species-poor into the bargain.

Up to this point, the lover's reactions to each scene have included a rather forced allusion to Laura. But before he turns towards the green

---

[56] This species, the creeping willow, is actually a low bush. But it seems unlikely that Crabbe means the true dwarf willow, *Salix herbacea*, a mountain plant.

[57] Grigson, *Englishman's Flora*, p. 110.

pastures where his betrothed grew up, his thoughts place her fairly and squarely at the centre of the desolate scenery that represents the life he is offering her. He only draws a line at the smelly salt marsh, exchanging it in his imagination for the kind of heathland bog made fragrant by the sweet gale (sweet myrtle) that figured in the opening of *The Borough*:

> 'Various as beauteous, Nature, is thy face,'
> Exclaimed Orlando; 'all that grows has grace,
> All are appropriate – bog, and marsh, and fen,
> Are only poor to undiscerning men.
> Here may the nice and curious eye explore,
> How Nature's hand adorns the rushy moor;
> Here the rare moss in secret shade is found,
> Here the sweet myrtle of the shaking ground;
> Beauties are these that from the view retire,
> But well repay th'attention they require;
> For these my Laura will her home forsake,
> And all the pleasures they afford partake.   (lines 129–40)

These lines form a climax to the story's autobiographical subtext. Its narrrative peak comes later when, after striking inland, the lover arrives at Laura's home, only to discover she has left it to visit friends. Here Crabbe is at his entertaining best as a storyteller. The couplets quicken into a convincing mixture of train-of-thought with verbal exchange, behaviour that at first surprises proves on reflection to be true to life (the confrontation we have been expecting turns into an embrace) and as the lovers subsequently journey home together, momentum is maintained in a rapid re-wind of the scenes the lover has passed through but which are now 'viewless' to him, cocooned as he is in happiness.

In all this, Crabbe the botanist has not disappeared. The bitter comments the lover makes on the verdant inland landscape reflect not only the character's disappointment, but also that often experienced by his creator. What is the beauty, he demands to know, of 'vile beans with deleterious smell' and 'deep fat meadows'?

> I hate these long green lanes; there's nothing seen
> In this vile country but eternal green.   (lines 260–1)

This is a countryside in which every landowner could boast, with Richard of *Tales of the Hall*, that 'to land like this, no botanist will come' because weeds 'have no – what? – no *habitat* with me'.[58] Crabbe complained, when

---

[58] *Tales of the Hall*, book IV, lines 82, 87.

he had drawn up his list of plants in Framlingham, that this inland parish had a limited flora, 'there being no great diversity of soil, nor any extensive morass, or other uncultivated land'.[59] And when the reforming bishops finally compelled him to return to Leicestershire, he had to exchange easy access to all that Gerard Manley Hopkins in 'Inversnaid' would praise as 'wildness and wet . . . the weeds and the wilderness' for life in what George termed 'a clayey desert':[60] a monotonous landscape of enclosed corn and turnip fields, where the only safe haven for wild flowers was Crabbe's own garden.

We do not know how far ahead of its publication in 1812 'The Lover's Journey' was written, but Crabbe's description of the salt marsh suggests that, at the time of composition, he was at some remove from such scenery, both in time and place. There is a nostalgic overtone, and there are oddities in the double catalogue of plants: Crabbe writes 'arrowhead' (a freshwater aquatic) for 'arrowgrass';[61] and that thrift, i.e. sea-*pinks*, should be blue is hardly conceivable.[62] The probability is that he wrote the poem some years after the family's return to the Midlands in 1805. This would mean that it belongs to a time when his wife's condition had worsened into dementia, so that when he turned to her it was to find that, in a very real sense, she was no longer there. 'Mrs Crabbe only lived to the present', he later confided to a friend. 'We could not speak of the past. We could not hope together for the future.'[63] But Crabbe himself could speak of the past in his poetry, and in so doing recall a time when there had been hope for the future. Some forty years previously, at the end of a long, hot journey, he had sought 'Mira' and found her not to be there: even, he thought in a panic of jealousy, lost to him forever. But then he had only to struggle on a little further to regain her, and for good it would seem, since that was at a time when, as in his quest for little-known flowers, patience and persistence could expect to be rewarded. Despite this, in the end 'happiness was not granted',[64] as he was to write, many years later, in a blank space of a letter

---

[59] *History of Framlingham*, p. 449.   [60] *Life*, p. 191.

[61] Crabbe in his footnote refers to this as part of the 'herbage', as distinct from the water-plants, so he must mean *Triglochin maritima*, marsh arrow-grass. Arrowhead proper – *Sagittaria sagittifolia* – gives trouble to other writers in this book: Clare before he learns its real name calls it frogwort, and Ruskin confuses it with water plantain. Lawrence wisely leaves it unnamed in a memorable passage of *Women in Love*.

[62] Perhaps Crabbe was remembering the white variety of sea-thrift that still grows on the coast a little south of Aldeburgh.

[63] *Selected Letters*, p. 118.

[64] Thus in the original letter in A. M. Broadley's grangerised *Life of Crabbe*. George in referring to the letter writes 'happiness was denied'.

that Sara had sent him in the early days of their marriage. It is perhaps fitting that now the flowers have also gone. Sundew and sweet gale have vanished from Aldeburgh's heaths.

After Sara's death in 1813, Crabbe lost interest in his wild flower garden, and readily accepted the offer of a living in the west of England. There he virtually abandoned botany in favour of geology. Though he bought Patrick Keith's *Physiological Botany* on its publication in 1824 and placed it on his sitting-room shelves next to his Linnaeus, he complained of it being too specialised a work.[65] Botany was showing the first signs of becoming a laboratory science: something very different from the process of search and discovery that, for this reserved man, had constituted a passion that he instinctively called upon in his poetry to strengthen the expression of his deepest feelings. In 'The Lover's Journey' the evocation of a happiness that was later withdrawn is powered by Crabbe's recall of the unique flora from which he was later exiled, just as in other places vivid memories of that flora give strength and substance to – 'fix' as it were – a major concern of his life and work: the misery of poverty as he had himself experienced it and as he exposed it in *The Village* and *The Borough*.

[65] Catalogue of books at one end of UC Adds. 4426; *Selected Letters*, p. 305.

CHAPTER 4

John Clare: bard of the wild flowers

John Keats could not see the flowers that surrounded him as he listened 'darkling' to his Hampstead nightingale, although from their scent he guessed them to be hawthorn, sweetbriar, sweet violets and 'the coming musk rose'. A few miles away, in Epping Forest, but two decades later in time, John Clare was to listen to another nightingale singing, as the species mostly does, by daylight – the light of a long May evening in which the poet's eye would distinguish, below the intense green of young beech and hawthorn leaves, a ground layer of bracken, orchids and foxgloves, 'where mugwort grows like mignonette'.[1] Mugwort was familiar to Keats from his medical studies. But it is difficult to imagine him giving it a place in his verse; whereas the flicker of self-mockery in 'like mignonette' suggests that Clare knows *Artemesia vulgaris* to be as much at home in his poetry under its common name as sweetbriar is in Keats's ode under its pastoral name of eglantine. As honest, sturdy mugwort, it takes its due place, alongside ragwort, fleabane and sow thistle, among the 370 plants that Clare actually names in his poetry and prose.

This is an astonishing tally. Indeed the list is so comprehensive that when Clare fails to mention a common wild flower we find ourselves asking why. What of red campion, subject of the first ever poem written by his fellow-Midlander, D. H. Lawrence? A glance at the distribution map for *Silene dioica* shows it to be ubiquitous in central England *except* for an area south of the Wash and extending to Clare's village of Helpston. Of the plants Clare does name, about a fifth are cultivated, for he was a gardener

---

[1] 'To the Nightingale' ('I love to hear . . .'). My quotations from Clare's poetry are from the Oxford Standard Authors edition: Eric Robinson and David Powell (eds.), *The Early Poems of John Clare* (1989); Eric Robinson, David Powell and P. M. S. Dawson (eds.), *John Clare: Poems of the Middle Period, 1822–1837* (1996, 1998 and 2003); Eric Robinson and David Powell, *The Later Poems of John Clare* (1984). In quoting Clare and his correspondents, I have normalised spelling and, to a very small extent, punctuation. Poem titles are as given in the consolidated index of titles and first lines in volume V of *John Clare: Poems of the Middle Period*. When a poem is untitled or a title is duplicated, I give the opening words. I also give line numbers for poems over 100 lines in length.

by training, by definition ('gardening' was given as his usual occupation when he was admitted to the Northampton General Lunatic Asylum in 1841), and above all by choice; his letters home during the asylum years repeatedly and touchingly ask after his garden. Besides relishing cottage garden favourites such as bear's breeches and summer sultan, he had aspired to grow 'florist' flowers. 'Made a new frame for my auriculas' he recorded in his journal for 25 May 1825.[2] But the words that immediately follow, 'found a large white orchis in Oxey Wood', point to his real priorities. Like Dorothy Wordsworth and George Crabbe, Clare made his garden a refuge for wild flowers; the inside cover of a standard work on the cultivation of auriculas and other fashionable plants served him as a handy place in which to list the individual orchids of over a dozen species that he had transplanted to the shelter of his privet hedge. His practice of giving these introduced plants plenty of their original soil seems to have ensured their survival against all the odds, although his neighbours, knowing nothing of orchids' dependence on mycorrhizal fungi, simply declared him 'a wonderful man with flowers'.[3] Affection, as the most scientifically minded gardeners would covertly agree, may well have played its part, and Clare's primary affection was for the native plants he had known since his childhood. Asked, after years of institutional living, for verses to be inscribed on the back of his portrait, he wrote of himself as 'Bard of the wild flowers / Rain-washed and wind-shaken'.[4] That aspect of Clare's poetry is the theme of this chapter.

I

Clare's father was a thresher: in Northamptonshire speech, a whopstraw. In the poet's third publication, *The Shepherd's Calendar* (1827), his father is to be found shut away from the flowers of May as he toils in a dusty barn. But he must have been working for once out of doors, probably making hay in an open field in the south-east of Helpston parish, when he sent his teenage son to refill his water bottle from a spring that issued from the field as a willow-fringed stream. By Clare's reckoning, the date on which he performed this very ordinary errand was around 1809: at a time, that is, when he had discovered poetry through reading James Thomson's *The Seasons*

[2] Eric Robinson and David Powell (eds.), *John Clare by Himself* (1996), p. 230. (Hereafter *Himself.*)

[3] J. W. and Anne Tibble, *John Clare: a Life* (1972), p. 304. The most recent and authoritative biography of Clare is Jonathan Bate's (*John Clare: a Biography* (2003)), to which I am very much indebted in this chapter, as I am also to Margaret Grainger's *Natural History Prose Writings of John Clare* (1984).

[4] 'By Clare – to be placed at the back of his portrait'.

and had made the further discovery that he could write verses himself. For what made the day memorable to Clare was that, as he came and went to Round Oak Spring, he composed one of his earliest poems.

'Noon' owes something to Thomson's description of a heatwave, though its scampering seven-syllable couplets suggest that Clare was already reading poets of the rural scene who preferred the lighter measure of Milton's *L'Allegro*. But the heart of the poem is a completely non-bookish response to a group of heat-stressed brookside plants. The once pink flowers of ragged robin are burnt black and its leaves crumble at a touch; the normally exuberant and upstanding meadowsweet is 'drowking', that is, wilting; and, surest sign of drought conditions, 'the dew is parchèd up / From the teasel's jointed cup'. Writing a lifetime later for an urban readership, Richard Jefferies would dwell at length on the water-holding capacity ('as much as two or three wine glasses')[5] of that jointed cup, formed by the conjuncture of paired leaves round the stem of the wild teasel. Clare, who is in a hurry, must capture the plant's distress in the briefest of images: soon he is at the springhead and, looking towards the heath south of the field, he calls upon its parched birds to leave 'the shadeless gorse' for these cool waters:

> There your little feet may stand
> Safely on the printing sand,
> While in full possession, where
> Purling eddies ripple clear,
> You with ease and plenty blest
> Sip the coolest and the best.

Clare tells us that he made many changes in the early poems included in the collection that he succeeded in getting into print in 1820 as *Poems Descriptive of Rural Life and Scenery*. But however much he may have altered 'Noon', the poem has retained in all its purity the experience of thirst and exhaustion, of *drowking*, as man shares it with bird, beast and flower. The intimacy of that sharing and the specificity of the plants together offer a foretaste of Clare's poetry at its best, making the poem stand out in a rather conventional collection. Apart from a handful of garden flowers, of which a scabious 'so chocolately dusk'[6] is the most memorable, the plants named in this first volume are limited to the spring blossoms and cornfield weeds that had been the staple of late eighteenth-century pastoral and bucolic verse. By 1820 the generalised language of this

---

[5] Quoted by Richard Mabey, *Flora Britannica* (1996), p. 351.   [6] 'The Wish', line 155.

kind of poetry had become deadening in its effect, so that when the first of the hundreds of primroses in Clare's poetry starts up 'between / Dead matted leaves of ash and oak' it has to struggle against such dead matted phrases as 'thy presence beautifies the ground' and submit to being gazed at by 'the meek shepherd' and plucked 'with rude delight'. This sonnet, 'The Primrose', was however very much to the taste of the Town; quoted time and again in reviews and reprinted in magazines, it helped *Poems of Rural Life* to achieve a fourth edition within fifteen months.

This sunshine of public acclaim brought out an astonishing profusion of wild flowers in Clare's second collection, *The Village Minstrel* (1821). But it is in *The Shepherd's Calendar*, in which the poet recreates the pre-enclosure world of his parents, that the grassroots affinity between man and plant implicit in 'Noon' and a few other early poems is most fully developed. Here, flowers appear in their communal aspects, as weeds to be eradicated or herbs to heal, as a part of children's games or of courtship bouquets – including, in 'June', a clipping-posy that Shakespeare's Perdita might have carried to an earlier sheep-shearing feast. One passage in particular, from 'May', deserves quotation at length because it so vividly represents the awareness of plant life with which Clare grew up:

> Each morning now the weeders meet
> To cut the thistle from the wheat
> And ruin in the sunny hours
> Full many wild weeds of their flowers:
> Corn poppies that in crimson dwell
> Called 'headaches' from their sickly smell;
> And carlock yellow as the sun
> That o'er the May fields thickly run;
> And 'iron weed' content to share
> The meanest spot that spring can spare –
> E'en roads where danger hourly comes –
> Is not wi'out its purple blooms
> And leaves wi' pricks like thistles round
> Thick set, that have no strength to wound,
> That shrink to childhood's eager hold
> Like hair; and with its eye of gold
> And scarlet starry points of flowers
> Pimpernel, dreading nights and showers,
> Oft called 'the shepherd's weather glass',
> That sleep till suns have dried the grass
> Then wakes and spreads its creeping bloom
> Till clouds or threatening shadows come,
> Then close it shuts to sleep again

Which weeders see and talk of rain
And boys that mark them shut so soon
Will call them 'John go bed at noon';
And fumitory too, a name
That superstition holds to fame
Whose red and purple mottled flowers
Are cropped by maids in weeding hours
To boil in water milk and whey
For washes on an holiday
To make their beauty fair and sleek
And scour the tan from summer's cheek;
And simple small forget-me-not
Eyed wi' a pin's-head yellow spot
I' th' middle of its tender blue
That gains from poets notice due.
These flowers their toil by crowds destroys
And robs them of their lonely joys,
That met the May wi' hopes as sweet
As those her suns in gardens meet;
And oft the dame will feel inclined
As childhood memory comes to mind
To turn her hook away and spare
The blooms it loved to gather there.   (lines 147–92)

Scenes of field labourers at work were part of the bucolic tradition. James Hurdis, whose poems were known to Clare, has one in *The Village Curate* (1788). But Hurdis's weeders are picturesque touches of colour in the landscape, viewed from a safe distance at which the chatter he condemns as idleness cannot offend his ear. He is, after all, in holy orders, besides being Oxford's Professor of Poetry. Clare, by contrast, is right in there among the weeders, engaged in what is known across the Atlantic as stoop labour; indeed, the 'dame', who appears to have kept her weeding hook from a time when seed was scattered broadcast, must be bent double. Seed drills were in use by Clare's time, so conceivably the younger members of the gang are hoeing abreast between the rows, and their desultory talk gives the passage its garrulity. If you smell *that* flower you'll get a headache. Look, these ones have closed up – it must be going to rain. Keep those, they make a good face wash.

It all sounds agreeably unhurried. Yet the gang know that their daily bread depends on their quick recognition and destruction of each threat to the young crop. Like many other passages in Clare's poetry, the passage in 'May' is grounded in a peasant acceptance that human life is sustained by the exploitation of growing things: for fuel – in winter the 'stickers' are everywhere collecting firewood; for shelter – reeds and sedges must be cut for thatch; above all, for food. Clare and his childhood companions were sometimes so hungry that they took advantage of the farmer being in church to invade his field of peas and boil up a Sunday meal on a makeshift fire. In contrast to the boy Wordsworth who, carefully dressed in old clothes, pauses to luxuriate in the sight of laden hazel branches before he strips them, Helpston's urchins are genuinely ragged and ravenous, so that they fall like a flock of birds on whatever the hedgerows can provide: blackberries and dewberries, haws 'like sugar plums'[7] (the improbable comparison shows just how hungry they are) and other fruit too sharp even for them until they have been roasted by

> boys that sit right merry in a ring
> Round fires upon a molehill toasting sloes
> And crabs that froth and frizzle on the coals.[8]

Besides plants that could supply the basic needs for food and shelter, there were dozens that could be put to other uses. Playthings for the young were provided by the many-stalked cowslip clusters that were tied into balls and tossed over garlands strung from eave to eave in a May Day game; by celandines that, held under the chin, foretold a golden future; and by the seeds of mallow that furnished food for pretend feasts eaten off broken saucers. Poppies and cornflowers were bunched into military cockades, and in the same game of soldiers the hollow stems of wild angelica or hogweed 'made bugles spout their twanging sounds'.[9] A few years on, less innocuous amusement came from the spores of puffballs, which a girl might use 'To smut the brown cheek of the teasing swain'.[10] He for his part could retaliate by hiding the explosive seed-vessels of 'touch-me-not' among the flowers in a gift posy,[11] By this age girls – as the 'May' passage goes on to tell us – would be stripping the florets off knapweed and tucking the remaining knobs between their breasts, in the belief that, if their lovers were true, new florets would grow there.

Undeterred by this hard test, Helpston couples sometimes achieved an independent roof over their heads and duly safeguarded its thatch from lightning by planting it with house-leek (the southern name of which, 'welcome-home-husband-though-never-so-drunk', Patty Clare might have appreciated). Rafters beneath the thatch would be hung with dried plants, for as George Herbert had said in 'Life', flowers were 'fit while [they] lived

---

[7] 'Remembrances', line 22.   [8] 'The Shepherd's Fire'.   [9] 'The Last of Autumn', line 68.
[10] 'October' (*The Shepherd's Calendar*), line 65.   [11] 'The Sorrows of Love', lines 65–7.

for smell and ornament / And after death for cures'. Clare's Woodman, in the poem of that title, grows agrimony and self-heal with which to treat the cuts that are an inevitable part of his work. For the cure of other ailments he would have recourse to 'The Village Doctress', who searches for simples with a sharp eye for the distinctive feature of each species:

> self-heal flowering in a russet husk
> And scurvy-grass that pursy grannies prize
> With dwarf heath-mallow smelling faint of musk
> Bogbean too shining in its mozzly dyes
> Brooklime that on the shallow water lies
> With famous eyebright's slightly pencilled flowers.   (lines 127–32)

These are some aspects of the practical and everyday relationship with the plant kingdom represented in the passage from 'May' that I have quoted. But what gives the passage a Wordsworthian depth is the way Clare credits his weeders with a sensibility over and above the peasant common sense of their plant lore. Weeds must be hunted down but, as in all predatory situations, the hunter's need to understand his prey brings him into secret sympathy with its claim on life: here, with the 'lonely joys' of plant existence. In later poems, Clare would frequently raise his voice about man's trampling destructiveness. The voice we hear in this passage is however low-toned and not exclusively Clare's, since the poet alluded to is in fact Coleridge, whose 'blue and bright-eyed floweret of the brook' carries a footnote commendation of the name 'forget-me-not'.[12] Clare's own sensibility is here sunk in a common tenderness: any, or all, of the weeders might remember a child's pleasure in discovering that the leaves of the thistle-like knapweed are soft to the touch, or share the old woman's recollection of some eye-to-eye encounter in childhood with a wild flower.

For the awareness of plant life that Clare here records is communal in ways beyond the sharing of current purposes and pleasures. The permanence of the countryside's green mantle, together with the re-emergence spring after spring of its flowers, bind together past and present generations as well as the past and present of the individual. Hence the pain felt by Clare and his fellow-villagers at the disappearance of any tree to which village custom had given a landmark quality, and their much deeper pain at the changes wrought by the Enclosures in their community's way of life. Hence too, in his mature poetry, the linking of nature's green permanence with the continuity of verbal communication. Long before the boy David

---

[12] Coleridge, 'The Keepsake'.

became king of Israel, he sat composing his psalms on 'the seat of velvet hue' that moss provided:

> And David's crown hath passed away
> Yet poesy breathes his shepherd skill;
> His palace lost – and to this day
> The little moss is blooming still.[13]

A continuity such as this, in which 'the grass eternal springs / Where castles stood and grandeur died', and in which the flower that Eve showed to Adam blooms on through millennia – 'Ay still the child with pleasure in his eye / Shall cry "The daisy!"'[14] – is the way Clare and the community he came from saw eternity. *The Christian Year* and *The Shepherd's Calendar*, were published within months of one another in 1827, but culturally they belong to different worlds. Keble, the dogmatic theologian, celebrates the great creedal festivals in hymns that finish up resoundingly with the Church Triumphant. Clare, as is made plain in the poem called 'Apocalypse' which was written about the same time as *The Shepherd's Calendar*, is appalled at the prospect of the skies passing away like a worn garment. His earthbound religion has much closer affinities with that of the undogmatic majority who do not ask for a new heaven and a new earth, and whose thoughts of perpetuity today attach themselves to the sheaves of the harvest festival and the poppies of Remembrance Sunday.

2

In *The Shepherd's Calendar* Clare seems to share whole-heartedly in his neighbours' close-to-the-soil awareness of plant life. So it is mildly disconcerting to find that there are places in his writings where he dismisses his fellow-villagers as 'clowns' who are insensible to the beauty round them and contrasts their boorishness with the responses of the Man of Taste. Try as we may to adjust to the favourable Regency colouring of this last word – approximately 'an educated sensibility' – it is difficult not to feel a touch of the pretentious in Clare's apostrophe to Taste in 'A Ramble' (1819):

> O Taste, thou charm
> That so endears and nature makes so lovely,
> Nameless enthusiastic ardour thine!
> That 'wildered witching rapture 'quisitive
> Stooping – bent genius – o'er each object; thine

---

[13] 'The Flitting', lines 85–8.   [14] *Ibid.*, lines 215–16; 'The Eternity of Nature', lines 13–14.

> That longing pausing wish that cannot pass
> Uncomprehended things without a sigh
> For wisdom to unseal the hidden cause;
> That hankering gaze [i]s thine that fairly would
> Turn the blue blinders of the heavens aside
> To see what gods are doing.

This is very grand, not to say grandiose, and a long way from the poetic manner of 'Noon,' which must have been taking its final form about the same time. Most readers will find the voice of the 'real' Clare in 'Noon'; yet there is something quite as true to common experience in this other poem's reaching-out after the riches that lay beyond a basic literacy. This was the time in Clare's life when, he tells us, 'I puzzled over everything in my hours of leisure that came in my way: mathematics, astronomy, botany and other things . . .'[15] One of the earliest books he owned was John Hill's *Useful Family Herbal* (1754), a work that he said 'gave me a taste for wild flowers'.[16] But Hill's book, despite the pleasure it often expresses in the beauty of a flower, was of small use as a flora: it is a survey, arranged alphabetically, of those plants, as often as not exotics, that Hill held to have curative properties. In search of a further guide to his botanising, Clare turned to *An Introduction to the Science of Botany*, James Lee's 1760 outline of the Linnaean classes and orders, only to be mystified by what he calls a dark system. He may well have been struggling with the Linnaean names of floral parts when he wrote the lines that the Oxford editors are almost certainly right to include as part of 'A Ramble':

> And here beside the dead bent's rustling tuft
> A blossom hides its beauties from the world;
> And such a one as Nature's happiest hand
> Ne'er took a tool to scoop and hollow out
> One of more curious interesting form.
> Its speckled petals calyx burnished gold
> Inmixed with sombre hues, exactly forms
> A living insect for industry famed.
> And hence this Nature's solitary gem
> That numbers in her calendar of curiosities
> Gains its distinguishment, though near unknown:
> The 'Bee Flower' – apt characteristic name.

At this point, the poem peters out in erasures. Its confusions of syntax and scansion suggest that Clare is no happier with James Thomson's

---

[15] *Himself*, p. 59.   [16] *Ibid.*, p. 61.

weighty blank verse style than he is with terms like 'calyx', as he stoops ('bent genius') to examine *Ophrys apifera*. To purloin a phrase of Dryden's: Clare needed not the spectacles of books to read nature. His instinctive way of looking at flowers is that represented by the phrases he uses for the commoner species of orchid, especially early purples: 'gaping, speckled cuckoo flowers', 'the pouched-lipped cuckoo bud' and, most effective of all in calling to mind the way two sepals rise wing-like on either side of the petals, 'little cuckoos creeping from their hood'.[17] Given this kind of feeling for the essential character of a flower, something as instantly recognisable as a friend's laugh or turn of the head, Clare could have little use for procedures that would consign it to order *Gyandria*: class *Monandria*: genus *Orchis*: species *mascula*. For him it was not a dried and labelled specimen but a living neighbour. Hence his greatest need was for a name to greet it by. 'When we notice flowers', he once wrote to an unidentified botanist – and to 'notice' was for him to realise intensely – 'we feel a desire to know their names as of so many friends and acquaintance.'[18] And herein lay the problem that he sums up when he writes of Helpston's wild flowers that 'I find it would require a second Adam to find names for them in my way and a second Solomon to understand them in Linnaeus's system.'[19] Villagers, Clare told his publishers, could put names to only a limited number of plants. There are quite a few 'nameless' flowers in his early poetry. He even addresses a whole poem to one, and several years later this 'little white starry flower with pale green grassy leaves'[20] is still anonymous. So too, later still, is an even smaller blossom he describes as 'chickweed 'sembling' (a mouse-ear?) with which he shares his growing realisation that he for his part may also become nameless:

> Then may thy little lot attend
> On me till life shall close:
> To meet the notice of a friend
> And be unknown to foes.[21]

It was not just that Clare had no names for the less common plants. The names by which he had always known the more common ones often did not match the ones he found in books. In Hill's *Family Herbal* early purple orchids are 'fool's stones' ('what a silly name for such beautiful flowers'[22]

---

[17] 'Summer' ('the oak's slow opening leaf . . .'); 'Recollections after a Ramble', line 227; 'May Noon'.
[18] Mark Storey (ed.), *The Letters of John Clare* (1985), p. 284. Hereafter *Letters*. [19] *Himself*, p. 62.
[20] Margaret Grainger (ed.), *The Natural History Prose Writings of John Clare* (1984), p. 23. Hereafter *Natural History*.
[21] 'Thou little tiny nameless thing'. [22] *Natural History*, p. 16.

says Clare) and 'cuckoo flower' is an alternative name for lady's smock. This last however was for Clare the name given by children to the wood anemone. *His* name for Hill's lady's smock was 'lilac', a name that he did not find easy to transfer to the showy garden shrub whose flower-spikes, because of their resemblance to the Prince of Wales's crest, were for him 'princifeathers'. In the end he was prepared to join Shakespeare and Chatterton in calling *Cardamine pratensis* 'lady smock'. But *Orchis mascula*'s right to the title of cuckoo flower he defended against all other claimants, including Shakespeare's 'yellow cuckoo buds' (which are presumably buttercups). He does, however, appear to have accepted a Shakespearean name when he uses 'long purples' for purple loosestrife – erroneously as it happens, since Shakespeare meant (and here the wheel is come full circle) early purple orchids: Clare's cuckoos.

It is not surprising that Clare, despite his belief that 'the vulgar are always the best glossary',[23] sometimes turned to the poets for plant names: many poets of the late eighteenth century, responding to the period's craze for botany, were lavish in enumerating country flowers and supplying Linnaean binominal names, and often descriptions as well, in footnotes. Among those familiar to Clare was John Scott of Amwell, who celebrated the floweriness and fecundity of a landscape not unlike Clare's own. Others such as Thomas Gisborne and James Hurdis were more in the didactic *Georgics* tradition than the pastoral one. As dependent on Linnaeus as Thomson had been on Newton, Hurdis gave *The Favourite Village* the flavour of a botanic text book: his marshy dells are lined with 'sumptuous caltha' (Clare stuck to 'horse blobs'), archangel stems are 'quadrangled tubes' and his snowdrops have 'fair tripetalous dependent flowers'.[24]

Clare was in dire need of guidance through this Babel of local, popular, horticultural, scientific and poetic names. Fortunately members of his own community who were far from being clowns were able to come to his aid. Three friends of his youth had the advantage of 'big house' connections, at a time when a local lad, provided he possessed or could get hold of enough book learning in addition to his in-service training, might hope to attain the post of Head Gardener to some aristocratic family: a position in which he would have access to his employer's library and sufficient means to acquire botanical and horticultural works for himself – as could have been Clare's own ambition when, as a garden boy at Burghley House, he somehow managed to buy one such book. Typical of these early friends was Thomas Porter, who had inherited botanical books from his

<hr>

[23] *Ibid.*   [24] *Poems* (1808), vol. III, pp. 165, 166, 151.

great-grandfather, sometime steward at Walcot Hall. The facts that it was Porter who had put Clare in the way of getting the job at Burghley House, and that he was still collecting books on horticulture in 1825, suggest that he too may have been a member of the big-house gardening fraternity. What we know for sure is that he was a close and trusted friend. For some years before his marriage Clare went every Sunday to Porter's cottage in nearby Ashton, whence the two of them would often set out to hunt for rare flowers and especially for orchids. When, in 1828 or soon afterwards, Clare recorded on a list of native orchids the places where each could be found, he named many spots within a couple of miles of Ashton. Bee orchids, for example, were 'quite plentiful' at Ufford and Ashton stone pits and in the quarry area slightly to the south-east known as Swordy Well.[25] Some poems in or contemporary with Clare's first two collections read like records of those outings. Porter could not only help Clare with the names of unusual plants from his own knowledge; he could also provide facts about them from what Clare calls his heirlooms: 'works of Ray, Parkinson and Gerard' which, by comparison with Lee's Linnaean schemata, were for Clare 'like meeting the fresh air and balmy summer of a dewy morning after the troubled dreams of a nightmare'.[26]

Thanks to knowledgeable friends such as Thomas Porter and to the pre-Linnaean botanical works to which they gave him access, Clare, in his second collection, *The Village Minstrel*, is emboldened to call many wild flowers by their delectable local names – lambtoes, horse blobs, totter grass and the like – and to name and particularise many more, such as agrimony, ploughman's spikenard and pellitory, that were nameless to the average villager. Sometimes in these poems we can detect the echo of an informative voice or informative printed phrase. 'Oddly rude, misshapen, tawny flowers'[27] suggests an attempt to put the poet right on the origins of the fluffy fruits of *Clematis vitalba* that he mistook for flowers (if so, it did not succeed: for the rest of his life he would call the old-man's-beard festooning hedgerows a flower). But this occasional prosiness has a kind of angular

---

[25] *Natural History*, p. 302. After half a century as a rubbish dump, this area has been rehabilitated – and Peter Marren has recorded ('Restoration of a Poet's Corner', *Daily Telegraph*, 10 April 2004) the reappearance of bee orchids.

[26] *Himself*, p. 62. Robert Heyes suggests to me that Clare is here confusing John Ray, whose botanic works are in Latin, with the florist John Rea, whose *Flora: seu, de florum cultura, or a Complete Florilege . . .*, first published in 1665, was just the kind of book Porter's great-grandfather might have handed down. 'Gerard' probably means Thomas Johnson's 1636 enlarged version of the Elizabethan herbal. Thomas Parkinson's *Theatrum botanicum* (1640) would have delighted Clare by its loving descriptions and lavish woodcuts.

[27] 'The Wild Flower Nosegay'.

5 Early purple orchid (*Orchis mascula*), called 'cuckoo flowers' by Clare and 'long purples' by Shakespeare, photographed in Rice Wood near Clare's village of Helpston.
© Peter Moyse A. R. S. P.

'Saw three fellows at the end of Royce [Rice] Wood who I found were laying out the plan for an 'iron railway' from Manchester to London . . . I little thought that fresh intrusions would interrupt and spoil my solitudes after the Enclosure. They will despoil a boggy place that is famous for orchises at Royce Wood end.'

(John Clare, Journal, 4 June 1825)
(Fortunately this very early railway plan came to nothing.)

charm much to be preferred to the literary bookishness that sometimes mars Clare's first collection. Porter had no taste for poetry but he could, and did, tell Clare when he had got his details right, and this gives an authentic, conversational note to a number of flower-strewn walk-in-the-country poems.

The botanic largesse of *The Village Minstrel* led one admirer to write that Clare's element was 'under a hedge, among the various grasses and herbs and mosses'.[28] To many readers this would not have been a high recommendation. This second collection met with nothing like the acclaim that had greeted Clare's first, and its comparative failure coloured his long tussle with his publishers over the poems intended for *The Shepherd's Calendar*. What delights a present-day admirer as his 'pellmell succession of vividly accurate impressions ... the inexorable one-after-the-otherness of the world'[29] was, in John Taylor's eyes, wearisome enumeration: disapproval that may have provoked the ingenuous lines that follow the weeding episode in 'May' in Clare's manuscript:

> My wild flower catalogue of flowers
> Grows in my rhymes as thick as showers.
> Tedious and long as they may be
> To some, they never weary me. (lines 193–6)

Though this is artless, the 'catalogues' themselves are not. The flower passages in *The Village Minstrel* are ordered by pre-Linnaean divisions of the plant kingdom ('Hollywell') or by season ('The Wild Flower Nosegay') or by habitat ('Solitude'), while in the narrative poem, 'The Cross Roads', they are grouped to dramatic effect: wild flowers gathered by its heroine prepare us, by their echoes of Ophelia's flowers, for her death by drowning, and their fragility contrasts with the vigour of those that have till now bloomed in her mother's garden – as in their turn these contrast with the docks and henbane, nettles and thistles of its present desolation. All the same, the plant lists of Clare's earlier poems, reflecting as they do the eager head-hunting of the tyro botanist as well as the rhetoric of the Georgic and pastoral traditions, convey, as he concedes, less to the reader than they do to the writer. In his mature poetry, he both sees his beloved wild flowers more clearly and presents them more tellingly, That he is able to do so is in large part thanks to further friendships.

---

[28] Letter in *The Literary Chronicle* quoted by Mark Storey, *Clare: the Critical Heritage* (1973), p. 147.
[29] Seamus Heaney, 'John Clare: a bicentenary lecture', in Hugh Haughton and Geoffrey Summerfield (eds.), *John Clare in Context* (1994), p. 136.

Clare once observed that every friendship he made grew into a warm attachment. That was certainly true of those he formed in 1822 with two members of the staff of Milton House, Northamptonshire home of the Fitzwilliam family. Edmund Artis, the house steward, and Joseph Henderson, the head gardener, were well-educated men who won public recognition for their scientific work. Beside a book on his archaeological finds at Castor, Artis published a pioneer work on palaeobotany. Henderson, who has been called 'one of the earliest of the great fern specialists',[30] earned associate membership of the Linnean Society through his published papers on cryptogams. More importantly for Clare, both were excellent all-round naturalists and both shared his range of interests, from natural history to contemporary poetry. Henderson's letters to the poet show us Clare collecting birds' nests, ferns and native orchids for Henderson and passing on journals to him; Henderson identifying plants and insects for Clare, sending him plants for his garden, encouraging him to draw (he was a first-rate draughtsman himself) and criticising his poetry with care and insight. Above all he responded with understanding to Clare's swings of mood. 'Had a visit from my friend Henderson of Milton who brought "Don Juan" in his pocket', Clare records in the journal that he kept for about a year from September 1824: 'I was very ill and nursing my head in my hand but he revived me ... We talked about books and flowers and butterflies.'[31]

Clare's depression in the autumn of 1824 had other grounds beside the debility following a long illness. John Taylor, although he had more than enough material for a third collection of Clare's poetry, was dragging his feet: he did not think much of parts of *The Shepherd's Calendar*, and verse was going out of fashion. This last trend may have shifted Clare's inclination at this time towards prose, and his new friendships would have guided his thoughts to natural history. Within a week of beginning his journal, he was planning to follow in the footsteps of Gilbert White with 'A Natural History of Helpston', to take the form of a series of letters to Taylor's partner, Hessey.[32] In fact Hessey had already, a year before this, received one such letter, as the result of his having sent Clare a copy of *Flora Domestica*, Elizabeth Kent's guide, anonymously published in 1823, to container gardening. What Clare most enjoyed in this book were its descriptions of the wild form of many plants, together with their popular names and relevant quotations from the poets, including Clare himself. Flattered, he responded with a plant-by-plant commentary on Kent's

[30] David Elliston Allen, *The Victorian Fern Craze* (1969), p. 6.   [31] *Himself*, p. 174.   [32] *Ibid.*, p. 172.

work, which is his most detailed piece of botanical writing. And a year later he returned to her book in his journal, noting down the resolution:

If I live I will write one on the same plan and call it *A Garden of Wild Flowers* ... An English Botany on this plan would be very interesting and serve to make botany popular, while the hard nickname-y system of unutterable words now in vogue only overloads it in mystery.[33]

There were few wild flowers out in late October, when this entry was made. But ferns were conspicuous in the bare woods, 'shining rich and resolutely green'[34] as Clare put it in a poem, and soon he and Henderson together were so 'passionately bent'[35] on fern collecting that transplanted specimens covered the end of Clare's garden. Some of these were gifts from Henderson, although when Clare went to see his friend's collection he could not forbear noting down that it was 'far from complete',[36] and before long he had the satisfaction of sending rare ferns the other way. It must have been on the same visit to Milton in December 1824 that Henderson showed Clare a beautifully illustrated work of Linnaean botany.[37] In so doing he in all probability discovered that the Swedish botanist's classification and nomenclature bewildered his friend, since we find him, ten days later, urging Clare to study systematic botany, not just in order to name a particular plant, but to learn 'the wonderful provisions of nature for its protection and propagation'[38] and the construction of its various parts which, by their variation from those of all others, would enable Clare to trace it to its class and order. And he ends by offering to send his friend 'an Introduction to Botany'.

That Clare remained unconverted is suggested by another letter written some three months later, in which Henderson rejects, on the grounds that it met neither his views nor Clare's, the idea of their collaborating on a flora of the neighbourhood – presumably the *Garden of Wild Flowers* Clare had had in mind the previous autumn. For Henderson, it would have been unthinkable not to arrange such a work on the Linnaean system with each plant assigned its scientific name and 'proper place', whereas for Clare these details would have been mere pedantry. So in its stead Henderson revives a plan, which the friends appear to have formed much earlier, for a

---

[33] *Himself,* p. 189. [34] 'The Spindle Tree'. [35] *Letters,* p. 313. [36] *Himself,* p. 202.

[37] Clare calls it 'a fine edition of Linnaeus's *Botany*', but Linnaeus's works in their original Latin are not illustrated. Dr Heyes has however tracked down what is probably the actual volume that Henderson showed Clare: John Miller's *Illustratio systematis sexualis Linnaei... An Illustration of the Sexual System of Linnaeus,* 1777, bequeathed to Lord Milton's father in 1804.

[38] Quoted by Robert Heyes, 'Looking to futurity: John Clare and provincial culture' (unpublished London University thesis, 1999), p. 214.

collaboration in which Clare would stick to what he did best: the portrayal of flowers *in poetry*.

> I have been thinking that if you were to take as the subject and title of a poem *The Poet's Flower Garden*, you would lay the best foundation for the scheme. The woods and the fields, where Nature is gardener, would furnish your materials and in it you might embody all the local names you are acquainted with and when we make our long talked of excursion I shall perhaps be able to help you to others, I would even go so far as to coin a few, for there are many of our most beautiful wild flowers that have no familiar English name. On these and the plants mentioned in your works generally I would write notes, giving the botanical name and any other remark that might be thought interesting, which with your own observations might follow on as an appendix to your works[39].

Clare's reaction to this proposal that Henderson should annotate the allusions to flowers in his poetry is hinted at by a journal entry made on the same day: 'Intend to call my Natural History of Helpston "Biographies of Birds and Flowers".'[40] This suggests that when Henderson expressed unwillingness to collaborate on a flora Clare immediately reverted to the idea of a Gilbert White-style work – and in fact a month later he records that he has resumed his letters on natural history. He may have turned to his other friend from Milton for help over this, since later in March 1825 another of Clare's correspondents, replying to something in a letter to her, tells him, 'it will do you good to be employed with Mr Artis in a History of your favourite birds and flowers'.[41] But there is nothing in all this to suggest that Henderson's plan for an annotated edition of Clare's Works – prestigious word – was unwelcome. On the contrary, it must have helped to restore Clare's confidence in his future as a poet at a time when his publishers appeared to have lost theirs. Only a week after receiving Henderson's letter, he bought the manuscript book into which he began to copy his best poems, and which would be the basis of the collection he made a few years later under the title of *The Midsummer Cushion*.

Artis left Milton in 1826, but Clare's friendship with Henderson continued as warmly as ever. Lord Milton had a passion for orchids, and Clare, who had been collecting native species ever since his orchid forays with Porter, delighted Henderson with the specimens he sent to Milton House. 'Where the devil did you find the fly orchis? – for the *musifera* it certainly

---

[39] *Ibid.*, p. 219.   [40] *Himself*, p. 217.

[41] Quoted by Heyes, 'Looking to futurity', p. 182. Dr Heyes believes that Henderson, rather than Hessey, is the projected recipient of some of these letters. This allusion to Artis, by the widow of Clare's friend Octavius Gilchrist, raises a further possibility.

is',[42] Henderson writes in June 1827. Three summers later, Clare's finds are still giving pleasure: 'The plants of *apifera* are splendid – where did you get them?'[43] Meanwhile Henderson persisted in his efforts to interest his friend in systematics. In April 1827 he invited Clare over to 'a day or two of very interesting work'[44] with the thirty-six volumes of James Smith's *English Botany*, (known as 'Sowerby's Botany' after its illustrator), presumably borrowed from Lord Milton's library. A further attempt at persuasion came from another friend, Marianne Marsh, wife of the bishop of Peterborough, who in October 1829 sent Clare a pocket microscope, which (she said) would help him 'ascertain the place which a plant ought to have in the system'.[45]

It may be that Clare was yielding to the gentle pressure of these friends when he acquired the *Compendium of the English Flora* (1829) by the arch-Linnaean James Smith, and noted down titles of other botanical works. But there is no evidence that he read these, nor that Henderson ever succeeded in making a systematic botanist of his poet friend. It is true that Clare, in an essay written around 1825, speaks of the 'happiness in examining minutely into the wild flowers as we wander amongst them to distinguish their characters and find out to what orders they belong in the artificial and natural systems of botany',[46] but, as Margaret Grainger observes, this portrait of the man of taste has reservations that make it verge on the satiric. The same reservations are much plainer a few years later, in the poem called 'Shadows [i.e. varieties] of Taste', in which the pleasure that 'the man of science and of taste' gains from his interests is, by implication, compared unfavourably with the pleasure felt by those who 'in recordless rapture love to breath / Nature's wild Eden' where 'Associations sweet each object breeds':

> But take these several beings from their homes
> Each beauteous thing a withered thought becomes.
> Association fades . . .[47]

Such was the fate, it must have seemed to Clare, of Artis's stuffed birds and Henderson's dried mosses.

But collector and classifier as Henderson was, his main task as a gardener was to make plants grow; and as a botanist he was no less concerned with

---

[42] Quoted by Robert Heyes, 'Some friends of John Clare: the poet and the scientists', *Studies in Romanticism* 2 (1996), p. 102.
[43] *Ibid.*, p. 103.   [44] *Ibid.*, p. 102.   [45] *Ibid.*, p. 106.
[46] *Natural History*, p. 284 and headnote on p. 283.
[47] 'Shadows of Taste', lines 107, 125–6, 133, 147–9.

their way of life. Thus he not only mastered the recently discovered skill of propagating ferns from spores, but also attempted, in a paper published in 1837, to discover their method of reproduction.[48] This awareness of the living plant would have made him a wonderful companion in the country-side; one from whom Clare, as they roamed pasture, woodland, heath and marsh together, learnt to recognise with new confidence the species adap-ted to each habitat that, for a poet so acutely aware of 'association', was a plant's only proper place. Clare several times quotes Henderson as an authority when writing his comments on Elizabeth Kent's book, com-ments in which he distinguishes eight or nine kinds of cuckoo flower and half a dozen species of mallow, and also tells apart the very rare lesser centaury from the common one. On occasion his eye is sharper than that of his mentor. His journal records that he is sure, whatever botanists may say, that there are four kinds of bramble, even though 'Henderson will have it there is but two.'[49] He must have been gratified, when he acquired James Smith's *Compendium*, to find the botanists on his side: Smith lists over a dozen species (which Victorian 'splitters' were to divide into a couple of hundred sub-species).

Because of this increased awareness of plants as living entities in Clare's poetry and prose after 1822, there have been some rather ponderous attempts to link him with the history of biology, for example by attributing to him an awareness of the importance of photosynthesis or claiming that he provides 'striking examples of what today would be called cybernetic ecology'. But Clare's resistance to the dark system has shown us that he did not have the scientific cast of mind: he was instead a gifted natural historian. So, with hugely better resources of education and money, was Charles Darwin, and several of the aspects of plant behaviour that Darwin was to study captured Clare's interest as well. When Henderson showed him that honeysuckle twines to the left and old man's beard to the right he was feeding his friend's fascination with the rooted creation's often star-tling powers of movement: powers revealed not only in the burgeoning force of growth but also in the protective mechanisms known at the time as the sleep of plants. Among Clare's many sleeping flowers are dandelions

---

[48] Sadly, he reached the wrong conclusion: 'there is no impregnation' ('Observations on the germina-tion of ferns', *Magazine of Zoology and Botany* (subsequently *Annals of Natural History*) 1 (1837), p. 340). Henderson did not have a microscope that was powerful enough to show the sperm and egg cells on the tiny leaf-like structure that develops from the spore. Their discovery in the 1840s led Wilhelm Hofmeister to formulate the idea of an alternation of generations in all plants, flowering and non-flowering: the most significant advance ever made in botany and comparable with Mendeleev's Periodic Law in chemistry.

[49] *Himself*, p. 205.

that 'closed like painter's brush',[50] much as they do in Dürer's own Midsummer Cushion, *The Large Piece of Turf.* By contrast, in 'The Evening Primrose', a small lyric of Caroline delicacy, this 'shunning-hermit of the light', opens at night only to fade and wither the next morning 'at the gaze it cannot shun'.

Another kind of movement, that of wind-shaken flowers, always fasci-nated Clare. If he is sharp in his comment on a poet who made bluebells dance – his own bluebells are 'quiet hanging blooms' in 'The Flitting'– it is because he knows that movement has meaning in nature: by spreading pollen or dispersing seed, wind can be the breath of life to a plant, as he shows in his notes on the single-sex flowers of trees such as oak and ash.[51] But these notes, if they are the essay on the sexual system of plants[52] referred to in his journal, indicate that he was still indifferent to the notion that most flowers were bisexual. Floral sex, '[Erasmus] Darwin's prying thought',[53] remained largely an irrelevance in Clare's eyes. And patient as were his observations of insects, they never revealed cross-pollination to him. Had they done so, he would have had further evidence of the interdependence of plant and animal life of which he shows a profound awareness both in his natural history writings and in the 'habitat' poems of *The Midsummer Cushion*: an element not found in his early poetry for all their wild-flower catalogues and one that was perhaps the finest fruit of his friendship with Joseph Henderson.

3

Because much of Clare's botanical awareness was roused in the give-and-take of friendship there is, in his best poetry – written for the most part in his thirties and collected at the end of that decade into *The Midsummer Cushion* – an easy confluence between the villager's and the informed naturalist's view of the green world. One way in which this shows itself is in some of the revisions he made in his poems during the time his friend-ship with Artis and Henderson was at its most active.

Clare had an idiosyncratic way of re-writing. For him, 'true poetry' was 'not in words / But images that words express':[54] images that already existed out in the natural world, so that he can speak of the landrail's cry as 'one of the most poetical images in rural nature'.[55] It follows that revision is not a matter of putting things better but of seeing them better. He jots down, for instance, a couplet about the riotous growth in summer hedgerows,

---

[50] 'A Rhapsody', line 86.   [51] *Natural History*, pp. 101–2.   [52] *Himself*, p. 172.
[53] 'Morning Walk' ('Come lovely Lucy').   [54] 'Pastoral Poetry', lines 1–2.   [55] *Letters*, p. 282.

where 'now in all their glory twine / Bryony, wild hop, pale rose and streaked woodbine'. But when he incorporates these lines in the June section of *The Shepherd's Calendar*, completed late in 1834, the flowers have become 'Large bindweed bells, wild hop and streaked woodbine' (lines 7–8). Clare has reminded himself that wild roses do not twine, but clamber with the help of thorns, and being then left only with the showiness of honeysuckle (there is not much glory about the flowers of black bryony and hops), he brings on the arch-twiner, greater bindweed – risking the prosaic 'large' to show that he means its big white trumpets and not the pink-flowered trailing bindweed that runs over furrows.

Similar botanical exactitude is at work in the changes Clare made to a poem, called simply 'Spring', which in 1823 he hoped to include in the April section of *The Shepherd's Calendar*. Among the joys it celebrates is the pleasure of watching trees come into leaf or flower. When he recast the poem as 'The Pleasures of Spring' five years later, it appears that he went back to the trees for a closer look. This time, his perceptions sharpened by all the natural-history activity of the interim, he saw that the hawthorn 'unseals' rather than 'uncurls' its shoots; that the pussy-palm willow is studded, not with 'golden down' as he first wrote, but with a 'golden dust' of pollen that transforms the appearance of the downy white catkins; and that elm flowers are more accurately described as 'hop-like pale' than 'hop-like green'.[56] Elsewhere, however, in the recast poem this movement towards clearer definition is balanced by one towards a more telling use of the human associations that are basic to the villager's way of looking. The lesser celandine, or spring buttercup, figures in the first version, but not memorably: the lowly equivalent of the proud summer buttercup, it still has a sun-like or star-like beauty, and – a botanical fact – it closes up in a fading light. There are echoes here of two undistinguished apostrophes to the same flower that Wordsworth wrote in 1802. Two years later, however, the elder poet returned to the celandine's 'sleep' and made out of the fading flower's inability to protect itself by closing a wholly memorable poem about the enforced stoicism of old age. And in revising his own poem Clare does something equally effective. Picking up from the first version the image of the closed flowers resembling 'childern tired of play' (line 124), he recalls the game in which children pick the light-reflecting flowers and hold them under each other's chins:

> And he who seems to win the brightest spot
> Feels future wealth and fortune as his lot.

---

[56] 'Pleasures of Spring', lines 11, 16, 20. Compare 'Spring' ('How beautiful . . .'), lines 27, 32, 44.

Ah happy childhood with that sunny brow
No wealth can match what nature gives thee now,
And like these blossoms of the golden bloom
Thy spring *must* fade, though summer's wealth *may* come.

(lines 241–6)

Not least because Clare himself now longer looks to find a crock of gold, the new lines give an extra dimension to the passage, casting a reflection of their own back onto his description of the spring buttercup's unassuming brightness and the haughtiness of its summer successor, 'Which proudly leaves the grass to meet the sun' (line 57).

Clare's perception of a living plant is thus dual. He sees it in the light of recently gained botanical knowledge, as if for the first time; he sees it also, as the weeding party might see it in 'May', as part of the intercourse of his own and past generations with the natural world. Verbalised, this dual perception imposes a duality of discourse, a denotative clarity alongside of the connotative, figurative language that links what the poet sees to his circumstances. This holds for even such casual prose as – by way of example – the postscript he adds to the long letter he wrote Hessey about *Flora Domestica*:

PS. I must mention another now, it's so beautiful and grows nowhere else about here but on Barnack Heath. It is perennial. The vulgar call it 'sweet mullein', from the violet scent of its flowers. Its leaves are exactly like the foxglove, and its flowers grow on stalks like soldiers' feathers or the double larkheel, as thick as they can stand by each other, of a bright yellow with purple threads in the middle. It's nothing like the flannel mullein.[57]

Some of this detail is denotative, as in a flora's key to identification: bright (not pale) yellow petals, purple (not yellow) stamens, leaves like the foxglove's (not woolly and stem-hugging) together serve to distinguish the plant from great mullein, so that it was instantly recognisable to Margaret Grainger when she came to edit the passage. This is dark mullein, *Verbascum nigrum*, to the life. But that life inheres primarily in Clare's double comparison of the flower to shako plumes (with which the recruiting officer would cut a dash in the village) and to the dense flower-spikes of garden larkspur: 'as thick as they can stand by each other' suggests the pride of the flower show exhibitor.

Clare's nature poetry everywhere displays this blend of the exact and the evocative. Trees, shrubs and herbs announce their individuality through sharp definition of colour, form and pattern: the startling red of a water

---

[57] *Natural History*, p. 23.

dock's leaves where the eye expected only summer greenery, or the vivid green of spurge laurel against the browns of a wood in winter;[58] the 'barbed leaf' of arrowheads 'be-thread with lighter vein' and the 'gashed' leaves of sycamore 'burnished o'er with honied dew';[59] the pied beauty of 'bloodwalls glowing in rich tawny streaks' along with a host of other 'mozzled' flowers, all 'pencilled o'er with workmanship divine'.[60] Other senses provide impressions that are no less delicate and distinctive: Clare can detect privet in woodland air already heavy with the scents of dog rose and honeysuckle; his fingers explore, and transfer to his verse, a whole range of leafy textures from the oiliness of water-lily leaves to the razor sharpness of sedge.[61]

This sensory precision, typical of the botanising 'man of taste', does not however replace the grassroots familiarity that, for the poet, endows every plant with its aura of associations. The fact that certain flowers have morphological safeguards against bad weather in no way undermines – rather it adds to – the appeal of Clare's aconites with 'green leaf frilling round their cups of gold / Like tender maiden muffled from the cold'[62] and of his lilies of the valley –

> White beading drops on slender threads
> Wi' broad hood leaves above their heads
> Like white-robed maids in summer hours
> 'Neath umberellas shunning showers.[63]

Such personification nearly always takes the form of figures from village life: 'sleepy clowns' recalled by gaping snapdragons, or the 'green neighbours in white caps' represented by nodding white umbellifers glimpsed through a hedge[64]. And the everyday circumstances of these people provide a wealth of images. Willows in spring are 'mouse-eared with leaves', maple fruits are 'like wings o' dragon flies', the spear thistle is 'the very wasp of flowers', the 'tawny knopples' of burnet are 'like little honeycombs', dogwood stems are 'red as stockdove's claws' and 'button knapweed' has 'knobs like red toppings on fore horses' heads'.[65] Surprisingly, the poet jettisoned this last image, which captures so well the head-tossing boldness

---

[58] 'A Walk in the Fields', line 93; 'The Spindle Tree'.
[59] 'The Meadow Lake'; 'Spring' ('How beautiful ...'), lines 362–3.
[60] 'Pleasures of Spring', line 426; 'A Woodland Seat'.
[61] 'Summer Evening' ('How pleasant ...'); 'Spring' ('How beautiful ...'), line 313; 'Wanderings in June', lines 203–5.
[62] 'March', lines 241–2.   [63] 'May', lines 135–8.   [64] 'June', line 127; 'Evening' ('How beautiful ...').
[65] 'Come! come in the fields'; 'The bonny maple tree'; 'The Fear of Flowers'; 'Rhymes in the Meadows', lines 45–6; 'Pleasure of Spring', line 97; 'Valentine Eve', lines 136–7.

with which the plant flaunts its topknot. Perhaps botanical accuracy acted as a check. It is the greater knapweed, the one favouring limey uplands – what Clare elsewhere calls 'knapweed blood red on the hill' – that is described in floras of the time as crimson or bright red; the common knapweed he is here writing about is purple.

Clare's indications of colour are worth pausing over, for they take us to the heart of his endeavour to put into words his encounters with flowers. The bald statement of a flower's colour often reflects the act of identifying. Thus 'yellow flags' are water irises as distinct from the dark-flowered reeds and rushes Helpston villagers thought of collectively as 'flags'. Similarly 'yellow house-leek' suggests that what was planted on Helpston roofs was a distinctive variety of the common house-leek, which is red. Colour statements such as these record the poet–botanist's act of recognition: 'ah, there you are'. That however is only half the story. There is a response, 'here I am', that arises from Clare's associative form of perception. Flowers 'sing and talk of their delights', telling the poet 'of what they felt and I did feel / In springs that never will return'.[66] The reader, mildly embarrassed, may dismiss such passages as the legacy, shared with other Romantic poets, of eighteenth-century notions about plant sentience. Actually, Clare is more ready than Wordsworth is to declare such thoughts fanciful. Yet it is also a biological fact that a plant has to declare its presence if it is to reproduce: flower colour is the most effective way of doing this, and once the seed is ready the fruit may employ its own colour code to signal 'eat me' (or 'don't eat me' if that serves its purpose better). Even the top mammal succumbs to some of these blandishments and it could be that animal responses to plant colour have in human social life been refined into or replaced by the aesthetic delight Clare calls 'a pure unselfish love':[67] the kind of pleasure that most naturally expresses itself in heightened, connotative, metaphorical language.

The attempt to communicate colour as a joy-giving property and not merely an identifying 'character' puts the poet, however, in a quandary, because metaphor is apt to interpose itself between the reader and the purity of the prime experience. Is there any way to conjure up the colour of violets other than to say they are violet-blue? Clare does not try to solve this particular problem in his early verse, where the violet serves him in the way it had served poets for centuries as an emblem of modesty or humility or seclusion. In the poetry of his thirties it appears, frequently but fleetingly, as a passing glimpse of colour: a reminder, not a revelation. We scarcely

[66] 'The daisy wan the primrose pale'.   [67] *Childe Harold*, line 43.

expect better of the asylum poems, because in these Clare's reaching after metaphor is often strained. Yet it is among the poems transcribed for Clare in Northampton Asylum that the violet's epiphany at last occurs in 'Spring Violets':

> Push that rough maple bush aside!
> Its bark is all ridgy – and naked beside –
> But it stands in the way of the flowers that engross
> My eye, in bloom by its stump of green moss.
> How green is the moss and how purple the flower!
> I'll not pluck thee, sweet violets, in thy own sheltered bower.
>
> The first sunny day they were nought but green leaves
> When the bush threw another bush on the dead leaves
> So perfect and true, and such shadows I love,
> That it seemed an ink-drawing of the maple above:
> The moss it looks greener, the flowers are so blue
> While the gold sun of spring looks delightfully through.
>
> There's no flowers more red than the flower of the larch,
> And none are so sweet as the violets of March,
> In their dead leafy beds, how intensely dark blue
> By the moss maple stump where the sunlight looks through.
> Those sweet flowers that look up in their beautiful bloom
> Will ne'er live to see the bright maple leaves come.

This is a poem that could be summarised in three words: violets? yes, *violets* – the mark of interrogation implying the poet's search for the flowers, and the italics implying the epiphanic moment, the sense of something shown forth and *given* by their colour. It opens in Lawrence's 'living present'; a command expressed in six staccato stresses within eight syllables, and a close-up of the sheltering tree, together suggest a keen-eyed and determined search. The poet has been watching this spot as the strengthening sunlight has cast ever-sharper patterns of light and shade on the undergrowth, a sunlight that now floods in to make the purple blossoms 'blue'. And once the flowers have been revealed, Clare's 'I'll not pluck thee' creates the space in which they can declare themselves: he lets them be, and to let something *be* in this way is itself a fiat, calling it into poetic life. Conventionally, violets shrink from attention. Clare's boldly 'look up'. In many other poems, the metaphor of eye-contact serves him to express his recognition that plants as well as animals lead vigorous and distinctive lives: thus we find the brunny (brown) eye of the primrose, the silver eye of speedwell, the yellow eye of the forget-me-not, the golden eye of the pimpernel, the blue eye of butterwort and, of course, the silver-grey eye of the violet itself. But in this poem he appears bent on the flower's colour being expressed in no terms other than its own. The larch flowers that open the third stanza, momentarily an irrelevance, are Clare's way of saying that the perception of colour is too basic an experience to be put into figurative language. The old rhyme says it all: roses are red and violets are blue – only, this being March, the red is that of larch flowers (brilliant but minute, so that they too deliver a shock of discovery), and the contrast renders the violets 'intensely dark blue', with an intensity that is also the poet's as he savours a beauty that he knows to be only one phase of the woodland cycle. Already the moisture that the moss shows to have gathered at the maple's root, and the sunlight still able to pass through its lower branches, have acted together to bring the violets first into leaf and now into flower. Tomorrow they will cause the maple to break bud in its turn, and in its thickening shade the undergrowth will revert to dimness and fecund decay.

With its sense of the past and the future folded into a present joyous moment, 'Spring Violets' is one of the many poems that refute the old accusation that Clare's poetry describes but does not signify. The poem is however unusual in his work by reason of its concentration on one plant; something that tends to happen only when a single species lights up for him what would otherwise be a colourless prospect. It occurs in the mono-chrome fenland landscape of late summer, when he comes upon yarrow's swarming pink-and-white umbels 'defying dreariness', or ragwort's 'waste of shining blossoms' that 'richly shields / The sun tanned sward in splendid hues that burn'.[68] A similar effect occurs in woodland when a pussy willow breaks into bloom:

> Like sunshine in dark places and gold veins
> Mapping the russet landscape into smiles
> At spring's approach,

but by the end of this sonnet, 'The Sallow', the poet's eye has been caught by the 'brunny eye' of a primrose at the tree's foot. Elsewhere a field maple (such as sheltered the spring violets) is brought to life by Clare not only in its own details of tassel flowers, staghorn-shaped seeds, scalloped leaves and bark 'ribbed like corduroy',[69] but no less in the plant community, from moss to towering hemlock, that is nourished by its litter: something that

---

[68] 'The Yarrow'; 'The Ragwort'.   [69] 'The Maple Tree'.

Clare, as a worker on the land had always understood, and that the gardening books he read were beginning to explain in chemical terms.

Clare, then, has a lively awareness of the interdependence of life forms, animal as well as vegetable, whether such interdependence occurs in what we would now call a micro-habitat, such as a solitary spear thistle provides, or in a whole woodland's provision of shelter and sustenance ('birds have gardens of their own'[70]) to unnumbered species. His most famous bird poem, 'The Nightingale's Nest', guides us through a sleeping-beauty thicket of blackthorn, old man's beard, hazels, ferns, brambles and wood-grass to a nest that turns out to be made largely from oak leaves – elsewhere he notes that he never found a nightingale's nest without them – and lined with moss. The effect of seclusion and security must have been even more complete at a time when the construction of a human home also largely depended on materials from the plant world.

Clare's moorfowl, the subject of 'The Moorhen's Nest', depend likewise on vegetation for their survival; in their case on

> an aged tree
> Whose roots are bare – yet some with foothold good
> Crankle and spread and strike beneath the flood.

One such root provides the birds with a safe place in the river to build their nest of reeds and there raise a 'sooty brood' of chicks that are no sooner hatched than they take to the even safer refuge of 'bulrush forests'. This description, some score of lines in length, which first appeared in print in 1935 when J. W. Tibble extracted it from a much longer poem, is one of the most beautifully exact in Clare's writing. At the same time it is one of the most emotionally charged. 'Safety' is a recurrent word: but although the tree root may afford a refuge from predators and allow the birds to 'sweetly dream / On their shelfed nests', danger is always present and not least for the tree itself which is so undermined by the current that it seems on the point of falling.

This effect of survival against all the odds is doubled when we read the poem in its entirety as it appears in the *Midsummer Cushion* manuscript, from which it was first printed intact in 1967. For it begins with Clare contemplating his own survival as a poet and the way in which his hopes are repeatedly dashed and yet renew themselves with each returning year. It is not that either bird or poet is a metaphor for the other. Both are builders, and in their different modes of building both display terrestrial life's

---

[70] 'Walks in the Woods', line 84.

amazing resilience. And it is this resilience that drives the speaker, after his sombre and ruminative start, to set out afresh. 'And then I start and seek for joys again.' At first his pace is leisurely:

> And so I glad my heart and rove along,
> Now finding nests, then listening to a song,
> Then drinking fragrance,

a fragrance of summer rain on new-mown hay, which slows him down further into a reverie about the sweet-scented manna that nourished the Israelites in their wanderings, in an age when the patriarchs were blessed 'With angel answers if a trouble calls'. This thought of a speedy response brings comfort and stimulates him into a brisker pace – 'And then I walk and swing my stick for joy' – so that impressions begin to flit past him with cinematographic speed:

> A gate whose posts are two old dottrel trees,
> A close with molehills sprinkled o'er its leas,
> A little footbrig with its crossing rail,
> A wood gap stopped with ivy-wreathing pale . . .

It is as if he has now found an objective. As indeed he has, both in the moorhen's nest that demonstrates life's resurgence and in the poem's climax that proves his own power of poetic self-renewal.

Clare's peripatetic poetry, like his habitat poetry, draws equally upon his keenness of observation and his awareness of the associative power of what he observes. He misses nothing: not even slugs; not even blanket weed. At the same time most of this seeing is, as Elizabeth Helsinger has put it, 'reconceived as *heeding*':[71] he takes what he sees to heart. So if these poems sometimes suggest an informative nature trail, this more pedestrian quality is offset by the welcoming tones of Clare as host in his home parish, showing us things that have had lifelong meaning for him and his companions. For these are sociable poems. 'The Holiday Walk' is taken with Clare's three eldest children, and the voice in which he shares his country lore with them is a caring one. Only when the Oxford edition gave us Clare's poetry in its entirety was it revealed that this poem, like the outing it envisages, is a much cut-down version of 'A Walk in the Fields', which in all probability was written some years earlier in anticipation of a visit to Helpston in 1825 from Clare's loyal and helpful (if sometimes officious) friend Eliza Emmerson. This walk, which one can still follow on the ground, leads the poet and his

---

[71] 'Clare and the place of the peasant poet', *Critical Inquiry* 13 (1987), pp. 507–31.

companion through the fields to the north of the village and then southwards
into the woods and onto the heath, until rain drives them back to the
Helpston cottage, where they take down from the shelf the poems of
Thomson and Cowper who also 'roamed out of doors for their verses'
(line 553): a reminder that there was a century of peripatetic verse behind a
poem such as this. Whereas 'The Holiday Walk' focuses on insects and other
things of interest to young children, birds and flowers dominate the original
poem; there are two particularly rich 'botanical' passages. It may be that
Clare was challenging Mrs Emmerson's view that he was 'capable of higher
subjects than talking of birds and flowers',[72] by talking to her of both with an
involvement that showed that, for him, the significance of an experience was
embedded in the perception that gave rise to it.

The projected walk was too long (Mrs Emmerson, when she came,
sensibly hired a chaise and piled the children into it) and so was the
poem, even when Clare cut it into two, with an imagined midday rest at
his cottage. Given nature's inexhaustible variety, Clare's problem always
was how to know when to stop. That he was himself aware of this is
suggested by 'Sonnet to x.x.x.', written in 1832, in which he recalls how, in
his early days, he 'walked with poesy in the sonnet's bounds', but then left
that 'little garden home' and

> went sweet nature's wilderness to trace:
> A stretching landscape where the fading sight
> Skimmed like a bird and found no resting-place.

But the reader needed resting places, even if the poet could live on the wing.
In returning to the sonnet – *The Midsummer Cushion* has some 200 – Clare
aimed to limit his roving sensibilities to just as many sights and sounds as
could be contained within fourteen lines. Admittedly, he kept open the
option of starting on another fourteen, and another after that, if discoveries
crowded upon him. But the best of these sonnets of his maturity are single,
and their close-packed images, in Clare's special sense of the beings he
encounters, convey even more successfully than his habitat poems and
peripatetic poems his sense of the interpenetration of plant and animal
existences. A single example must suffice here, and I take one in which the
plant life is of the kind most of us pass by but was very much there for Clare
who, like Thomas Hardy, was a man who used to notice such things.

'First Sight of Spring' has, after its first two lines, few allusions to plants,
and those few are subdued and brief: dead wood, fungus on a tree trunk,

---

[72] Letter to Clare, 8 December 1826, British Library Egerton MS 2247, folio 238.

moss, lichen. But they have been made fully operative by the opening image: 'The hazel blooms in threads of crimson hue / Peep through the swelling buds and look for spring.' This is not quite what was printed in 1835, by which date, attempts to publish *The Midsummer Cushion* by subscription having failed, a publisher had been found for a selection called *The Rural Muse*. As she edited the copy for this, Mrs Emmerson, tut-tutting at the notion that flowers could look for anything, altered 'look for' to 'speak of' and then changed that again to 'foretelling'. Clare, however, is writing about an expectancy which, although not sentient, we might today carelessly say is there in the genes: unimpeded by foliage, the hazel's red stigmas await the fertilising pollen which will ensure that the ovaries below them (Clare's 'buds') bear the nuts by which the species will renew itself. This is the true rite of spring, an act of faith completed long before green leaves and birdsong send out reassuring signals of the season's return. As yet there are no songs, only the 'harsh toned notes' of woodpeckers, and their presence 'on the old touchwood tree' suggests that like other creatures at the end of winter they are hanging on to life, getting what energy they can from the insects which likewise have lingered on beneath the dead bark. There is vitality too in another sound, the crack of a stockdove's wing, suggestive of a mating display, and in the vigour with which a squirrel 'sputters' (exact if unglossable verb) up the oak powdered with the fine fungus that is one more sign of life's persistence in this lifeless-seeming landscape. Yet for all his liveliness, the squirrel too is hanging on precariously, and the sound of the woodman's 'understroke' (the oblique downward cut of an axe) is a threat to its existence: coppicing, almost certainly of hazels, is in progress, and that means the destruction of fertilised flowers and so of some part of the squirrel's expectations for the year ahead. In spite, indeed in defiance, of this, the sonnet ends with a double assertion of the tenacious hold that animals and plants retain upon life, as the squirrel leaps through branches clad in the mosses and lichens that have seized the opportunity for growth given by the tree's winter bareness. So, in a hairspring balance between delight and apprehension, the sonnet celebrates the determined drive for survival. No theme could be more congenial to Clare, who had himself hung on through years of literary misjudgement and neglect, faithful both to his vision of the natural world and to his vocation to put that vision into words.

This is the sonnet:

> The hazel blooms in thread of crimson hue
> Peep through the swelling buds and look for spring
> Ere yet a whitethorn leaf appears in view

Or March finds throstle pleased enough to sing.
On the old touchwood tree woodpeckers cling
A moment and their harsh-toned notes renew;
In happier mood the stockdove claps his wing;
The squirrel sputters up the powdered oak
With tail cocked o'er his head and ears erect
Startled to hear the woodman's understroke,
And with the courage that his fears collect
He hisses fierce, half malice and half glee,
Leaping from branch to branch about the tree
In winter's foliage, moss and lichens, dressed.

4

There was a time in Clare's life when pleasure in flowers all but vanished from
his poetry. Except for an isolated recall of the way buttercups 'shut up green
and open into gold' and a passing mention of 'the glorious sight of sinkfoin
[sainfoin] grounds in flower'[73] (the ready-made phrase perhaps echoing some
well-intentioned attempt to rouse his interest), the bald, inventorial sonnets
that he wrote in the two years preceding his mental collapse present a world
no longer in bloom. The change is evident in a chilling sonnet about a flower
foray such as had often given him pleasure in the past. Then, the quest had
typically been for richly coloured wild columbines, 'stone-blue and ruby-
red'.[74] Now, a sortie into the alien fen yields colourless plunder:

We went a journey far away.
The path was often ill to find.
The cows from strangers turned away
And turned a careless look behind.
We passed the stupid staring horse;
The farmer eyed us with dislike;
And where we found no brig to cross
We pulled each other o'er the dyke.
The men were burning shoaf around
And thick the ashes seemed to fall;
The smoke went over half the ground
And rolled along and hid us all.
We found the columbine so black
And dug and took a bundle back.

---

[73] 'I hate the very noise of troublous man'; 'The dreary fen a waste of water goes'.
[74] *Natural History*, p. 18.

From such desolate scenes Clare was himself transplanted in 1837 to Matthew Allen's private asylum at High Beach in Essex. 'I meet with great kindness, the country is the finest I have seen',[75] he writes, in the voice of the cooperative patient; and his poetry flowers again as he sets out on 'The Botanist's Walk' under the hornbeams and beeches of Epping Forest. But the song of a nightingale, a 'stranger' like Clare, brings back the Northamptonshire names that flowers had when he 'went in woods / To look for nests and hear the nightingale': the mask of the happy flower-seeker slips, and the verse becomes hesitant and repetitive. This homesickness, overt in other poems written at High Beach, presages his heroic tramp back to Northamptonshire in 1841. Home once more, he continued to work on a sequence celebrating his first love, Mary Joyce, whom he now believed to be his wife, although in fact she had died three years previously. Flowers in this sequence are as sparse as they had been in the poems he wrote just before his breakdown, and when they occur they tend to have a phantasmagoric brilliance.

At the end of that year Clare was removed to the Northampton General Lunatic Asylum, where he would spend the rest of his natural life. Treated with consideration by the staff ('especially as he was a POET'[76] one of them wrote), he had the good fortune to find among them an amanuensis, W. F. Knight, who transcribed most of the verse that he wrote in the 1840s. He was also at liberty for much of his time to wander out of doors. Flowers were plentiful in the Nene valley, and among them were some, such as naturalised daffodils, that were new to Clare. There must also have been a grand Victorian shrubbery in the asylum grounds, where he could enjoy the spring splendour of 'rich laburnums' and the autumn brilliance of sumachs 'all on fire / Like hot coals amid the green', and round off the year by watching 'Sweet chestnuts brown like soling leather turn'.[77] Novel flowers such as cyclamens grew under these trees, alongside old favourites including the hepatica that, in one of Clare's last poems, preserved in his own hand (Knight had by then left), appears as 'patty kay':[78] namesake of the wife he had not seen for almost twenty years.

Flowers reappear in profusion in Clare's asylum poems. In many lyrics they provide a setting for his praises of a beautiful girl. The girls named in fact outnumber the flowers, and it is difficult to believe that more than a

---

[75] *Letters*, p. 642.
[76] Quoted by Kerith Trick, 'Clare's asylum experience', in Richard Foulkes (ed.), *John Clare: a Bicentenary Celebration* (1994), p. 39.
[77] 'The healthful mind that muses'; 'Stanzas' ('The passing of a dream'); 'The winter's come'.
[78] 'Valentine' ('The morning is up'); 'The spring is come and spring flowers coming too'.

few of them were or had ever been known to Clare. Robert Heyes is almost certainly right to see them as poems, often valentines, written on request and for a small consideration.[79] A 'Valentine to Mary' written in the early spring of 1844 is one of the better examples. It starts in the asylum garden, and the phrase 'these laurels of ours' hints at Mary being a fellow-inmate. Here are to be found snowdrops, aconites, an early crocus and, protected from the February wind by lavender cotton, 'red primroses' or polyanthuses. But the poet soon wanders into the country in quest of wild flowers; and there, it would seem, Mary is transformed into his first love Mary Joyce and the flowers he gathers for her – primroses, violets, daisies, a forward cowslip and 'pilewort like sunshine' – grow where they picked them together as children, 'on the very same spot, as no changes had been'. The resultant nosegay of flowers, as 'young, fair, and simple, and pleasingly shy' as their recipient, constitutes a poem that, though it may be gift-album verse, has grace and charm. But few of these girl-in-a-prospect-of-flowers lyrics come up to this standard. Their lilt hardly ever fails, but their wording tends to be insecure and their flowers perfunctorily listed, making them, for all their celebratory tone, a reminder of Clare's changed circumstances. For one reader at least they make even sadder reading than the outcries of abandonment and separation that are what people usually have in mind when they speak of Clare's asylum poetry.

That Clare's fantasies should have taken the form of associating women and flowers is of course significant. Sexual deprivation, the worst aspect of his segregated existence, is contrasted with the fulfilment that a plant proclaims in its flowering:

> The gillyflower's a gillyflower
> And nature owns the plan;
> And strange a thing it is to me
> A man can't be a man.[80]

Clare also felt deeply the lack of intelligent friendship such as Henderson had provided in the days when he could always rouse Clare from depression by suggesting they take a botanising walk together. All the same, there must have been some fellow-patients at Northampton, as there had certainly been at High Beach, with whom Clare could talk about his

---

[79] 'Clare would sit on his seat outside All Saints and would be approached by someone wanting him to write a poem for a girl friend, fiancée, or wife. Clare would make a note of the name in his pocket book, go away and think about it, and come back a day or two later with the finished item.' (Personal communication.) Jonathan Bate makes the same suggestion: *John Clare*, p. 496.
[80] 'To Miss B.'

gardening and botanical interests. There were also visitors who tried to meet his needs. For instance Mary Howitt, herself a poet and an admirer of Clare's work, came with her husband William, whose *Book of the Seasons* she presented to Clare. This was a pedestrian work of natural history (the Howitts were writers of the type dubbed 'indefatigable'), but its month-by-month lists of wild flowers may have proved useful as a reference guide. Other visitors remarked on the fact that Clare was well provided with books. As Joanna Ball has shown,[81] the Northampton libraries of this period fed up-to-date books and journals into the asylum library on a scale that today's long-stay patients might envy.

From books and talk, then, Clare at Northampton was in a position to satisfy much of his lifelong curiosity about plant names. At last, it would seem from a mention of stitchwort, he learnt the identity of the 'little nameless flower' that had been the subject of one of his early poems. And now for the first time he was able to give names to plants that in villagers' eyes were too insignificant to merit a name of their own. That very common composite, sow thistle, is one such; others are the wayside crucifers, jack-by-the-hedge and yellow rocket, better known today as garlic mustard and weld. A plant for which he knew no generally accepted name in 1823, though Helpston children called it 'tassel flower', he now knows to be 'meadow rue', while another that he once misnamed by calling it 'frogwort' reappears at Northampton under its rightful name of 'arrow-head'. Other plants for which Clare already had local names acquire in this late poetry the common names used in his hearing by speakers from all over Northamptonshire and even farther afield. 'Buttercup' for *Ranunculus ficaria* may have seemed imprecise to Clare's companions and 'celandine' too literary, so he settles, as the 'Valentine to Mary' shows, for 'pilewort', which as it happened was an alternative Helpston name. More often, however, the shift is from a popular name to something more elegant, thereby reflecting both the tendency of Victorian books of popular botany to prettify and gentrify everything rural, and the fact that in the asylum's Gentlemen's Gallery, Clare found himself in a middle-class ambience. Already, at High Beach, 'cowslips' (i.e. cowslaps, cowpats) had become 'paigles', and in the Knight transcripts woodbine sometimes figures as 'honeysuckle', bindweed as 'bell flowers' and ragged robin as 'meadow pink'. To the reader's relief, none of these changes proves irreversible.

---

[81] See ' "The tear drops on the book I read": John Clare's reading in the Northampton General Lunatic Asylum, 1841–1864', *The Wordsworth Circle* 34 (2003), pp. 155–8.

Indeed, a feature of Clare's late poems is the number of flowers in them that are given two or more names.

Alternative names are of course a boon to the poet, for they widen his metrical and rhyming choices, offering him, say, 'mouse ear' for forget-me-not, or 'water skeggs' for flags. But the coexistence in Clare's asylum poetry of common and local names has a greater importance, for it is a pointer to the significance that plants had for him in these last decades of his life. The appeal to him of exotics in the asylum garden, 'a place so daintily dressed', is limited: its spanish chestnuts 'are not the trees / Under which I used to play' and the flowers in its borders count for little in comparison with 'the weeds along the fen'.[82] But the wild flowers of the surrounding countryside were, as the variations in their names implied, by turns painfully alien and comfortingly familiar. If on the one hand they heightened the contrast between his present surroundings and

> The scenes where my children are laughing at play
> The scenes where my memory is fading away,

they could also bring consolation:

> I always see a bit of home in every likely thing:
> A whitethorn hedge or bramble bush or pollard willow tree
> Brings me my own snug homestead.[83]

From such mixed responses arises the total recall, shot through with longing, that gives us the exquisite natural-history detail of 'The Round Oak', in which Clare is back forty years in the setting he had once given to 'Noon': aware even of the exact kind of feathery grasses that he picked as he watched the to-and-fro darting of small fish between the spring and the shallows. That Clare could still, in 1846, write such satisfying habitat poetry was in large measure due to the evocative power that wild flowers continued to have for him: a power that, a year or so earlier, he had sought to define in a line of verse which he also wrote down,[84] in slightly amended form, on a scrap of paper and handed to the doctor in charge: 'Where flowers are, God is; and I am free.'

---

[82] 'Stanzas' ('The passing of a dream'); 'Sleep of Spring'.
[83] 'Stanzas' ('The spring is come forth'); 'Recollections of Home'.
[84] P. R. Nesbitt quoted by Edmund Blunden, *Sketches in the Life of John Clare* (1931), p. 41.

CHAPTER 5

Ruskin's flowers of evil

17 June 1844 started badly for John Ruskin. 'Set off about eight, to show my father and mother the fall of the eau de Bérard, but they were neither of them well, lost their tempers and spoiled all.' His diary entry does not however begin with this family spat, but with 'Today high up above the val d'Entragues, Cout[t]et pointed out to me a flower of the Soldanella which had actually pierced the snow, and was budding in the midst of it.'[1] For later the same day, Ruskin had been able to escape to clearer air. The Swiss guide showed concern for his safety on the snow-covered slopes, but whereas the protectiveness of his parents was irksome, that of Joseph Couttet, henceforth often to serve as a surrogate father (pro-papa is Ruskin's term), was fortifying. Moreover, he knew all about alpine plants. Two weeks previously, he had identified a small purple flower that still reposes in Ruskin's album of dried flowers, and told him that it was the first species to pierce the snow in spring. Now, above the Val d'Entragues, it was doing just that, breaking free in a thrust of self-affirmation that aroused in Ruskin a deeply empathic response.

Soldanella, the alpine snowbell, reappeared at another time of family tension four years later. Ruskin and his bride of two months had joined his parents for an intended tour of English cathedrals. But at the point of departure wife and mother fell out over the matter of what he should be given for a bad cold. Ruskin appears to have sought refuge in sketching the leaves of a potted *Soldanella*, which he must have taken home with him when the tour was abandoned because, on the couple's departure for Normandy in August, it and another alpine were left in the

---

[1] Joan Evans and John Howard Whitehouse (eds.), *The Diaries of John Ruskin* (1956), p. 285 (hereafter *Diaries*; page numbers run through the three volumes). Quotations from this edition have been checked against the British Library's microfilm copies of the original diaries owned by the Ruskin Foundation, Ruskin Library, Lancaster University, and passages not in Evans are quoted from the microfilms.

care of a friend, to whom he wrote: 'I shall be happy in thinking that my poor pets, in my exile, have at least the consolation of some share in Miss Mitford's regards.'[2] Even in a whimsical context, 'exile' was an odd term to use of his first journey abroad with his young wife. But then Ruskin, high in the Alps, had bonded with *Soldanella* as he was never to bond with Effie Gray; and the eloquent record of that bonding was already in print in the second volume of *Modern Painters* (1846), where the fragile blossom is his chosen example of vital beauty in the natural world.

These two encounters with *Soldanella* are characteristic of the strength of Ruskin's response to plant life. It was a lifelong predilection. From a rather sheepish note in 1841 – 'taken up botany; stupid, very; but useful for one's stones vegetables [i.e., fossils] and amusing for the present'– to one of his last diary entries nearly half a century later – 'Botanized on ragged robin coming home'[3] – his diaries and letters yield a copious *biographia botanica*. Yet when he attempted a book wholly devoted to plants, the result was an embarrassment for his admirers. *Proserpina* is a wreck, strewn with a few descriptive pearls. In large part, of course, its confusions are those of a mind that was both alienated and failing. Whereas flowers brought a liberation of spirit to Clare in his asylum years, the storm cloud that darkened Ruskin's later life rendered any plant that was the subject of Darwinian theory detestable to him. But even the earlier chapters of *Proserpina*, like a good deal of writing on plants in his other books, bewilder and disappoint the reader. It follows that my account of Ruskin as botanist is going to be a sad tale, though one that needs to be told because his influence on the way people looked at the natural world and thought about the natural sciences was both widespread and long-lasting. It is also an involved story, since Ruskin's responses to plants were as much entangled (witness *Soldanella*) with his personal relationships as they were with the perturbations of nineteenth-century biology. For the sake of clarity, I focus here on four pieces of writing, each from a different phase of a very varied career: the discussion of vital beauty in *Modern Painters II* (1846); the section 'Of Leaf Beauty' in *Modern Painters V* (1860); the second chapter of *Queen of the Air* (1869); and *Proserpina*, which was issued in parts between 1876 and 1884.

    [2] E. T. Cook and Alexander Wedderburn, *Works of John Ruskin* (1903–12), vol. XXVI, p. 89.
    [3] *Diaries*, p. 169; *ibid.*, p. 1148.

I

Ruskin's claim that his mental make-up was a 'balanced unison of artistic sensibility with scientific faculty'[4] though hard to justify at the point in his later life when he made it, is certainly borne out by his activities as a young graduate in the 1840s. In May 1842 there occurred the deep change in his way of looking at the natural world that in his 1884 autobiography, *Praeterita*, he attributes to the effects of a dual epiphany. On two separate occasions, the act of sketching a growing plant culminated in the realisation that beauty was not a quality to be mentally abstracted from the visual but was inherent in every specific natural form: "'He hath made everything beautiful, in his time", became for me thenceforward the interpretation of the bond between the human mind and all visible things.'[5]

Ruskin's response to what he felt as a transformation in his way of seeing was twofold. The primarily artistic response was an eagerness to get down on paper every detail of the humblest vegetation:

On fine days, when the grass was dry, I used to lie down on it and draw the blades as they grew, with the ground herbage of buttercup or hawkweed mixed among them, until every square foot of meadow, or mossy bank, became an infinite picture and possession to me, and the grace and adjustment to each other of growing leaves, a subject of more curious interest to me than the composition of any painter's master-piece.[6]

Another response, distinct from the artistic one though closely linked to it, was that Ruskin now 'took to careful botany',[7] beginning in a Swiss pine wood, where he for the first time observed

One delicate white leaved flower with blue veins, five leaves, the left hand edge of each usually overlaying the next. Centre yellow, passing into green. Cannot count stamens; two sets, upper and under, good many, white and small, growing out of delicate green calyx. Leaf formed of three separate heart shapes joined at centre where stalk is inserted. I have three leaves on the plant in water; one has its leaves extended flat and regular . . . another has each petal folded close in the vertical line dividing the heart shape, the third has them thrown back on the stalk.[8]

In *Proserpina*, Ruskin dates his study of Alpine botany from the drawing that accompanies these notes. Not surprisingly, wood sorrel retained a lifelong fascination for him.

---

[4] *Fors Clavigera*, Letter 67, § 11. Ruskin numbered his works in small divisions (§) usually of one to three paragraphs in print. I give references according to these numbers when possible, rather than to the thirty-nine volumes of the Cook and Wedderburn *Works*, which are not widely available.
[5] *Praeterita*, vol. II, § 77.   [6] *Ibid.*, § 199.   [7] *Ibid.*, § 78.   [8] *Diaries*, p. 225.

It was in Switzerland also that Ruskin, stung by the contempt shown to Turner in the English press, decided to write a defence of the artist and of other modern landscapists. He was deep in this task in the early months of 1843; yet he still found time to read Liebig's *Organic Chemistry* and an essay written then reflects his awareness of the breakthrough it achieved in the understanding of plant nutrition.[9] Even after the favourable reception given to *Modern Painters I* on its publication in May 1843 had set him on course as an art critic, he continued to follow a formidable schedule of study that spanned arts and sciences; making, for instance, daily drawings of plants, then scrutinising them with the help of a lens and ascertaining their botanic names. For he believed that however spontaneous a great artist's grasp of the phenomenal distinctiveness of natural forms might be, it was incumbent on his critic to study that distinctiveness with scientific care, in order to demonstrate the artist's fidelity to nature.

As Ruskin's categories of true-to-life painting widened to include many artists of the sixteenth century and earlier, the accuracy and delicacy with which these artists painted plants became for him a touchstone of their powers. In the National Gallery, he discovered 'laborious botanical fidelity'[10] in the wild flowers that spring up around Raphael's St Catherine and in the irises and columbines beneath the chariot of Titian's Bacchus. These details are pressed into the service of the argument, vigorously set out in the Preface to the second, 1844, edition of *Modern Painters I*, that the generalisation of natural forms as advocated by Reynolds and exemplified in Claude's landscapes was a blasphemous distortion of the God-given, and that the true ideal of landscape is the expression of 'the *specific* characters of every object in their perfection':[11] not rocks in the abstract, but gneiss and sandstone; not unidentifiable herbage, but such recognisable species as the *Crambe maritima* or common sea colewort which Ruskin held to be the plant with 'sinuated leaves and clustered blossoms' growing by the Sea of Galilee in Raphael's cartoons.[12] The possibility of such identification was the test of a painting's truth.

Entries made later the same year in Ruskin's diary show with what thoroughness he went on to explore the foreground detail of paintings in the Louvre. The year following, on his first tour abroad without his parents, he studied paintings with a floral guide to hand if not actually in his hand, finding that works in the Pitti Palace were 'full of flowers, of

---

[9] *Works*, vol. I, pp. 475–87.   [10] Preface to the Second Edition (1844), § 23.   [11] *Ibid.*, § 20.
[12] *Ibid.*, § 23, and compare *Diaries*, p. 265. *Crambe maritima* is a good guess; but in fact it is an Atlantic species that Raphael can never have seen.

which I cannot state whether they are truly drawn or not until I go to my field book'.[13] When the printed guide failed him, he called on the knowledge of Couttet, who scoured the Tuscan countryside for the originals. In Fra Angelico's *Deposition*, however, Ruskin had no difficulty in recognising a foreground rich in wood sorrel. And in the church of the Madonna dell'Orto in Venice he discovered that the lovingly painted wall plant beside St Peter in Cima da Conegliano's group of saints was the very *erba della Madonna* that grew on the marble steps outside. Henceforth *Cymbalaria muralis*, or ivy-leaved toadflax, was '*my* flower' for Ruskin, and in the third edition of *Modern Painters II* he incorporated Cima's use of it, along with his other 1845 observations upon flowers in paintings, into his discussion of 'finish' or detail.

Given the importance that Ruskin attached to the critic's botanical knowledge, it comes as a surprise to find him, in the 1844 Preface, declaring the 'mere botanist's' perception of a flower to be ignoble in comparison with that of the painter. Whereas the one 'counts the stamens, and affixes a name, and is content', the other considers 'each of its attributes as an element of expression', and so

seizes on its lines of grace or energy, rigidity or repose; notes the feebleness or the vigour, the serenity or tremulousness of its hues; observes its local habits, its love or fear of peculiar places, its nourishment or destruction by particular influences; he associates it in his mind with all the features of the situations it inhabits, and the ministering agencies necessary to its support. Thenceforward the flower is to him a living creature, with histories written on its leaves, and passions breathing in its motion. (§ 30)

Any plant scientist's hackles must rise at the falsity of this opposition, for even if the 'expression' of a flower is mainly the artist's concern, its life processes as they are affected by habitat and environment are prime concerns of the biologist, whose subject is by definition the living creature. But at the root of Ruskin's evaluation is not a science-versus-art dichotomy (that would come later) but a reproach to the botany of the time for failing to be a true life science. In the 1840s, plant study in England still meant first and foremost the classification and naming of species preliminary to their preservation in herbaria. There were historical reasons for this, as we have seen in earlier chapters. The acquisition of Linnaeus's collections and the founding of the Linnean Society, together with Kew's importance as the collecting point for new species pouring into the country from the

[13] Harold I. Shapiro (ed.), *Ruskin in Italy: Letters to his Parents, 1845* (1972), p. 130.

expanding Empire, ensured the dominance of systematics over all other aspects of the science.

Ruskin's feeling for the growing plant strikes us as in every way more in line with botany as we know it today. Admittedly, once the Preface was in the press and Ruskin settled with his parents in Chamonix for the summer of 1844, he busied himself like any other 'mere botanist' with collecting and drying plants. But the notes accompanying each of these relics concern life as the plant knew it: the altitude, soil and aspect of its habitat, the microclimate such as might perhaps have been created by an overhanging rock, the other species associated with it. Ruskin himself blossomed in the course of these studies: the long June days spent with Couttet scrambling over moraines in pursuit of flowers were, his diary records, among 'the most delicious and most instructive days I ever spent in my life',[14] and some months later one of them furnished him with a particularly telling image in the first part of *Modern Painters II*.

This section of the work attempts to define the qualities in the natural world that arouse a perception of beauty in the beholder. Whereas inanimate aspects of landscape such as clouds, rocks and snow display what Ruskin terms *typical* beauty because they offer types or symbols of such divine attributes as infinity and purity, what is found beautiful in plants and animals is the 'appearance of felicitous fulfilment of function in living things'.[15] To make the transition from the one to the other, Ruskin draws on a recent experience:

I have already noticed the example of very pure and high typical beauty which is to be found in the lines and gradations of unsullied snow: if, passing to the edge of a sheet of it, upon the Lower Alps, early in May, we find, as we are nearly sure to find, two or three little round openings pierced in it, and through these emergent a slender, pensive, fragile flower whose small, dark-purple, fringed bell hangs down and shudders over the icy cleft that it has cloven, as if partly wondering at its own recent grave, and partly dying of very fatigue after its hard won victory; we shall be, or we ought to be, moved by a totally different impression of loveliness from that which we receive among the dead ice and the idle clouds. There is now uttered to us a call for sympathy . . . (Chapter 12, § 1)

Knowing, as we do from Ruskin's diary, the circumstances in which he first saw *Soldanella* piercing the snow, we can understand this stress on fellow-feeling. The climber who has negotiated a glacier and the snowbell whose metabolic warmth has cleared the snow round it are both defying entropy.

---

[14] *Diaries*, p. 277. The dried 'Flora of Chamouni' is MS 65 in the Ruskin Library.
[15] *Modern Painters II*, 'Of the theoretic faculty', chapter 3, § 16.

Together they can be said to have come through: they have indeed felicitously fulfilled their function. The climber's discovery of the plant is thus a moment of biophilia, of life recognising itself, such as I have suggested is a fundamental experience of artist and biologist alike, and this appears to be what Ruskin is aware of when he writes 'There is now uttered to us a call for sympathy' and when, in the next chapter, he enlarges on this sympathy as an instinctive delight in the appearance a plant gives of enjoying the air it breathes: 'Every leaf and stalk is seen to have a function, to be constantly exercising that function, and as it *seems*, *solely* for the good and enjoyment of the plant.'[16]

But at this point in his discussion of the beauty of vitality, Ruskin introduces a qualification that in effect drives a wedge between the painter's experience and the biologist's. The pleasure we feel is diminished, he argues, the moment we think of that vitality in terms of 'mechanism', of inner processes creating the appearance of joyful life. Plant examples of such mechanisms will spring to the reader's mind,[17] but Ruskin goes straight to animal ones, arguing that the 'high sense of organic power and beauty' that we have as we watch the rise and fall of a shark's dorsal fin is lost once we investigate the fin's structure and discover 'the ingenuity of the mechanical contrivance'[18] that effects its movement through water. There are of course no solid grounds for this exclusion. One only has to turn to Stubbs's animal paintings to find depictions of organic power and beauty that draw their strength from the imaginative grasp of underlying mechanisms. That this grasp is an emotionally satisfying and even an aesthetic experience is borne out by the undertone of joy in much scientific writing, a tone akin to Ruskin's own earlier delight in the mechanics of the nitrogen and carbon cycles. The onlooker has a sharper sense of a plant's vitality when he is aware of the beautifully ordered biochemical processes taking place within its tissues. Scientists today may fight shy of the term 'beauty', but they work the term 'elegance' very hard; and the word 'contrivance', fiercely derogatory as used by Ruskin, was for Charles Darwin an approbatory term. For Ruskin, however, the scientific knowledge required of art critics and their readers was to be, in the distinction he would eventually draw in *Modern Painters III*, a 'science of aspects' and not a 'science of essences'. This would have far-reaching effects on his later

---

[16] *Ibid.*, chapter 12, § 4.
[17] One that Ruskin could have used, photosynthesis, he had already used in excluding all ideas of utility from the perception of vital beauty, utility in this case being designed usefulness to man, which was the way the 1840s thought of the gas-exchanges of the world's vegetation (chapter 12, § 5).
[18] *Modern Painters II*, 'Of the theoretic faculty', chapter 12, § 7.

writing about the plant world: effects matched here, in *Modern Painters II*, by others derived from the emphasis he now goes on to give to a second component of Vital Beauty.

In order to concentrate on Ruskin's recognition of the biophilic impulse, and on his limitation of it to outward appearances, I had to break off my quotation of the *Soldanella* passage in mid-sentence. Besides uttering a 'call for sympathy', the passage goes on, the alpine snowbell presents 'an image of moral purpose and achievement'. Ruskin's claim is that we feel a living organism to be beautiful not only because we delight in its air of vital happiness, but because our moral nature grasps the lesson it has been created to teach: in the case of plants, the exemplification of such virtues as

humility, and modesty, and love of places and things, in the reaching out of their arms, and clasping of their tendrils; and energy of resistance, and patience of suffering, and beneficence one towards another in shade and protection; and to us also in scents and fruits. (Chapter 12, § 11)

In short, 'fulfilment of function' in the plant kingdom consists not, as we might expect, in a plant's ability to survive, grow and multiply, but in the performance of its God-appointed duty towards the rest of creation and to man in particular, even when that duty makes impossible the well-being that comes from physical perfection. The 'poor and feeble' *Soldanella* that pierces the snow strikes the beholder with its beauty in a way that its flourishing counterparts below the snow line fail to do; stunted trees that 'fill up all the spaces where greenness, and coolness, and ornament, and oxygen are wanted, and that with very little reference to their comfort or convenience'[19] can still exemplify an ideal beauty.

At this point today's reader feels a great gulf opening between his or her thought processes and Ruskin's. Even in 1845 few would so ardently have asserted that everything in nature was designed for man's instruction. The emblemising view of creation had long since faded from the higher and drier reaches of eighteenth-century Anglicanism, and had not as yet been revived by mid-Victorian Anglo-Catholics. But it retained its strength in Evangelical circles of the kind Ruskin grew up in. It has to be remembered that, at the time of writing *Modern Painters II*, he was toying with the idea of becoming a lay preacher – stationed, it need hardly be added, in Florence or Rome. And the same habit of mind persisted with him long after his conventional religious beliefs had given way to social concerns. Two

---

[19] *Ibid.*, chapter 13, § 11; § 9.

decades on, as he pored over a zinnia's bracts half-metamorphosed into florets, he would declare them 'all useful in their imperfection – and *appointed to it* – how full of teaching!'[20] For though Ruskin would in time come to regard as pious insolence the confidence with which, in the 1840s, he interpreted God's intentions, he never surrendered his anthropocentricity. One striking instance of it is in the use to which he put a passage in his diary for 1846. In the original entry he describes a rich community of flowers near Champagnole in which wood sorrel is dominant, and associates each species with a previous encounter ('the delicate blue flower that I found on the granite rocks of the glacier des Bois'[21]) or with a poem or a painting. But when, in order to demonstrate the power of association in landscape, he incorporates this diary entry into *The Seven Lamps of Architecture*, he prefaces it with words that muddy the purity of the original experience.

Under the dark quietness of the undisturbed pines, there spring up, year by year, such company of joyful flowers as I know not the like of among all the blessings of the earth. It was spring time, too; and all were coming forth in clusters crowded for very love; there was room enough for all, but they crushed their leaves into all manner of strange shapes only to be nearer each other . . . (Chapter 6, § 1)

Outrageously sentimental as is this portrayal of a plant community in which competition for resources appears to have been intense (and every gardener knows how hard the sorrels would have fought), the passage, like the section on Vital Beauty in *Modern Painters II*, leaves us less irritated than apprehensive. For with hindsight we recognise the vulnerability of this view of the natural world. When the final volume of *Modern Painters* appeared in 1860, the periodic press was already agog with *The Origin of Species*, and those readers who had revelled in Ruskin's earlier volumes would soon have to come to terms with Huxley's *Man's Place in Nature* and Darwin's own *The Descent of Man*.

I have treated the opening of the Vital Beauty section of *Modern Painters II* as seminal because it presages Ruskin's later quarrel with the scientists. But at this stage, the quarrel is primarily with himself. Puritan and fundamentalist by upbringing, he combines a strong dread of the forbidden fruit of the tree of knowledge with a passionate curiosity about organic structures that lie beyond the reach of everyday observation. In fact, in the chapter succeeding the one in which he excludes all grasp of 'mechanical' contrivance from our apprehension of the beautiful, he demands that the

---

[20] Ruskin Library MS 12, p. 146. [21] *Diaries*, p. 325.

artist study 'the inward anatomy of everything'.[22] And in the last volume of *Modern Painters*, some fourteen years later, he will seek the source of a tree's beauty in whatever the botanists can tell him about the manner of its growth.

2

The summer of 1847 found Ruskin unwell and unhappy at Leamington Spa, and seeking relief from the tedium of hydrotherapy by studying the local flora. His diary observations on this reflect his shift in interest around this time from painting to sculpture and architecture: a wayside plantain covered in dust 'might have been turned into bronze on the instant, and put Ghiberti to shame'.[23] He dissected water plantain (*Alisma plantago-aquatica*) in order to work out the ratios between the whole inflorescence and its individual parts: measurements that he would use in *The Seven Lamps of Architecture* (1849) to demonstrate that architects could not do better than adopt the proportions of the natural world. His recorded examination ('with my smallest lens'[24]) of the structure of this and other flowers shows all the obsessiveness of the lover in Rossetti's poem about the wood spurge's 'cup of three' – and for much the same reason, since Ruskin's unhappiness at the time was due in large measure to his believing himself crossed in love. In the end, however, his parents came round to his marrying Effie Gray.

The years of Ruskin's marriage were also years of intense architectural study. Botany had to be set aside entirely while the volumes of *The Stones of Venice* (1851 and 1853) were in preparation. This perhaps explains why, when he sprang to the defence of the Pre-Raphaelite painters exhibiting at the 1851 Royal Academy, he wrote, apropos of Charles Collins's 'Convent Thoughts': 'I happen to have a special acquaintance with the water plant, *Alisma plantago* . . . and I never saw it so thoroughly and so well drawn.'[25] Was no reader of *The Times*, in that botanically minded generation, prepared to tell him that the plants in the painting are not water plantains such as he had so laboriously studied at Leamington but arrowheads – *Sagittaria sagittifolia*?

If anyone had dared to point out the gaffe it would have been Pauline Trevelyan, an enthusiastic admirer of Ruskin's work and, like her husband Sir Walter Trevelyan, a keen botanist. Their friendship became firm in

[22] Chapter 13, § 13.   [23] *Diaries*, p. 352.   [24] *Ibid.*, p. 356.
[25] Letter to *The Times*, 13 May 1851. Compare *Seven Lamps of Architecture*, chapter 4, § 29.

1853, when Ruskin, his wife and John Millais spent a week with the Trevelyans on the way to their fateful holiday in Scotland. Other things were helping Ruskin back to the green world around this time: Pre-Raphaelite naturalism of the kind exemplified by the mallows and fleabanes of Holman Hunt's *The Hireling Shepherd*; the necessity, in preparation for the first public lecture Ruskin ever gave, to find names for the foliage he and Millais painted in the Highlands (it was posted leaf by leaf to Lady Trevelyan for identification); above all, renewed study of botany in preparation for the completion of *Modern Painters*, a part of which was to be devoted to the beauty of vegetation. We do not, however, know what prompted the other extraordinary botanic venture that he now embarked upon. This was nothing less than an attempt to re-classify the whole range of flowering plants.

Ruskin knew nothing whatever about systematics. The Trevelyans had to tell him that over the past sixty years a natural system, based on the totalities of affinities between species, had come to replace the artificial Linnaean system. They probably recommended the latest edition (1848) of John Lindley's *Introduction to the Natural System of Botany*, since Ruskin, who would quote this work several times in his subsequent writings, appears to be responding to such a recommendation when he tells Pauline Trevelyan: 'I have got a book by Lindley on Botany – which tells me larkspur and buttercups are the same thing – I don't believe it; and won't.'[26] This was *The Ladies' Botany* (1837–8): a popular work on the lines of Rousseau's *La Botanique* but based on a natural system, and in spite of its (rightful) inclusion of buttercups and larkspurs within the same family, it would remain a favourite with Ruskin. Undaunted, however, by Lindley's eminence, Ruskin went stubbornly ahead with his own classification, explaining to the Carlyles, in the autumn of 1855: 'I became dissatisfied with the Linnaean, Jussieuan, and Everybody-elsian arrangement of plants, and have accordingly arranged a system of my own. . . . I consider this arrangement one of my great achievements of the year.'[27] And although he admitted to Pauline Trevelyan that he had discovered shortcomings in his system, which had left him with 'a large class called Tiresomes, which were plants who didn't know their own minds', he was convinced that 'people will learn botany a great deal faster on my plan'.[28] At Christmas he sent her

[26] Virginia Surtees (ed.), *Reflections of a Friendship: John Ruskin's Letters to Pauline Trevelyan, 1849–1866* (1979), p. 90.
[27] George Allan Cate (ed.), *The Correspondence of Thomas Carlyle and John Ruskin* (1982), p. 68.
[28] Surtees, *Reflections*, pp. 107–8.

the completed classification, having already expressed the hope that she would tell him it was all right. She appears to have left it to her husband to tell him it was all wrong, since three weeks later Sir Walter sent it back to Ruskin 'with notes showing its unscientific and illogical nature'.[29] Ruskin remained uncrushed. Despite the self-irony of the letters I have quoted, he was in earnest, and twenty years later would flaunt his system, strangely elaborated, in *Proserpina*.

Whatever possessed him? Pure arrogance, one is tempted to say, brought on by the discovery that, already regarded by many as an oracle in print, he was a charismatic lecturer as well. In the letter from Paris on September 1854 in which he mentions Lindley he also announces 'I am going to set myself up to tell people anything *in any way* that they want to know, as soon as I get home',[30] adding a preference for artisan audiences of about 200. But arrogance can mask self-doubt. Four months after the humiliating annulment of his marriage, Ruskin may well have been seeking to escape the recent past by inventing for himself a new persona, that of the popular educator. And his concern with bringing an understanding of the beautiful to the disadvantaged was perfectly genuine; what he in fact settled for on his return to England was quiet and effective one-to-one teaching at the Working Men's College. The eccentricity of his approach to systematics lay, not in his wish to make botany accessible to the many, but in the notion that he could toss off in his spare time a classification that would replace the one that Antoine-Laurent Jussieu, Candolle, Robert Brown and others had given their whole careers to formulating.

There is no arrogance in Ruskin's most sustained and carefully planned piece of botanical writing, 'Of leaf beauty', which he began in 1858 and which was to form the first part of the final volume of *Modern Painters* (1860). An opening chapter surveys the various ways in which vegetation is essential to human life, presenting it as 'God's daily preparation of the earth' for man.[31] Next, he groups plants into 'builders with the shield' (broadleaved trees), 'builders with the sword' (conifers) and 'tented' or nomadic plants (the ground flora).[32] Of these three categories, only the first is important to landscape art: even Turner could not enter 'the spirit of the pine';[33] and Ruskin, for all his earlier delight in Italian Renaissance fore-grounds, has to admit that for a variety of reasons the greatest painters have avoided trying to portray the flowers of the field. So 'Of Leaf Beauty' is mainly an exploration of how broadleaved trees build and shape their

---

[29] *Ibid.*, p. 110, quoting Trevelyan's diary.   [30] *Ibid.*, p. 88.   [31] 'Of leaf beauty', chapter 1, § 3.
[32] *Ibid.*, chapter 2, § 2–3.   [33] *Ibid.*, chapter 9, § 7.

biomass, with only its last two chapters devoted to the beauty of conifers and of the ground flora. This scheme allows Ruskin to end with the wild flowers and mosses he loved, so that the celebratory tone of the peroration echoes that of the opening chapter and frames the whole section in Ruskin's gratitude for the green mantle enfolding human life:

No words, that I know of, will say what these mosses are. None are delicate enough, none perfect enough, none rich enough. How is one to tell of the rounded bosses of furred and beaming green, – the starred divisions of rubied bloom, fine-filmed, as if the Rock Spirits could spin porphyry as we do glass, – the traceries of intricate silver, and fringes of amber, lustrous, arborescent, burnished through every fibre into fitful brightness and glossy traverses of silken change, yet all subdued and pensive, and framed for simplest, sweetest offices of grace? They will not be gathered, like the flowers, for chaplet or love-token; but of these the wild bird will make its nest, and the wearied child his pillow.

And as the earth's first mercy, so they are its last gift to us. When all other service is vain, from plant and tree, the soft mosses and grey lichen take up their watch by the headstone. The woods, the blossoms, the gift-bearing grasses, have done their parts for a time, but these do service for ever. Trees for the builder's yard, flowers for the bride's chamber, corn for the granary, moss for the grave. (Chapter 10, § 24)

Between these two opulently written chapters comes Ruskin's main topic, tree morphology: a subject that follows on naturally enough from his attack, in the work's first volume, on the supposed old masters of landscape painting for their inability to grasp the 'Truth of Vegetation'. Turner alone knew and told the truth about trees; and now in this final volume Ruskin sets about expounding the laws of growth, of which he believed Turner to have had an instinctive understanding. The chapters on the beauty of shoots and leaves are Ruskin's science of aspects at its best: a wonderfully sensitive interpretation of visible form as the outcome of a tree's life history. Then he passes to the limbs and trunks of trees and turns to the botanists for an answer to the question 'How does a tree make its trunk?' In 1858, however, they did not all give the same answer; and the answer Ruskin accepted was wildly wrong.

A scientific error can often tell us more about the habits of thought of a particular generation, or of an individual thinker in it, than we can learn from its scientific discoveries. And the cast of Ruskin's thought around 1860 is responsible for his determined adherence to what, making use of his own image, we may call the silver cord theory of tree growth put forward early in the century by Aubert du Petit Thouars.[34]

---

[34] *Essais sur la végétation considérée dans le développement des bourgeons* (1809).

From every leaf in all the countless crowd at the tree's summit, one slender fibre, or at least fibre's thickness of wood, descends through shoot, through spray, through branch, and through stem; and having thus added, in its due proportion, to form the strength of the tree, labours yet farther and more painfully to provide for its security; and thrusting forward into the root, loses nothing of its mighty energy until, mining through the darkness, it has taken hold in cleft of rock or depth of earth, as extended as the sweep of its green crest in the free air. (Chapter 6, § 3)

This is beautifully expressed nonsense. German botanists of the 1840s had seen through their Zeiss lenses the ring of cambium cells whose division and differentiation effects the increase in a tree's girth, and the facts of their discovery, besides being set forth in the edition of Lindley's *Introduction* used by Ruskin, had been available in English since 1849 in M. J. Schleiden's *Principles of Scientific Botany*. But du Petit Thouars' fancies persisted in books that Ruskin owned,[35] and neither by upbringing nor by temperament was he equipped to discriminate between speculation and scientific demonstration; indeed, such discrimination, second nature to informed readers today, was far from being widespread in the mid-nineteenth century.

So when it came to explaining tree growth, Ruskin felt free to help himself to what he wanted. He did not want the cell-division explanation because it represented for him that prying into the mechanics of nature that he had already repudiated in his second volume. He *did* want the silver cord explanation because, in addition to accounting – or so he believed – for 'external and visible fact', it fitted with the other obsession revealed in *Modern Painters II*, the moral instructiveness of all life forms; this much is indicated in a footnote reference to Alexander Harvey's *Trees and their Nature* (1858). The interest of this maverick work is not so much that it cheerfully mixes the silver cord fallacy with the facts of cell formation (much as Ruskin himself was to do a year later when lecturing at the Royal Institute on 'Tree Twigs') as that it propounds something called 'the corporation theory of trees'.[36] For Harvey a tree is 'an aggregate of individuals ... a collection of perfectly distinct annual tree plants'.[37] This concept of a tree (or for that matter a buttercup) as a social rather than an individual entity, however erroneously employed by writers like Harvey, is itself perfectly viable. In 1858 Asa Gray advanced it in an authoritative

---

[35] Besides the book by Alexander Harvey discussed below, Ruskin owned Christopher Dresser's *The Rudiments of Botany* (1859) which contains a completely imaginary diagram of wood being formed on the Thouars principle; moreover Lindley appears in his *Introduction* (1848 edition) unwilling to relinquish the theory and in a footnote Ruskin refers to his restatement of it.
[36] Harvey, *Trees and their Nature*, p. xvi.   [37] *Ibid.*, p. xv.

and up-to-the-minute textbook that Ruskin also possessed. Moreover, it had special appeal for him at this time. The world round him was still rich in archetypes, but as his Evangelical faith waned, the interpretation of these archetypes in religious terms had begun to give way to a perception of social and political meanings. So it came about that Ruskin, who had already discovered an expression of communal values in Gothic architecture, now discovered them anew in the plant kingdom. The deflection of the lower leaves in a branch of laurel, in contrast to the directionless spread of elm leaves, demonstrated to him that 'when the community is small, people fall more easily into their places, and take, each in his place, a firmer standing than can be obtained by the individuals of a great nation'.[38] To such social virtues of harmony and obedience he joins sacrifice: the trunk's straight ascent is achieved through the withering of many branches. And the fact that, despite much apparent symmetry, two leaves of a tree are never identical, illustrates for him the 'delightsome inequality'[39] of individuals in a healthy society.

The modern reader, teeth already set on edge by what a friend termed Ruskin's talk-down-to-lower-intellects style (in large part the result of his association, around this time, with Winnington School for girls), is likely to have even greater difficulty with the substance of passages such as this. Ruskin appears not to be playing with analogies but claiming real equivalencies. In so doing he is seeking a validation of social values (some of them questionable) in conjectures about plant growth that are, biologically speaking, without foundation. What controls the growth of leaves is after all not a moral adjustment between individual caprice and the sense of fellowship, but the amount and direction of light they receive. Branches do not drop off out of a spirit of sacrifice but because of the decay consequent upon a loss of light. Given the general understanding of photosynthesis at that time, Ruskin's underestimation of the power of light to promote growth is puzzling in someone who was a gardener, a painter and a devotee of Turner – for whom the sun was God.

Yet it would require a very unsympathetic reader, and one with little historical sense, to take such a disparaging view of 'Of leaf beauty'. Under the influence of Pauline Trevelyan, perhaps the best friend he ever had, Ruskin shows himself genuinely and humbly ready to learn from the botanists; and though some of them misled him into regarding a tree trunk as a bundle of vessels descending from individual leaves, he does latch onto something interesting when he imagines this bundle, in richly

---

[38] 'Of leaf beauty', chapter 4, § 8.   [39] *Ibid.*, chapter 8, § 18.

Victorian terms, as 'a group of canals for the conveyance of marketable commodities, with an electric telegraph attached to each, transmitting messages from leaf to root, and root to leaf, up and down the tree'.[40] Twenty-one years later, Charles Darwin and his son Francis would postulate the existence of a messenger substance (now called auxin) between the light-sensitive tip of a shoot and the stem that curved in response to it – although it was not until this century that a leading geneticist could claim: 'We'd found that auxin from the shoot meristem . . . travels all the way down the stem and into the root, where it promotes root growth. That there's a connection between these two most distant poles of the plant.'[41]

What still has power to please in 'Of leaf beauty' is the empathy with growing things that, for all Ruskin's new social concerns, here yields less precipitately to his moral preoccupations than it did in *Modern Painters II*. The section's chapters are shot through with delight, amounting to an awareness of palpable presences, in the idiosyncrasies of form that reflect a leaf's 'life of progress and will' or a branch's 'fits of enthusiasm to which it yielded in certain delicious warm springs'.[42] And if this vitalist language irks the modern reader, delight minus the anthropomorphism can be savoured in the drawings that accompany the text. But the most telling evidence of how Ruskin could by word and pencil together enter into the life story of a tree comes from one of his students at the Working Men's College:

He explained that my tree did not tell its own story sufficiently, and, as he sketched, pointed out that the tree would naturally have grown upright, but being on the side of a steep bank, it declined a little from the perpendicular; as it grew higher and became heavier from increase of branch and leafage, it declined still further from the perpendicular, but the lower part of the trunk, being older and stronger than the upper part, was only a little out of the upright; as the branches grew, they naturally shot upward, those on the upper side have a free course and grow fairly well, but those on the under side of the trunk fall over with it and droop more and more the nearer they are to the ground; as they near the top, they get a better chance and grow in a more normal fashion, whilst the forms of the leafage on the two sides of the tree differ from each other in consequence of this difference in the growth of the branches. All this history of a life, as shown in the form of a tree, astonished at the same time that it convinced me of its truth, as he spoke and illustrated his meaning by his sketch.[43]

---

[40] *Ibid.*, chapter 6, § 4.   [41] Nicholas Harberd, *Seed to Seed: the Secret Life of Plants* (2006), p. 254.
[42] 'Of leaf beauty', chapter 4, § 17; chapter 8, § 11.
[43] Quoted by E. T. Cook, *The Life of John Ruskin* (1911), vol. I, pp. 382–3.

3

Ruskin's next sustained piece of botanical writing was the second section of *The Queen of the Air*, published in 1869: at the end, that is, of a stressful decade in which frustration after frustration added its residue of unhappiness until these built up into a deep sense of rejection. The social concerns which had made themselves felt even in the way Ruskin described the growth of a tree were stifled when editors stopped accepting his essays. Moreover his father, though publicly loyal, was privately appalled by his son's radicalism. To ease the strain in their relationship, Ruskin spent most of his time abroad, even planning to settle in Switzerland. His pleasure in the structure of the flowers he observed there – the set of a nasturtium on its stalk, the 'peculiar windmill form' of a periwinkle[44] – was one of the few subjects safe to write about in letters home. Loss of orthodox beliefs was another matter on which he could not express himself publicly: in 1861 he promised his Irish friend, Maria La Touche, that he would publish nothing on that subject for ten years.

Thus inhibited from airing either his political or his religious views, Ruskin found it 'wonderfully difficult'[45] to know what to do next. Letters of the time show him considering the claims of natural history. Gradually his interest in the plant world came to dominate, so that even after his father's death in 1864 set him free to write and lecture on social questions, his diaries and letters record a continuing and vigorous botanical activity. There are jottings about his proposed system of classification; there are notes from the botanical works that he bought almost as fast as the bookseller Quaritch could supply them; above all there are his own records of living plants, whether in drawings such as a delicate study of sow thistle leaves[46] or in descriptions such as this of a zinnia:

Within the great scarlet leaves [i.e., florets] which have each a large double-forked style, comes a row of smaller fringed leaves, each with a smaller forked style curled like an Ionic volute – Then, yellow star-shaped 5 foil flowers golden, covered with hairs, looking through lens like brushes of gold. Within these, a central group of purple and crimson fringes like (seen through lens) some splendid crustacean, purple horned. Four orders of flowers altogether, exclusive of external incipient leaf, and each so complex and beautiful it would take a day to draw them.[47]

---

[44] *Works*, vol. XXV, p. xxxiv.   [45] Cook, *Life*, vol. II, p. 22.

[46] Reproduced as Plate 39 in *Diaries*, but not, as there stated, a drawing of 'teazle' and not done in 1854; Ruskin used a blank page of an old diary to make the drawing in 1865.

[47] Ruskin Library MS 12, p. 146v.

Out of these activities came the determination to write a book on botany for the young: perhaps for the Winnington schoolgirls and certainly for one schoolgirl, not at Winnington, whose relationship with Ruskin was the greatest frustration of his life: Maria La Touche's daughter, Rose.

From the time of Ruskin's first stay with the La Touche family in 1861 when Rose was thirteen, her parents' mixed feelings about him – pride in the attention of so eminent a man, disapproval of his unorthodoxy and anxiety over the effect his infatuation could have on a daughter who was beginning to show signs of mental instability – rendered their own behaviour to him unstable. May 1868 brought a typical incident. On the point of giving a lecture in Dublin, Ruskin received a note from Rose to say that her parents had forbidden her to write to him or accept his letters. She tried instead to communicate through the language of flowers in a package delivered after the lecture; but though he could recognise the intent of a rose enfolded in a tangle of *erbe della Madonna*, the message as a whole was too complex for him to decipher. Two days later he wrote angrily to a friend: 'I am going to do my book on botany – and every word of it will be dead and lifeless – for ever – compared with what it would have been – because this wicked woman's commands are obeyed by her husband.'[48] He was even more distraught when he discovered the La Touches believed that a match with Rose, should it prove fertile, would contravene the annulment of his first marriage. A difficult summer followed. Ruskin doggedly kept up study for the planned book – the pages facing his laconic diary entries are full of botanical notes – and sought immediate consolation in the wild flowers of Normandy. But he was profoundly disturbed: a delirious night at Abbeville, in which the wallpaper turned into faces (and a move to a room with a frieze of white roses can scarcely have helped), was remembered by him in later years as the first intimation of insanity.

Diary entries for the closing months of 1868 show Ruskin still busy with his botany, but they record neither of the two visits he paid to Charles Darwin, who lived a few miles away across the North Downs, nor Darwin's return visits to him. The two men had met some thirty years earlier, in Ruskin's first year at Oxford, when they had 'got together and talked all the evening'.[49] We do not however know what they talked about in 1868. If the first visit to Down House included a tour of Darwin's greenhouse, Ruskin's botanic interests would have sprung to the fore. But the friend who

[48] John Lewis Bradley (ed.), *The Letters of John Ruskin to Lord and Lady Mount-Temple* (1964), p. 159. (Hereafter *Mount-Temple Letters*.)
[49] *Works*, vol. XXXVI, p. 14.

brought them together only recorded that their talk was scientific and 'afforded striking illustration of the many sympathies that underlay the divergence of their points of view'.[50] Certainly Ruskin found Darwin 'delightful',[51] and this sympathy may have made him receptive to theories that – as he wrote some months later in *The Queen of the Air* – 'Mr Darwin's unwearied and unerring investigations are every day rendering more probable'.[52]

How well (if at all) did Ruskin know *The Origin of Species?* There is no mention of its publication in November 1859 among his surviving papers, but then his diaries for that period are lost. The fact that he failed to understand the mechanism of natural selection, which he unwittingly travesties in several passages, tells us little. For all its beautiful simplicity, or perhaps on account of it, the theory eluded some of the best minds of the time. A passage from his correspondence has been taken to indicate that, whatever his misunderstandings of the letter of Darwin's theory, Ruskin grasped its spirit as early as 1861: he writes that he is contemplating devoting himself to natural history, but admits that he finds it a terrifying subject:

Not that natural history is in one sense, peace, but terrific. Its abysses of life and pain; of diabolical ingenuity – merciless condemnation – irrevocable change – infinite Scorn – endless advance – immeasurable scale of beings incomprehensible to each other – every one important in its own right – and a grain of Dust in its Creator's – it makes me giddy and desolate beyond all speaking.[53]

This angst can, however, have owed more to Robert Chambers's *Vestiges of the Natural Order of Creation* (1844) than to *The Origin of Species*. For though it is now possible to detect in the latter an underlying acceptance of blind chance, Darwin, having watched the professional scientists butcher Chambers at the 1847 British Association meeting, himself remained the most circumspect and cautious of writers. In *The Origin* he took care to stop short of speculating on the descent of man; and when Asa Gray hailed the work as the restoration of teleology, Darwin himself promoted the English sales of Gray's *Natural Selection not Inconsistent with Natural Theology* (1861). His caution paid off: many intellectuals of the 1860s, Ruskin among them, were at first surprisingly receptive to the idea of natural selection.

---

[50] C. E. Norton (ed.), *Letters of John Ruskin to Charles Eliot Norton* (1905), vol. I, p. 195.
[51] *Ibid.*   [52] *Queen of the Air*, lecture 2, § 62.
[53] John Bradley and Ian Ousby (eds.), *The Correspondence of John Ruskin and Charles Eliot Norton* (1987), pp. 65–6. (Hereafter *Norton Letters*.)

Just after Ruskin's first visit Darwin remarked to a botanical correspondent that 'natural historians'[54] valued observation far more than reasoning. Himself aware of the shortfall of demonstration in *The Origin*, especially regarding plant evolution, he had spent much of the 1860s, as we have seen, in observing and recording the adaptive successes of plants: watching, for example, the same stand of orchids hour after hour, until he discovered that the pollen-mass which the floral structure compelled a bee to carry away from a flower required *just the time of the bee's flight to the next flower* in order to reposition itself in such a way that the bee would perforce deposit it on the second flower's stigma. 'Unwearied and unerring' investigations indeed, and it is these, rather than anything in *The Origin*, that Ruskin has in mind when he speaks of Darwin's day-to-day work. The painstaking record of *Various Contrivances by which Orchids are Fertilized by Insects* (1862) was more than enough to convince Ruskin that there was transformation of species in the plant kingdom.

Ruskin insisted in later years that his hostility towards scientists was directed not against Darwin but against the Darwinians. Although this was scarcely an accurate statement once Darwin, in *The Descent of Man* (1872), had brought human origins into his scheme of things, Ruskin in the previous decade felt that the main threat to his humanist concept of man as the sun of the world came from the author of *Man's Place in Nature*, Thomas Huxley. He may too have felt a threat of personal dislodgement: Huxley was a spell-binding lecturer. One of his most brilliant performances, 'The physical basis of life', given at Edinburgh late in 1868, caused such a stir that the journal in which it was published in February 1869 had to be reprinted six times. In this 'lay sermon', Huxley threw down the gauntlet to all who held 'a conception of life as a something which works through matter, but is independent of it'.[55] Life, he maintained, inhered in the basic content of the cell, a nucleated mass of protoplasm which, reduced to its elements, was endlessly recycled into new organisms whose every activity, including the utmost refinements of human thought, was achieved through molecular change. It followed that inorganic chemical compounds stood no more in need, for their transformation into the driving powers of organic life, of a process or property called 'vitality' than oxygen and hydrogen required 'aquacity' to form them into an ice crystal.

---

[54] Frederick Burkhardt and Sydney Smith (eds.), *Calendar of the Correspondence of Charles Darwin, 1821–1882* (1985), item 6475.
[55] *Lay Sermons, Addresses and Reviews* (1870), p. 104.

At the time Huxley's lecture was published, Ruskin was himself preparing to give a lecture at University College, London. Because his sense of the
numinous now found its most satisfying expression in terms of pre-
Christian myths ('I mean to be religious again', he had said in 1862, 'but
my religion is to be old Greek'),[56] he sought in this lecture to recreate, in
terms of various legends about the goddess Athena, the Greek sense of a
spiritual power at work in the physical world as seen in the effects of air
upon water and rock. From there it was a natural step, such as he had taken
in *Modern Painters II*, to the work of the same power among forms of life.
Outrage at what he saw as the extreme materialism of Huxley's Edinburgh
lecture now compelled him to take that step and to present Athena, in the
second part of what would shortly be published as *The Queen of the Air*, as
'Athena in the Earth': the vital principle in organic nature. Huxley had
likened protoplasm to the clay of the potter: 'which, bake it and paint it as
he will, remains clay, separated by artifice, and not by nature, from the
commonest brick or sun-dried clod'.[57] To this Ruskin opposed the metaphor he had recently used in *Ethics of the Dust*: 'Discern the moulding hand
of the potter commanding the clay, from his merely beating foot, as it turns
the wheel.'[58] Athena is accordingly presented in the second section ('lecture') of *The Queen of the Air* as *Athene Keramitis*, 'fit for being made into
pottery': mythic equivalent of the power, traditionally spoken of as the
breath of God, which endowed matter, whether clay or protoplasm, with
shape and feeling. And just as was the case with the dramatic introduction
of *Soldanella* into *Modern Painters II*, the clearest evidence that Ruskin can
educe that a life-giving power exists is our response to the 'inner rapture' of
a plant at its moment of flowering: a moment at which 'the strongest life is
asserted by characters in which the human sight takes pleasure, and which
seem prepared with distinct reference to us, or rather, bear, in being
delightful, evidence of having been produced by the power of the same
spirit as our own'.[59]

From this empathy with the self-realisation of other life forms, Ruskin
passes, just as he did in the earlier work, to the moral response that he
believes we make to their variety. A lifelong respect for chemical fact
compels him to admit that protoplasm goes to the making of both
crocodiles and lambs; but, he argues, the distinctiveness of their aspects
and qualities, seen as the shaping work of Athena, has communicated to
humanity the awareness of evil and of good whereby they are associated

[56] Cook, *Life*, vol. II, p. 51 (quoting a letter to Mrs Hewitt).   [57] Huxley, *Lay Sermons*, p. 112.
[58] *Ethics of the Dust* (1866), § 108.   [59] *Queen of the Air*, lecture 2, § 61.

with myths of destruction and redemption. And Ruskin still has Huxley in his sights when he moves on to the two phyla most closely connected with Athena. In another lecture, delivered earlier in 1868, Huxley had made use of *Archaeopteryx* and other intermediate fossil forms to argue persuasively for the dinosaur origin of birds. Ruskin in reply seizes upon the association of both birds and snakes with Pallas Athene in order to exert all his rhetorical skills on the total incompatibility of the two kinds of being: the one embodying the very spirit of the air, the other a 'divine hieroglyph of the demoniac power of the earth'.[60] Against Huxley's demonstration of anatomical continuities, Ruskin attempts an emotionally charged evocation of the distinct life force in each creature as expressed through its movement. This eloquence would, of course, cut no ice with the Darwin circle who, except when Ruskin attacked Tyndall a few years later, appear to have paid no heed to his views in either their public or their private writings. But as Ruskin expatiates on avian grace and reptilian repulsiveness, the reader begins to realise that something more is at stake than the writer's misgivings about the Darwinian account of the transformation of species: something that is implied when Ruskin speaks passionately of the human race as 'still half-serpent, not extricated yet from its clay; a lacertine breed of bitterness – the glory of it emaciate with cruel hunger, and blotted with venomous stain'.[61]

'Lacertine' means lizard-like, not serpent-like. So much was noted in the margin of her copy by one reader who was in a position to grasp the significance of Ruskin's usage: 'Poor green lizards!...Why not say serpentine?'[62] For Lacerta was Maria La Touche's nickname: a pleasantry in 1861 ('the grace and wisdom of the serpent, without its poison'[63]) that became anything but pleasant once Maria set herself to keep Rose (author of the pencilled note) and Ruskin apart, as she did from the early months of 1867. Ruskin's deep frustration intrudes on his more cerebral but still strongly felt unease at the Darwinian notion of birds having evolved from dinosaurs. How could the bird-spirit Rose have descended from such a reptile as Lacerta? And its force carries him on to consider other supposedly evolutionary relationships in the natural world: this time, among the flowering plants.

What he has to say at this point has generally eluded his critics. His Edwardian editors, in their synopsis, reduce it to a vague phrase: 'The distinctions of species in the plant world in their moral aspect'.[64] More

[60] *Ibid.*, § 68.   [61] *Ibid.*, § 71.
[62] Quoted by Tim Hilton, *John Ruskin: the Later Years* (2000), p. 157.
[63] *Ibid.*, p. 20.   [64] *Works*, vol. XIX, p. 422.

recently one of his most serious admirers has called it 'a slough of Ruskinian ethical botany'.[65] Certainly it has little relevance to Athena. But it is highly relevant to Ruskin's wish to reconcile a qualified acceptance of the transmutation of species with his profound sense of their spiritually endowed distinctiveness. It is also relevant to feelings about Rose and Maria that were crying out for expression, as Ruskin admitted to a friend just after *The Queen of the Air* was finished:

There's a word or two here and there – which only ρ [i.e. Rose] will understand – a little botany about leaves that grow among ruins – which people will say is fanciful – and some Darwinian notes on origin – no – on distinction – of species – lacertine and others.[66]

The 'distinction of species' of flowering plants by sorting them into taxa of his own devising had occupied Ruskin's mind for a number of years and now he makes it public for the first time. As it happens, his groupings at this stage are not all that different from those generally accepted. Thus his Drosidae, or dew flowers, correspond to the order Liliales: monocot plants with regular flowers of which the parts are in threes or sixes; while his Draconidae, or dragon flowers correspond to the irregular, two-lipped flowers of the ill-named family Scrophulariaceae. Ruskin's innovation is his presentation of the two groups, with all the passion of a revivalist preacher, as mythological embodiments of good and evil; an opposition intensified in his own mind by thoughts of Rose and her mother. The Drosidae are associated with purity, virginity, chivalry (the fleur de lis), rural contentment (tulips), childhood (bluebells) and other good things; whereas the more or less serpentine Draconidae 'all agree in a tendency to decorate themselves by spots, and with bosses or swollen places in their leaves, as if they had been touched by poison'.[67] The spots on foxgloves are especially repellent. Is Ruskin remembering Millais's drawing of Effie garlanded with these flowers – Effie who, he believed, was conniving with Rose's mother to prevent his remarriage?

When he was reading the botany and the mythology he was to bring together in *The Queen of the Air*, Ruskin jotted down *Les Fleurs du Mal* as a book he wanted to buy.[68] It would seem that he assumed Baudelaire's poems to be about flowers issuing – like Rose – from evil, or even as evil in themselves. The idea had been with him from his early days, when he wrote of garden cultivars as 'corrupted by evil communication into speckled and

---

[65] Raymond E. Fitch, *The Poison Sky: Myth and Apocalypse in Ruskin* (1982), p. 570.
[66] *Mount-Temple Letters*, p. 197.   [67] *Queen of the Air*, lecture 2, § 86.
[68] Ruskin Library MS 15, p. 55v.

inharmonious colours'[69] and it accounts for the catalogue of repulsive blooms (named with Pauline Trevelyan's help) that contribute to Mountain Gloom in *Modern Painters IV*. Outbursts such as these help explain why hardly anyone now reads Ruskin. And yet, in this distaste for certain flowers, Ruskin could be said to be putting his finger on an aspect of everyday experience suppressed by Victorian sentimentality but given recognition in the work of several twentieth-century poets. There *is* often something disturbing about flowers that have evolved away from a simple radial symmetry and taken on the axial symmetry we connect with animals. The importance of this reaction for Ruskin, and perhaps one reason for his overstating it so violently, are that it made it possible for him to assent to Darwin's theory of floral adaptation while retaining a belief in perfect archetypes that had been there from the beginning. His way of eating his cake and having it is to regard the evolution of regular into irregular (zygomorphic) flowers as a process of degeneration. 'Which is the highest?' asks Darwin of his orchids before giving the palm to 'the magnificent Vandeae'[70] for the ingenuity of their mechanism of survival. But Darwin's highest is Ruskin's lowest. In his eyes there has been a fall of flowers, so that in almost every family there are species that have lost their regularity of form and purity of colour; and in his myth, as in the Genesis one, this corruption is the work of a serpentine power. Such a spirit, although it 'never once' touches the roses,

enters like an evil spirit into the buttercup, and turns it into a larkspur, with a black, spotted, grotesque centre, and a strange, broken blue, gorgeous and intense, yet impure, glittering on the surface as if it were strewn with broken glass, and stained or darkening irregularly into red. And then at last the serpent charm changes the ranunculus into monkshood; and makes it poisonous. It enters into the forget-me-not, and the star of heavenly turquoise is corrupted into the viper's bugloss, darkened with the same strange red as the larkspur, and fretted into a fringe of thorn. (*Queen of the Air*, lecture 2, § 87)

Steady on! cries the reader: the viper's bugloss has been called the most beautiful wild flower in existence. And at this point Ruskin's revulsion does begin to subside. All we are told of the supposed transmutation of asphodels into spotted orchids is that it is accomplished through 'a strange insect spirit'. Deference for Darwin holds Ruskin back, though only for the present.

---

[69] *Works*, vol. I, p. 209 (*The Poetry of Architecture*).
[70] Charles Darwin, *The Various Contrivances by which Orchids are Fertilized* (2nd edn, 1877), p. 264.

Moreover, as he goes on to admit, the symbolism offered by mythology can be ambiguous. Just as the serpent is a symbol of healing as well as of destruction, 'there is an Æsculapian as well as an evil serpentry among the Draconidae'. Lacerta might, one day, change into the benign friend she had once been. That personal feelings are near the surface, and that personal messages are being sent, becomes evident when Ruskin ends this section with his 'little botany about leaves that grow among the ruins':

and the fairest of them [i.e. the Draconidae], the 'erba della Madonna' of Venice (Linaria Cymbalaria,) descends from the ruins it delights in to the herbage at their feet, and touches it; and behold, instantly, a vast group of herbs for healing – all draconid in form, – spotted, and crested, and from their lip-like corollas named 'labiatae', full of various balm and warm strength for healing.

The probability is that Ruskin, who must have been disconcerted to find that Our Lady's herb was a snapdragon, is here reminding Rose that he has long since left his eminence as a writer on architecture in order to teach young girls how to bring balm to society. These private meanings elude us today, though they would have been understood by Rose, who replied also in code; later that year she sent Ruskin a botanical book with a single rose leaf and a sprig of *erba della Madonna* pressed between pages dealing with the Dioscoridae – of which the sole British species is the strangling and poisonous black bryony.

Whatever the coded message, it is a relief when Ruskin returns to his real subject: the shaping spirit behind the diversity of organisms. Leaves in their growth, the botanists tell him, are seeking for something they want – presumably the light that will enable them to produce sugars. But why do they assume so many forms in their quest?

What made them seek for it thus? Seek for it, in five fibres or in three? Seek for it in serration, or in sweeping curves? Seek for it in servile tendrils, or impetuous spray? Seek for it, in woolly wrinkles rough with stings, or in glossy surfaces, green with pure strength, and winterless delight? (§ 88)

Much the same question had been asked (of flowers, not leaves) by, of all people, Huxley: 'Who has ever dreamed of finding a utilitarian purpose in the forms and colours of flowers?'[71] Darwin's orchid book gave him his answer. But for Ruskin,

There is no answer. But the sum of all is, that over the entire surface of the earth and its waters, as influenced by the power of the air under solar light, there is

---

[71] Quoted by Adrian Desmond and James Moore, *Darwin* (1992), p. 509.

6 Ruskin's drawing of ivy-leaved toadflax, *Cymbalaria muralis*. He regarded the plant,
l'erba della Madonna that flourished between the stones of Venice, as his personal emblem.
Reproduced from a photogravure in *The Works of John Ruskin*, 1903–1912.

'Venice. 16th September, 1876 . . . I am weary, this morning, with vainly trying to draw the
Madonna-herb clustered on the capitals of St Mark's porch; and mingling its fresh life with
the marble acanthus leaves which saw Barbarossa receive the foot of the Prince of
Christendom on his neck.'

(*Fors Clavigera 70*)

developed a series of changing forms, in clouds, plants, and animals, all of which have reference in their action, or nature, to the human intelligence that perceives them; and on which, in their aspects of horror and beauty, and their qualities of good and evil, there is engraved a series of myths, or words of the forming power, which, according to the true passion and energy of the human race, they have been enabled to read into religion. (§ 89)

This is splendid eloquence. When Henry James heard Ruskin deliver the first part of *The Queen of the Air,* he was deeply impressed. Yet when he met the lecturer socially, he decided here was a man in flight from reality.[72] And sadly, once the resonances of Ruskin's prose in this section of the book die on the inner ear, the reader has to concur. What at first appeared to be an attempt to come to terms with the transmutation of species ends in high-sounding evasions.

There was so much that should have made Ruskin receptive to Darwin's ideas: his geological knowledge; his instinct for patient and accurate observation, such as compelled him to spend two days drawing a marsh orchid; his eagerness for demonstrative proofs; the biophilia they had in common; his recent liberation from religious dogma. But he could not share Darwin's self-effacing objectivity, and it was shrewd of Charles Waldstein, in one of the first books on Ruskin as thinker, to contrast Ruskin's 'prophetic and denunciatory violence' with Darwin's 'charitable and unselfish statement of a great continuous effort in a long laborious life': a contrast echoed by Darwin's widow, when she read it, in the words 'Ruskin never forgets himself.'[73] Nor could his extraordinary upbringing and the circumstances of his adult life, so strongly contrasted with those of Darwin, allow Ruskin to be anything but self-absorbed. In the 1860s in particular, he was in both his public and private life nursing a deeply wounded ego, and this made him emotionally resistant to the evolutionists' view of the two kingdoms from which man had been dethroned; where Wallace's birds of paradise and Darwin's orchids flaunted their beauty, not to please human eyes, but to perpetuate their phenotype.

4

At the time of Ruskin's visits to Down House in 1868, the theory of natural selection had found the widest acceptance it would ever attain before it was

[72] Letter from James quoted by Tim Hilton, *John Ruskin: the Later Years* (2000), p. 153.
[73] *The Work of John Ruskin: its Influence upon Modern Thought and Life* (1894), p. 156; Emma Darwin, *A Century of Family Letters, 1792–1896* (1915), vol. II, p. 303.

verified by the findings of twentieth-century genetics and molecular biology. But during the next few years it was subjected to several powerful attacks from within the scientific establishment itself. These resulted in so much attenuation of the original theory in the sixth edition of the *Origin of Species* that pure Darwinism might be said to have been, if not in retreat, at least in temporary withdrawal by the autumn of 1872, which was also the beginning of the third year of Ruskin's tenure of the Chair of Fine Art at Oxford. On assuming the post he had to 'throw up the botany' – meaning by this the book begun in 1867 and recently named (perhaps with *Soldanella* in mind), '*Cora Nivalis*: Snowy Proserpine'.[74] Botany continued, however, to be much in his mind in the next year or two, both in his arrangement of his teaching materials and in lectures that attracted crowds such as Oxford had never seen before. Regrettably, this popularity encouraged Ruskin to play to the gallery. After the publication of *The Descent of Man*, his lectures abounded in tiresome misrepresentations of Darwin's ideas. And to his attacks on 'filthy heraldries which record the relation of humanity to the ascidian and the crocodile'[75] he added many similar outbursts in *Fors Clavigera*, the monthly letter that he for many years addressed to 'the workmen of England'.

But if Ruskin encouraged the mob, academic and otherwise, in its growing hostility to the theory of natural selection, he remained reluctantly persuaded that, where flowers were concerned, Darwin was right. There was as we have seen only one escape from so unpalatable a fact: to view adaptations not as progress but as regress. So in the autumn of 1874, after his friend Sir John Lubbock had made him miserable by an article giving Darwin's discoveries about pollination fresh currency, he declared, in *Fors 46*, that 'the Fly God of Ekron himself superintends – as you may gather from Mr Darwin's recent investigations – the birth and parentage of the orchidaceae'. Three years later, the appearance of a second edition of *Various Contrivances* provoked an even more intemperate allusion to 'the assumption, rendered so highly probable by Mr Darwin's discoveries respecting the modes of generation in the Orchidaceae, that there *was* no God, except the original Baalzebub of Ekron, Lord of Bluebottles and fly-blowing in general'.[76]

These passages disturb the modern reader because they are themselves charged with a deep disturbance that presages Ruskin's first devil-haunted attack of mania early in 1878. The Slade Professor might be adulated in

---

[74] *Norton Letters*, p. 182; *ibid.*, p. 180. [75] *Love's Meinie* (1873), § 61.
[76] *Fors Clavigera*, letter 77, § 1.

Oxford, but no acceptance there could compensate for his rejection as a lover. Rose La Touche, now come of age, treated Ruskin with cruel capriciousness in the name of religion. The language of flowers grew abusive: wounded by her savage reply to a renewed proposal, Ruskin demanded back his drawing of an olive branch, offering in its place drawings of hemlock, belladonna and monkshood. They made it up after a fashion, but the happiness of their few subsequent meetings was soon undermined by the realisation that Rose was terminally ill.

On the day of Rose's death Ruskin was occupied in describing two stages in the blossoming of hawthorn. When it was fully in bloom there was revealed, at the centre of each white flower,

a faded, yellowish, glutinous, unaccomplished green; and round that, all over the surface of the blossom, whose shell-like petals are themselves deep-sunk, with grey shadows in the hollows of them – all above this already subdued brightness, are strewn the dark points of the dead stamens – manifest more and more, the longer one looks, as a kind of grey sand, sprinkled without sparing over what looked at first unspotted light.

Against this picture of the full-blown flower's imperfection Ruskin sets the bud, 'with all its sweet change that one would so fain stay', its petals 'pouting, as the very softest waves do on flat sand where one meets another; then opening just enough to show the violet colour within'.[77]

It is not difficult to recognise in these passages the contrast between the gentle, sensitive adolescent that Rose had once been and the deeply flawed nature of the grown woman (affected with the 'green sickness', the male organs rendered 'dead' by her frigidity), nor to grasp the relevance of the allusion to Darwin which separates the two descriptions: 'Undeveloped, thinks Mr Darwin – the poor, shortcoming, ill-blanched thorn blossom – going to be a Rose, some day soon; and what next – who knows? – perhaps a Paeony!' All that Darwinism yielded in the end to Ruskin was support for his own tragic realisation that the best could degenerate into the worst. The rest, in company with a large part of the British public, he continued to dismiss, and it was against this background of hostility to the new biology that he took up again the writing of his botanical book, now to be called *Proserpina*.

It goes without saying that the work pays no heed to the spectacular advances in knowledge of plant physiology that were being made in German laboratories. Instead, in *Proserpina*, Ruskin avoids, and urges his

---

[77] *Proserpina*, vol. I, chapter 8, §§ 2 and 3.

'girl-readers' to avoid, 'all study of floral genesis and digestion'.[78] His 1872
Oxford lectures on science and art take the obscurantist view that science
should be 'the proper grasp of facts already known'.[79] But there were
obstacles to Ruskin writing even an old-fashioned book of natural history.
He had too many irons in the fire: in 1875 he was trying concurrently to
write seven books. Some of these, including *Proserpina*, were issued in
parts, which meant that under pressure he was tempted to cobble together a
new part by drawing on something he had written years before, without
troubling to ask himself if it had become outdated. His work suffered too
from the fact that he was now virtually his own publisher, with no editor or
press reader to question his assertions. Yet with this erratic and piecemeal
mode of composition went inflated notions of the importance of what he
was doing: *Proserpina* was to be nothing less than a 'classical' educational
work for which many parents and children would thank him.[80]

At other times, Ruskin was willing to admit his ignorance, especially on
the subject of plant morphology with which, following the usual plan of a
botanical textbook, *Proserpina* begins. So he clutched at a chance of expert
help that Fors put in his way. His *Fors Clavigera* letter of May 1871 began
with a hearsay account of a botanical lecture given at the Natural History
Museum in which the lecturer was alleged to have said that there was no
such thing as a flower, only whorls of modified leaves. Taking a sideswipe
as he wrote at Darwin's supposed reduction of man himself to a transitional
form, Ruskin in reply characteristically asserted that the flower was the be-
all and end-all of the plant because of the pleasure it gave to human eyes.
The lecturer, who was Daniel Oliver, Professor of Botany at University
College, London, as well as Keeper of the Herbarium and Librarian at
Kew, wrote to protest that he had been misrepresented. Ruskin won him
over with a handsome apology followed by requests for advice on planting
round a memorial fountain, and early in 1875 there began between them a
three-year correspondence about the problems Ruskin was encountering in
writing *Proserpina*: problems that, it can be assumed, also came up during
visits to Oliver at Kew.

Oliver's letters, so far as is known, have not survived, but from Ruskin's
side of the correspondence[81] it would seem that one of the first things he

---

[78] *Ibid.*, vol. II, chapter 1, § 42.   [79] *The Eagle's Nest* (1872), § 37.

[80] *Norton Letters*, p. 364; *Works*, vol. XXV, p. xli (quoting letter to Dean Liddell).

[81] T 30, Ruskin Foundation, Ruskin Library, Lancaster University, is a typed transcript, made for or by
Oliver's son, F. W. Oliver, of Ruskin's letters to his father.

demurred at was Ruskin's resolve to rename all those plants whose accepted names gave him offence. He got a magisterial reply:

Modern botanical nomenclature is *absolutely* ephemeral. It *cannot* last above ten years more – it is entirely unscholarly – and it is founded on imperfect knowledge, hastily and competitively fitted with names. It is in many ways disgusting and cannot be translated to girls.[82]

Showing remarkable freedom from professional touchiness, Oliver, who may have shared (as who has not?) some of Ruskin's dislike of ugly and cumbersome botanical names, appears to have made a suggestion or two for new ones. What he would have found more disturbing than Ruskin's innovations was the other's use of outdated and unreliable sources. He was himself the author of a school textbook that strikes even today's reader as essentially modern, both in its Darwinian viewpoint and in its awareness of the importance of cell biology: cells are 'the workshops in which all the secret and wonderful operations of plants are carried out'.[83] Ruskin airily waved aside this approach with 'I shall never, myself, understand anything about cellular tissue.'[84] In consequence, although Ruskin submitted to Oliver his chapters on the leaf and the flower and their final, published form shows some signs of his influence, he is in no way inhibited by the caution Oliver's own book displays in dealing with the still largely unexplored processes of plant nutrition. Instead, he launches confidently into an account of 'that strange vital power – which scientific people are usually as afraid of naming as common people are afraid of naming Death', by means of which 'the tree gives the gathered earth and water a changed existence' in the form of sap which descends and re-ascends so that 'the tree becomes literally a fountain, of which the springing streamlets are clothed with new-woven garments of green tissue, and of which the silver spray stays in the sky – a spray, now, of leaves'.[85]

Oliver may have viewed this and similar passages as poetic licence, their wildness the downside of the empathy that elsewhere in the book produces a description of the poppy that was to inspire Gerard Manley Hopkins, as well as the compelling (and surely autobiographical) evocation of the same flower in bud –

When the flower opens, it seems a deliverance from torture: the two imprisoning green leaves are shaken to the ground; the aggrieved corolla smoothes itself in the

---

[82] Letter 11, 19 January 1875.
[83] *Lessons in Elementary Botany* (1864), p. 107. Oliver gave Ruskin a copy on his first visit to Kew.
[84] Letter 14, 11 February 1875.   [85] *Proserpina*, vol. I, chapter 3, §§ 17, 18.

sun, and comforts itself as it can; but remains visibly crushed and hurt to the end of its days.[86]

But the rambling third part of the work, published early in 1876, indicated that Ruskin really was losing his grip; and when his letters of that spring showed him to be struggling with outdated and incorrect notions of stem growth, Oliver tried to refer him to more reliable accounts of the process. Ruskin, who had a few weeks previously subscribed himself 'Ever your grateful and troublesome and knownothing pupil',[87] now retorted with

I don't want more *authorities* than you. My business is popular education – and for that purpose I must recommend readable, not scientific, books. The facts I will work out with your help, as far as the botany goes; but I am also concerned with the art; and Figuier's is the only book by a man who could draw![88]

The same division of labour is implied by a reference, in the *Fors Clavigera* letter of that December, to 'the friend who is helping me *in all I want* [my italics] for *Proserpina* – Mr Oliver'. The trouble was that Ruskin did not rely on Oliver even for matters of fact. In the book's fourth part, published that August, he repeats the silver cord fallacy, merely appending to it the airy comment that his good friend Mr Oliver has told him that

all the increment of tree stems is by division and multiplication of the cells of the wood, a process not in the least to be described as 'sending down roots from the leaf to the ground.' I suspected as much in beginning to revise this chapter; but hold to my judgment in not cancelling it. For this multiplication of the cells is at least compelled by an influence which passes from the leaf to the ground and *vice versa*.[89]

Another theme of Ruskin's letters that must have troubled the Kew botanist even more than his friend's obstinate adherence to outdated theories about plant growth was his long-standing obsession with the 'evil' of certain flowers. In the course of arranging his first visit to Kew he confessed that

My feeling about the orchids is complicated with many moral and spiritual questions wholly overwhelming to me ... I have notions which I dare not print for fear of the world's thinking me mad, and I never yet was so sane ['sure' in the transcript] in my life as I am now – though threatened I think with brain disease from fatigue if I don't slack work.[90]

---

[86] *Ibid.*, chapter 4, § 19.   [87] Letter 28, 25 April 1876.
[88] Letter 32, 31 May 1876. Louis Figuier's *Histoire des plantes* (1865) is rhetorical and unreliable.
[89] *Proserpina*, vol. I, chapter 9, § 14.   [90] Letter 13, 3 February 1875.

And in one of his last letters in the correspondence, he covers his *idée fixe* with the thinnest veil of self-mockery: 'The reason I wanted to see Arum Triloba is because it is detestable. I am studying the laws of Immorality in Plants as in Animals.'[91]

This obsession is on full display in the parts of *Proserpina* that Ruskin wrote when he returned to the work after his serious breakdown of February 1878; returned too soon, it would appear, for a second attack followed in 1879, and he was still showing the effects of this when he exchanged friendly visits with Darwin, who was holiday-making near Ruskin's Lake District home at Coniston. Darwin's daughter Henrietta, noticing Ruskin's distressed look as he talked of baleful new clouds in the sky (another obsession of these years), concluded that 'his brain was becoming clouded'.[92] The saddest evidence of decline is a chapter of *Proserpina* in which, free from the disapproval of Oliver who now, as he tactfully put it, was sparing Ruskin the agitation that letters might cause, he turned to his beloved Figuier to help him expound the creation of woody stems – only to end in a wretched muddle from which a few lines in Oliver's book could have saved him.

Yet he had gone back confidently enough to his book of botany, with a chapter setting out his scheme of classification. True, its distortions of the accepted groupings must have had the Trevelyans turning in their graves, especially as Ruskin invented new terms for the taxa themselves for good measure, avoiding, for example, the word 'species' as 'vulgarized beyond endurance'.[93] Thus the family Orchidaceae is renamed the Order of Ophryds ('on account of their resemblance to the brow of an animal frowning, or to the overshadowing casque of a helmet') and is arbitrarily divided into three Gentes, the most characteristic of which, Satyricum (the neuter ending indicating an association with evil or death), has members that are 'in the habit of dressing in livid and unpleasant colours; and are distinguished from all other flowers by twisting, not only their stalks, but one of their petals . . . and putting it far out at the same time, as a foul jester would put out his tongue'.[94] Finally the whole order is declared transitional to the orders of climbing, poisonous and sleep-inducing plants which belong to 'the Dark Kora of the lower world'.[95]

---

[91] Letter 36, n.d., but from Oxford where Ruskin lectured for three weeks in November 1877.
[92] Emma Darwin, *A Century of Family Letters*, vol. II, p. 238.   [93] *Proserpina*, vol. I, chapter 11, § 21.
[94] *Ibid.*, § 7; *ibid.*, § 9.   [95] *Ibid.*, § 32.

It is clear that by now Ruskin had the Immorality of Plants fairly on the brain. Nothing, he told hearers of what purported to be a lecture about snakes, is more mysterious

than the relation of flowers to the serpent tribe, – not only in those to which, in *Proserpina*, I have given the name Draconidae ... but much more in those carnivorous, insect-eating, and monstrous, insect-begotten structures, to which your attention may perhaps have been recently directed by the clever caricature of the possible effects of electric light, which appeared lately in the *Daily Telegraph*.[96]

This allusion to the *Telegraph*'s triffyds is a red herring. Ruskin was trying, in view of their recent friendly encounter, to veil the fact that he has two works by Darwin in mind: the book on orchids and the one on insectivorous plants which, when it was published in 1875, caused Ruskin to write in his own copy of the first part of *Proserpina*: 'needs a note about nasty carnivorous vegetables'.[97] *Movement in Plants* (1868) would also have been in the minds of Ruskin's hearers when he went on to talk of vegetable stranglers (a serpent is 'a honeysuckle, with a head put on it'), though here his ostensible target was Huxley, with whose theories on the evolution of reptiles the lecture openly engages: 'That there is any difference in the spirit of life which gives power to the tormenting tendrils, from that which animates the strangling coils, your recent philosophy [i.e. the material basis of life] denies.'[98]

The second volume of *Proserpina* concerns itself for the most part with a selection of wild flowers from Ruskin's classification, among them a fair number of those that he had, in *The Queen of the Air*, described as touched by the spirit of the Draconidae. When he describes a flower which was very dear to him, *Brunella*, or self-heal, his tone is more one of sorrow than of anger: 'it is not the normal character of a flower petal to have a cluster of bristles growing out of the middle of it, nor to be jagged at the edge into the likeness of a fanged fish's jaw, nor to be swollen or pouted into the likeness of a diseased gland in an animal's throat'.[99] A few months on, however, in the period of restlessness and extreme irritability which followed a severe mental collapse early in 1881, the tone becomes frenetic as he writes of plants which 'may by this time have furnished the microscopic malice of botanists with providentially disgusting reasons, or demonically nasty necessities, for every possible spur, spike, jag, sting, rent, blotch, flaw, freckle, filth, or venom'.[100] The genus prompting this outburst is,

---

[96] *Deucalion* (1879), vol. II, chapter 1, § 32. [97] *Proserpina*, vol. I. chapter 2, § 3, footnote.
[98] *Deucalion*, vol. II, chapter 1, § 19; *ibid.*, § 32. [99] *Proserpina*, vol. II, chapter 5, § 10.
[100] *Ibid.*, chapter 1, § 8.

unbelievably, *Viola*; and once again Darwin is at the root of Ruskin's distress. The fertilisation of violets and the structures that facilitated it had figured in Darwin's most recent book, *The Different Forms of Flowers on Plants of the Same Species* (1877). And although Ruskin goes on to insist that 'with these obscene processes and prurient apparitions the gentle and happy scholar of flowers has nothing whatever to do', the occurrence among violet species of the dull but useful ground-cover plant *Viola cornuta* turns the residue of his rage into whole paragraphs of abuse that are the reverse of gentle and happy. *Viola cornuta*'s flower is 'a nasty big thing, all of a feeble blue' producing 'various fanged or forked effects, faintly ophidian or diabolic', its flower stalk is 'like a pillar run thin out of an iron foundry', its stem 'a still more stubborn, nondescript, hollow angular, dog's-eared gaspipe' and its leaves 'so crumpled and hacked about, as if some ill-natured child had snipped them with blunt scissors'. All told, 'clearly no true "species" but only a link'.[101]

This preposterous outburst may have had therapeutic value, since Ruskin never again worked himself into such a frenzy over an 'evil' flower. By 1883, when he wrote the chapter on the genus the botanists call *Pedicularis* and the rest of us lousewort, but which he re-named *Monacha* or the nun, he had even begun to wish he could take such members of the Draconidae out of the power of the Dark Kora – though in the end, finding one species of *Pedicularis* to be the parasitic red rattle, he decided to leave them in this floral sin bin. Such flowers perhaps appeared less lacertine after his reconciliation with Maria La Touche, with whom he hunted at Coniston that summer for the bog pimpernel, reminded of Rose by its brilliance and delicacy and wayward habit of growth. He also made his peace with Lubbock, pleased at being forgiven by him 'for all the ill-tempered things I've said about insects and evolution'.[102] At Coniston too he could invite the village children into his garden for a botany lesson followed by a good tea, and when they had gone have 'fine talks with the anemones, in their tongue' or capture their brilliance for a flower-loving neighbour in a haiku-like phrase: 'I have some anemones from Florence which are marvellous in their exquisitely nervous trembling and veining of colour – violin playing in scarlet on a white ground.'[103]

This mellowing is reflected in Ruskin's diaries of the 1880s. Whereas the botanic notes in his 1877–8 diary (some of which were inserted in the

[101] *Ibid.*, §§ 18; 19; 20; 25.   [102] *Works*, vol. XXXVI, p. 590.
[103] Charlotte Quaritch Wrentmore (ed.), *Letters of John Ruskin to Bernard Quaritch 1867–1888* (1938), p. 80; Helen Viljoen (ed.), *The Brantwood Diary of John Ruskin* (1971), p. 383.

difficult year 1881) show him still wrestling with the much-resented 'authorities', the ones he made on his autumn journey abroad in 1882, despite the odd flash of petulance ('the nastiest and dismallest abortion of a plant I ever saw'),[104] are a record of painterly delight in some forty species in their natural surroundings. *Brunella* reappears, no longer draconid: 'its round compact head of divine purple is the glory of foregrounds high above Talloire on the banks of the old path where the pervanche [peri-winkle] is rich in spring, and low in the dell of the Fier, bright through perpetual rain'.[105] From Lucca he writes to Mary Gladstone about cyclamens massed beneath the grey and silver olive boughs: 'vividest pale red-purple, like light of evening'.[106] He would come across these most enchanting of autumn flowers again six years later at Champernole, on his last Continental journey, and associate them with 'the true love which may be felt, if we are taught by the Muses, for the beautiful earthbound creatures that cherish and survive our own fleeting lives'.[107] A few months later, he was himself earthbound. By an irony of Fors, Ruskin's old age prolonged itself into a vegetative state.

Long before that, *Proserpina* had faltered, and come to a stop. What can be regarded as the first attempt at an inter-disciplinary work, bridging what were by the 1880s beginning to be perceived as distinct cultures, had been a sorry failure. But I must not fling aspersions from the insecurity of my own half-finished glasshouse. Better to remind the reader of the many trium-phantly successful attempts that Ruskin made, in sketchbooks, letters and diaries, to capture with pen and pencil the inner rapture of flowers: attempts that, whether already published or hitherto unpublished, ought to be brought together one day as the real *Proserpina*.

---

[104] Ruskin Library MS 23, p. 51.   [105] *Ibid.*, p. 41.   [106] *Works*, vol. XXXVII, p. 413.
[107] *Works*, vol. XXXV, p. 641 (a passage intended for *Dilecta*, Ruskin's planned supplement to *Praeterita*).

CHAPTER 6

D. H. Lawrence, botanist

When D. H. Lawrence and Earl Brewster met in an olive grove, in a drift of poppies, the American thought Lawrence 'looked like a man who lived devoted to the study of such life – a botanist'.[1] This was remarkably perceptive. Lawrence had a lifelong interest in plants, and he is unique among major English writers in having studied botany as a university subject. In another way, though, Brewster was wide of the mark. What Lawrence devoted his writing life to was '*the* problem of today, the establishment of a new relation, or the re-adjustment of the old one, between men and women'.[2] Every reader knows that he writes wonderfully about flowers, whether in his novels – the moonlit lilies in *Sons and Lovers* perhaps come first to mind – or in essays such as 'Flowery Tuscany', or in many poems of which 'Bavarian Gentians' is the most anthologised. But when Connie Chatterley and her lover deck each other's body hair with forget-me-nots, it is an odd reader (and a southerner into the bargain) who wonders how they have come by forget-me-nots in the middle of a wood – before remembering that there is a woodland species, *Myosotis sylvatica*, and that it grows abundantly in Derbyshire.

Is, then, the floweriness of Lawrence's fictional worlds – the 145 named species in his first novel, for instance – to be regarded simply as by-work? He did not himself think of it in this way. When he wrote that 'the business of art is to reveal the relation between man and his circumambient universe, at the living moment', he made Van Gogh's 'vivid relation between himself, as man, and the sunflower, as sunflower' his prime example of what he calls 'pure relationship ... between me and another person, me and other people, me and a nation, me and a race of men, me

---

[1] Edward Nehls, *D. H. Lawrence: a Composite Biography* (1959), vol. II, pp. 57, 60. For biographical material this chapter is much indebted to the three-part Cambridge biography of Lawrence: the first volume by John Worthen (*The Early Years*, 1991); the second by Mark Kinkead-Weekes (*Triumph to Exile*, 1996); and the third by David Ellis (*Dying Game*, 1998).

[2] James T. Boulton (ed.), *The Letters of D. H Lawrence* (1981–2001), vol. I, p. 546. (Hereafter *Letters*.)

and the animals, me and the trees or flowers . . .' before going on to state his
belief that, in art, 'the highest complex of subtle interrelatedness that man
has discovered' is the novel.[3] In Lawrence's writings, this sense of interrelatedness is the continuous strand by which he joins together the radii of
me-to-person, me-to-plant and the rest, into the web of being. In his
fiction, the web is wide-stretching and intricate. Even a brief poem,
however, can furnish accessible proof of its subtlety and strength.

'First Morning' begins from a seemingly ideal setting for the establishment of a new relationship between man and woman – the first night of
what is, to all intents and purposes, the poet's honeymoon. It has not,
however, gone well: 'I could not . . . free myself from the past, those others.'
But now –

> Now, in the morning
> As we sit in the sunshine on the seat by the little shrine,
> And look at the mountain-walls,
> Walls of blue shadow,
> And see so near at our feet in the meadow
> Myriads of dandelion pappus
> Bubbles ravelled in the dark green grass
> Held still beneath the sunshine –
> It is enough, you are near –
> The mountains are balanced,
> The dandelion seeds stay half-submerged in the grass;
> You and I together
> We hold them proud and blithe
> On our love.
> They stand upright on our love,
> Everything starts from us,
> We are the source.

The thought here is as finely poised as the dandelion clocks, syntax and
lineation balancing upon the fulcrum of 'It is enough, you are near.' On
one side of this statement of love's awareness is what the lovers see; on the
other is what they, in consequence, know. Along with the mountains, and
with the fragile plants that yet hold together the past, marked by the
sinuous line of their former seeding, and the future, contained in their

[3] *Study of Thomas Hardy and Other Essays*, pp. 171–2 of the Cambridge Edition. (Hereafter *Study*.)
Whenever possible, quotations from Lawrence's prose works are from this edition (1981–2004,
various editors), but dates, when given, are those of the original publication. Novels by Lawrence
in the Penguin Modern Classics follow the Cambridge text, and page numbers tally. Lawrence's
poetry is quoted from Vivian de Sola Pinto and Warren Roberts (eds.), *D. H. Lawrence: the Complete
Poems* (1977; hereafter *Poems*).

still undistributed seeds, they have all the time in the world. It is not that they are 'like' these contrasting aspects of nature; rather that lovers, distant Alps, and nearby plants are all joined in the same serene inevitability of natural processes. In fact the paragraph has only one metaphor in the conventional sense. It begins to form at the end of the first part, in 'bubbles' and 'ravelled', and defines itself at the end of the second part as the waters of life which, once the wind of the spirit has blown the seeds abroad ('Not I, not I, but the wind',[4] begins the cumulative poem of the series), will empower them to grow. Meanwhile, the lovers can afford to wait, knowing that they, the mountains and the flowers are all *there*, coexisting in their interrelatedness. Each validates the others.

The following pages are an attempt to explore the modes of perception that are suggested by this poem and that, over and over again, enable Lawrence to establish, delicately yet firmly, the interconnectedness of human and plant life. One is the biologist's way of looking, founded upon knowledge of structures and processes common to different life-forms. Another is the contemplative vision, a realisation of the beautiful that brings with it a sense of healing and renewal. Primarily the artist's vision, it reminds us that Lawrence was creative in more than one medium: 'blue shadow' and 'dark green grass' are painter's notes. A third mode of perception, one less easy to define, characterises Lawrence the traveller, who experienced the flora of four continents. To call it discovery lays the emphasis in the wrong place. It is more a receiving than a perceiving. A revelation occurs, for which his chosen word is 'utterance'. Though it often accompanies the shock of the new, it can also (dandelions grow anywhere) come from the familiar in a new setting. Rather than attending *to* the dandelions, Lawrence attends *upon* them: he is 'A man in his wholeness wholly attending'. The phrase comes from 'Thought', which is among those late poems in which the three ways of looking at the green world that I have here artificially separated strengthen one another, and I shall accordingly focus upon those poems in conclusion.

I

When the fifteen-year-old Lawrence began to visit the Chambers family at Haggs Farm, his confidence in naming wild flowers roused Jessie Chambers's scepticism. How did he know he was right? Lawrence flew

---

[4] 'Song of a Man who has Come Through'. The series was first published as *Look! We Have Come Through!* in 1917.

into a temper: 'I know *because* I know. How dare you ask me how I know?'[5] Adolescent rage can be baffling; on the face of it, there was no reason why Lawrence should have made a secret of the fact that he and a school friend liked to roam the countryside identifying wild flowers from the rather garish plates of a pocket guide acquired the previous summer. In this way, the friend would recall, they 'gathered, pressed and mounted specimens of every plant, shrub and tree to be found for miles around'.[6]

Lawrence would, however, have gained much of his knowledge of wild flowers earlier, in childhood; and here, perhaps, lies the reason for his rage. He hated to admit that his father had taught him anything. Yet Arthur Lawrence was informative about wild life, and Jessie's remark that his son knew the names and *qualities* of plants implies the kind of traditional lore that his father relied on when he gathered medicinal herbs. From him Lawrence would first have heard many local and country names for plants. Alongside of 'may-blobs' and the bookish 'marigold' ('marsh marigold' in the pocket guide), kingcups figure in Lawrence's poetry as 'water-blobs' and 'buttercups', both of them names used by another Midlander, John Clare. In the novels, ribwort plantains are 'chimney-sweeps', bird's-foot trefoil is 'eggs-and-bacon', and the greater burdock is 'Robin Hood's rhubarb'. Such names can be used to telling effect, as when, in *The Crown*, Lawrence writes of life's successive fulfilments 'from the delicate blue speedwells of childhood to the equally delicate, frail farewell flowers of old age':[7] 'farewell-summer' is a happier name than 'soapwort' for *Saponaria officialis*. Saws and sayings about plants also came easily to Lawrence's pen. Readers of 'The Wild Common' are expected to know that when gorse is out of bloom, kissing is out of fashion. Parsley must go 'seven times to the Old Lad' before it is warm enough to germinate, and there is a fine proverbial ring to Lawrence's comment on a stained glass window in which Eve is shown holding two apples – 'bet she ate the pippin and gave him the Keswick'.[8]

On top of this easy at-homeness with plants and their properties was superimposed the late-Victorian cult of natural history that sent the school-boy Lawrence plant hunting in the Derbyshire dales. Nature study was in vogue among educationalists. A School Nature Study Union, with its own journal, was founded in 1903, and it was on the crest of the subject's

[5] E. T. [Jessie Chambers Wood], *D. H. Lawrence: a Personal Record* (1935), p. 34.

[6] George Neville, *A Memoir of D. H. Lawrence*, ed. Carl Baron (1981), p. 40. The guide was W. T. Gordon, *Our Country's Flowers: and How to Know Them* (n.d.).

[7] *Reflections on the Death of a Porcupine, and other Essays*, p. 286. (Hereafter *Reflections*.)

[8] *Letters*, vol. I, pp. 47–8; vol. V, p. 565.

popularity that, in 1904, the pupil-teacher Lawrence wrote the earliest essay
we have from him. In it, he earnestly commends the new subject for its
encouragement of observation, reasoning and lofty thoughts – 'after
inspecting several times the wondrous adaptability of everything to carry
out the work allotted to it, a fresh young mind cannot fail to be struck with
awe at the wisdom and majesty of the Creator'.[9] But when he went on to
university, Lawrence discovered that not all educationalists shared his
enthusiasm. Nottingham's Professor of Education held that the subject
had no place in primary schools. 'Even *elementary* science requires a
knowledge of some general notions and general principles, and these are
beyond the ordinary child's grasp.'[10] This choice bit of class arrogance
helps explain Lawrence's dislike of the man. Fortunately the educational
authorities in Croydon, where Lawrence went on to teach, thought otherwise, and organised courses for teachers of nature study. A sympathetic
headmaster gave him a free hand to teach biology and for years afterwards
kept Lawrence's lesson notes, including watercolour drawings that were
'models of correctness and clarity'.[11] Did one of these depict the hazel twigs
that Louie Burrows sent Lawrence from the Midlands, their 'gynaecious'
flowers coloured red and their 'androgynous'[12] flowers yellow as advocated
by school inspector Birkin in *Women in Love*?

Birkin's jargon is a reminder that, at Nottingham's University College,
Lawrence followed a formal course in botany that took him beyond
mere nature study. But it did not take him as far beyond it as critics who
emphasise Lawrence's 'scientific training' sometimes imply. Teacher training at the time consisted of educational theory and practice together with
a topping-up of the conventional school subjects. The crowded timetable
left little space for an option such as botany, which was the sole responsibility of a lecturer, E. A. Smith, who was soon to shift to extra-mural work
in other subjects. For all his enthusiasm, Lawrence did not receive enough
exposure to the subject ever to acquire a habit of reasoning untrammelled
by the teleological cast of mind instilled in him by his reading of Carlyle
and Ruskin, even though, with time, his teleology became non-religious.
Moreover, there was little room for evolutionary theory in the strongly
practical syllabus in botany laid down by the Board of Education, and its
limitation to flowering plants excluded most of the evidence of evolution

---

[9] University of Nottingham MS La B 220.   [10] A. Henderson, *Some Notes on Teaching* (1904), p. 80.
[11] Quoted by Nehl, *D. H. Lawrence*, vol. I, p. 86.
[12] p. 36. Presumably Lawrence meant 'androecious', from *androecium*. By 1917 he was vague about
these evasive terms for 'female' and 'male'.

within the plant kingdom – though Birkin does know that daisies are high up the evolutionary scale.

Despite these limitations, the Board of Education's botany syllabus for 1907 has an up-to-date look. It emphasises plant physiology, in which great strides had been made during the second half of the nineteenth century, and relegates traditional systematics – dissecting flowers and assigning them to families – to a brief course in the summer term. In Lawrence's laboratory notebook for that term, we can glimpse him at work on flowers in season, from April's wild garlic to the cornflowers and poppies of June. But it was the earlier part of the course, an introduction to the anatomy and morphology, reproduction, nutrition and adaptations of plants, that accorded best with his empathy for growing things, for 'the rise of a poppy, then the after uplift of the bud, the shedding of the calyx and the spreading wide of the petals, the falling of the flower and the pride of the seed-head'.[13]

Time-lapse photography was unknown in Lawrence's day, yet his feeling for plant growth repeatedly creates its effect, as when Gudrun Brangwen responds to the thrust of arrowheads out of water, or Connie Chatterley to the unfolding of a hart's-tongue fern. In the first poem he ever wrote, 'Campions', forget-me-nots have 'climbed to the last / Rung of their life-ladders' fragile heights'; the lengthening of the flowerhead after it has uncurled is a distinctive feature of the woodland species. At the beginning of his time in Croydon, 'The Best of School' is the thought that he is giving support to growing minds:

> As tendrils reach out yearningly,
> Slowly rotate till they touch the tree
> That they cleave unto, and up which they climb
> Up to their lives – so they to me

– although he soon rebounds from this sentimentality, countering it in 'Discipline' with a vision of plant roots which 'cannot know / Any communion whatever' as they seize upon their personal space. Laboratory observation of the way that germinating seeds appear to burrow into the earth inspires 'End of Another Home Holiday', in which the nascent plant, as it 'draws down the earth to hide', is finding room for the process of selving to begin; something denied to the poet, subject as he is to 'inexorable' mother-love. He returns to the same image a year later, but in such

---

[13] *Introductions and Reviews*, p. 212.

desolation of spirit (Lydia Lawrence is dying) that he conceives of the seed as tortured by its inability to burst 'into new florescence'.[14]

These quotations suggest the persistence, but also the occasional awkwardness, of botanical ideas and terms in the poems Lawrence was writing during the four years after he left university. *Look! We Have Come Through!* (1917), the collection of poems written for the most part after he and Frieda Weekley left England together in 1912, makes a more carefully selective use of botanical language; 'pappus', for example, a word retrieved from his student notes, helps by its soft plosives to create the hushed expectancy of 'First Morning'. And in the novels Lawrence often finds strikingly appropriate use for textbook terms. Ursula, at the beginning of *Women in Love* (written in 1916), is like a dormant plant: 'Her active living was suspended, but underneath, in the darkness, something was coming to pass. If only she could break through the last integuments!' – exactly Lawrence's own state of mind towards the end of 1916, when he described himself to a correspondent as 'a seed that is shoving at its integument'.[15]

One term that occurs again and again in Lawrence's work is 'protoplasm', often shortened to 'plasm' (today's 'cytoplasm'). His early reading of popular works by Huxley and Haeckel would have familiarised him with the concept of a fundamental matter of life. Then, at Nottingham, practical work with a microscope gave him the opportunity to *see* protoplasm for himself: an experience anticipated in the notes, including a careful record of protoplasm's chemical constituents, which he made at what appears to have been 'Botany' Smith's introductory lecture.

Most of the plant tissues that Lawrence saw through his eyepiece would have been sectioned and then fixed by chemicals: in short, they were dead. Yet in his writings plant cells palpitate with life, from the 'shimmering protoplasm' suggested by Paul's painting in *Sons and Lovers* (1913), which reappears in the novel's Foreword as the rose's 'quivering, shimmering flesh of flesh ... called if you like Protoplasm', through the 'living plasm' which 'vibrates unspeakably' in the Introduction to *New Poems* (1918, American edition) where it is contrasted with fixed tissue that is 'only a hardened bit of the past', right down to the crocuses of the 1927 spring, their 'little cells ... leaping with flowery life'.[16] Most striking of all is a passage in the *Study of Thomas Hardy*, written in 1914. Lawrence there

---

[14] Published in 1918 as 'Reality of Peace, 1916', but actually written in 1910.
[15] *Women in Love*, p. 9; *Letters*, vol. III, p. 43.
[16] *Sons and Lovers*, p. 183; *ibid.*, p. 470; *Poems*, p. 182; *Sketches of Etruscan Places and other Italian Essays*, p. 230 (Hereafter *Sketches*).

likens the life of the essential self to the dividing cells of a plant's growing
tip – 'a palpitating leading-shoot of life, where the unknown, all unre-
solved, beats and pulses' – in contrast to the rest of that self's mental life,
which is perforce passed in the zones of cell growth and cell elongation, in
'that which is behind, the fixed wood, the cells conducting towards their
undifferentiated tissue'.[17]

Clearly Lawrence at some time had the opportunity to observe living
cells and found the experience profoundly revealing. And in fact the
standard botany textbook of the time does provide for students to observe
one form of visible movement in fresh plant tissue – the phenomenon of
'streaming', or movement along the strands of protoplasm that separate the
moisture-filled spaces within a plant cell called vacuoles. It is an arresting
sight and one that Lawrence may well have recalled in *The Rainbow* (1915),
where, explaining Ursula's fascination with botany, he wrote 'She knew
the pulse of the vacuoles'.[18] But he then went on 'and the quivering of the
cambium tissue' although in fact there was no way in which Ursula could
have observed cambium cells, from deep inside a plant's stem, in a living
state. Either because he realised this or because he felt the language was
becoming too technical, he removed the whole sentence in proof and
substituted the rather flat statements: 'She had entered into the life of the
plants. She was fascinated by the strange laws of the vegetable world.'[19] But
it is still worthwhile asking why, originally, Lawrence should have made
Ursula perform the impossible.

Like Ursula, Lawrence had gone to university 'to hear the echo of
learning pulsing back to the source of the mystery', and even when he
became disillusioned with other subjects, he continued, like her, to
believe that in botany 'the mystery still glimmered'.[20] His quest was for
nothing less than life at its fount: the activity of strands of protoplasm as
he may have watched them for himself in the living cells of
Tradescantia's[21] stamen hairs; the activity of cells multiplying at the tip
of root or shoot, producing primary growth, and in the cambium layer of
the stem producing secondary growth, as he envisaged them and, for a
time at least in the composition of *The Rainbow*, imagined Ursula actually
seeing them. And there were other cells even more suggestive of life at its

[17] *Study*, p. 34.   [18] *Rainbow*, p. 653. (Or is this *Paramecia*'s contracting vacuole? See below, p. 191.)
[19] *Ibid.*, p. 404.   [20] *Ibid.*
[21] 'No botanist, working with the microscope, who has watched the streams of protoplasm ebbing and
      flowing within the cell, or from vessel to vessel, can feel that plants are the inert and lowly organised
      objects popular opinion unquestioningly holds them to be.' J. Ellor Taylor, *The Sagacity and
      Morality of Plants* (second edn, 1904), p. 8, next to a drawing of a *Tradescantia* cell.

fount, in that evolutionists postulated something very like them as the common origin of both plant and animal existence: motile, single-celled organisms, or protista, such as he had Ursula study through her microscope in her final year:

She looked still at the unicellular shadow that lay within the field of light, under her microscope. It was alive. She saw it move – she saw the bright mist of its ciliary activity, she saw the gleam of its nucleus, as it slid across the plane of light. (p. 408)

But there is another puzzle here. Botany Smith's first lecture had touched on organisms that could be called plant-animals in that, while they photo-synthesise like plants, they also swim by means of 'long processes which lash about and propel [the] organism' (to quote Lawrence's notes).[22] Ursula's specimen, however, is not propelled by flagella, but by a bright mist of hair-like cilia. These make it a Ciliate, and as such, an animal: most probably *Paramecium caudatum*, the slipper-shaped creature with a big nucleus and a small second one that scientific films sometimes cause to glide, its contractile vacuoles gleaming, across our television screens. So what is it doing in a botany class?

There is a clue to the answer in the description of it as 'special stuff come up from London'.[23] Shortly before Lawrence wrote this, some *Paramecia* at Imperial College in the University of London became the object of study by his friend David Garnett – usually known as Bunny – who had taken a degree in botany but had then switched to zoology. Bunny's project, which reads like an Arts graduate's send-up of biological research, was based on the fact that *Paramecia*, although they reproduce by fission, can exchange the genetic material contained in those little second nuclei by conjoining one with another at what approximates to a mouth. Once he had set up his project, all Bunny Garnett had to do was visit the laboratory morning and evening, in order to ascertain if any individuals among those cultured in various solutions had embarked on a sixteen-hour kiss.

We have not strayed so far from Lawrence the botanist as may appear, for his friendship with Bunny was close at the time. Bunny's parents stood loyally by Lawrence and Frieda after they went to Germany in 1912, and the twenty-year-old Bunny joined them for part of their journey across the Alps. He was already a keen field botanist, and Lawrence helped him amass 200 alpine species in three days. 'Oh the flowers I see that I want you to

[22] University of Nottingham MS La L 9. [23] *Rainbow*, p. 408.

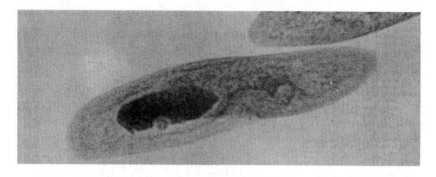

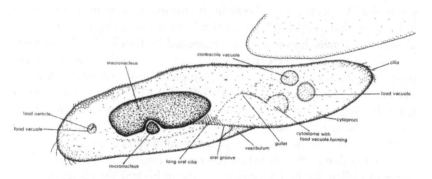

7 *Paramecium caudatum*, (above) as Lawrence would have seen it under David Garnett's light microscope and (below) as Ursula Brangwyn might have drawn it. (Reproduced from *Biological Studies through the Microscope: Book I, Motile Protista* by Marguerite D. Hainsworth (1972); photograph by J. Shillcock.)

'She looked still at the unicellular shadow that lay within the field of light, under her microscope. It was alive. She saw it move – she saw the bright mist of its ciliary activity, she saw the gleam of its nucleus, as it slid across the plane of light.'

(*The Rainbow*, chapter 15)

have',[24] he wrote after Bunny left. He missed him 'fearfully', for he had discovered that they had much in common besides a love of wild flowers, and it is thanks to this affinity that Ursula's experience as a student slips easily from being that of Lawrence at the Day Training Centre to being that of Bunny reading for Honours in botany, as he had begun to do on his return to England in 1912.

[24] *Letters*, vol. I, p. 445.

When Bunny began his research in the autumn of 1914, he kept in touch with Lawrence, who sometimes stayed at the Garnetts' London flat. Given Lawrence's fascination with life under the microscope, it seems inevitable that Bunny should have talked about his work, and highly probable that he took his friend with him on one of his late-night visits to the 'long empty laboratory'[25] in South Kensington. There would, for example, have been an opportunity for this between 21 and 23 November, at the time when Lawrence was coming to the end of the attempt to define his own world-view in his *Study of Thomas Hardy*, and was set to start on the closely related novel, *The Rainbow*.[26] That weekend, he stayed either with Bunny or with a zoologist friend of Bunny's, and they all went to the Zoo together. But whenever the opportunity may have arisen to take a look at Bunny's *Paramecia*, the description of the creature moving under Ursula's lens, written toward the end of February 1915, has the vividness and precision of a recent experience.

The context of Bunny's research would also have been meaningful for Lawrence. A Haeckelian biologist had claimed that he could make *Paramecia* conjugate at will, simply by changing the medium in which they were cultured. Bunny's supervisor, Clifford Dobell, got Bunny to test the claim by repeating the experiment. Very few conjugations occurred, and those mostly among the control specimens. This questioning of the assumption that an organism's behaviour was no more than a chemical reaction would have reminded Lawrence of his own mental fight, in his last year at university, against the belief, voiced in *The Rainbow* by Dr Frankstone, that life can be reduced to 'a complexity of physical and chemical activities';[27] a fight, incidentally, in which he enlisted the help of Botany Smith, whom he called his 'first live teacher of philosophy'.[28] Dobell too was opposed to Haeckel's idea of unicellular organisms as no more than (in Bunny's phrase) 'blobs of protoplasm',[29] and Lawrence, seizing upon the recognition that *Paramecium* was an animal of some complexity and capable of independent behaviour, originally had Ursula, at the point where she becomes aware of her protist's individual existence, embark on a long meditation in which

[25] David Garnett, *The Flowers of the Forest* (1955), p. 13, where the research is described.

[26] *The Rainbow* was a re-working of *The Wedding Ring*, written in the spring of 1914. There is no way of knowing if the heroine of the earlier book studied botany, but since the affair with Skrebensky was an addition in the re-working, the laboratory scene which forms its prelude was probably new as well.

[27] *Rainbow*, p. 408. Lawrence calls her 'a doctor of physics', but her original at Nottingham was the science faculty's only woman lecturer, a physiologist.

[28] *Letters*, vol. I, p. 147.   [29] David Garnett, *The Golden Echo* (1954), p. 230.

evolution was presented in terms of the will-to-be of countless individuals. When, however, he received back the typescript, he replaced this with Ursula's sudden intuition of her own will to achieve fullness of being, and tried to link this intuition to her earlier awareness of the life-force at work in the individual plant's two kinds of growing point:

> Suddenly she had passed away into an intensely gleaming light of knowledge, she was transfigured within the bright world of complete transfiguration. She could not understand what it all was. She only knew that it was not this limited mechanical energy, nor this base purpose of self-preservation and self-assertion. She was pushed with the growing tip onto the verge of Paradise. She felt the gleam of Paradise in the quivering cambium. She saw the light of Paradise in the nucleus under her slide. (p. 656)

Finally, at proof stage, Lawrence dropped both the biblical language derived from the abandoned 'evolutionary sermon' and the allusions to the growing points, or meristems, of plants, in order to concentrate upon Ursula's awareness, as she identifies with the moving speck under her microscope, of her own forward drive towards a realisation of her identity such as will carry her beyond the bounds of the selfhood to 'a consummation, a being infinite'. And at this point in her life, when she is waiting for Skrebensky's return, that affirmation takes the form of her resolve to accept him as her lover. That the creature under the lens has perhaps also been moving towards conjunction – its own evolutionary step forward – seems to linger in Lawrence's mind in the odd uses to which he puts the word 'nucleus',[30] when he goes on to describe Ursula's meeting with Skrebensky. It is as if he is unwilling to surrender, or let the reader surrender, the effect of Ursula's mind-changing insight.

Bunny Garnett's *Paramecia* were a godsend to Lawrence because it was easier for a reader to conceive of Ursula becoming aware of the life-force, the will-to-be, in an animal, however 'primitive', than of her receiving such illumination from plant cells. But for Lawrence himself, when he set out to define his personal philosophy in the opening chapters of his *Study of Thomas Hardy*, the culmination of the will-to-be in 'a consummation, a being infinite' presents itself most readily in the form of the flowering plant as it is ultimately shaped by all its cellular activity. His example of pure realisation is the poppy: an annual plant that directs

---

[30] 'Nucleus' recurs twice, and there is a nonce-word, 'nucleolating', presumably from 'nucleolus', which Lawrence may mistakenly have thought was the right term for *Paramecium*'s second nucleus.

all its energies towards the single day when 'transfigured into flower, it achieves at last itself':

The final aim of every living thing, creature, or being, is the full achievement of itself. This accomplished, it will produce what it will produce, it will bear the fruit of its nature. Not the fruit, however, but the flower is the culmination and climax, the degree to be striven for. Not the work I shall produce, but the real Me I shall achieve, that is the consideration; of the complete Me will come the complete fruit of me, the work, the children. (pp. 12–13)

We have been here before: in *Proserpina*. By focusing upon a flower that blazes through whole pages of Ruskin's writings, Lawrence revives one of Ruskin's most cherished ideas, his belief that what he called the inner rapture of a plant in flower is the be-all and end-all of its existence. But for the Victorian's conviction that the final end of a flower's beauty is the pleasure it gives to human eyes, Lawrence substitutes his sense of inter-relatedness: 'The world is a world because of the poppy's red... And I am I as well, since the disclosure.' In a later chapter, the sixth, Lawrence tries to expound and explore this human–plant interrelatedness by associating a plant's flowering with the self-transcendence achieved in a wholly ful-filling relationship between a man and a woman. But he fails, in part because he allows the fact of plant sex to intrude – 'the pollen stream clashes into the pistil stream'[31] – and thus confuses the image with what is imaged. Conceptually the chapter is a muddle, as Lawrence himself realised. The thinking behind the *Study* needed to be reshaped, and in the next three years he made several attempts to do this. There are traces of such re-shaping in the travel sketches he re-cast for publication in 1915 as *Twilight in Italy*, as well as in the evolutionary sermon in the manuscript of *The Rainbow*. But of Lawrence's several attempts at an ordered presentation of his philosophy, there survive from this period only the six essays entitled *The Crown* (1915).

The Crown too has its dominant botanic image, but now Ruskin's poppy is replaced by a less spectacular weed – the sow-thistle that had already, in its opportunist way, cropped up briefly in the opening chapter of the *Study*. It was a good choice. The sow-thistle had been the subject of one of Ruskin's illustrations to *Proserpina*; it was free of the literary accretions that had gathered round the poppy; and while, like the poppy, it was an annual that grew from a small seed, the yellow flowers rising above its massive foliage made it the perfect foil to the tied-down cabbages which for

---

[31] *Study*, p. 53.

Lawrence represented unfulfilled existence. Accordingly, it takes centre stage in *The Crown*'s second chapter:

Out of the dark, original flame issues a tiny green flicker, a weed coming alive. On the edge of the bright, ultimate, spiritual flame of the heavens is revealed a fragment of iris, a touch of green, a weed coming into being. The two flames surge and intermingle, casting up a crest of leaves and stems, their battlefield, their meeting ground, their marriage bed, the embrace becomes closer, more unthinkably vivid, it leaps to climax, the battle grows fiercer, fiercer, intolerably, till there is the swoon, the climax, the consummation, the little yellow disk gleams absolute between heaven and earth, radiant of both eternities, framed in the two infinities. Which is a weed, a sow-thistle bursting into blossom.[32]

   This is a difficult passage – *The Crown*, its author said, was 'no use for a five minutes lunch'[33] – but it has an underlying coherence. A metaphysical framework, the elementalism of the pre-Socratic thinkers whose writings Lawrence had recently encountered for the first time, now structures his often wayward thought processes. As a result, imagery that in the comparable sixth chapter of the *Study* flew apart in all directions is, in *The Crown*, unified into the clearest presentation yet of the vision that is at the source of both works as well as the Foreword[34] to *Sons and Lovers*. It is a vision, to which Lawrence's familiarity with Blake's *Marriage of Heaven and Hell* made him fully receptive, of existence at its richest as a conjunction of opposing elements. So, with an underlying wordplay upon 'iris', the rainbow flowers between earth and sky; sexual joy flowers between man and woman; and connecting these non-living and living worlds by creating organic life out of inorganic matter, the plant unites in its flowering the four elements of antiquity. Air and sunlight from above encounter the water drawn up, thanks to what Lawrence once called a plant's 'careful architecture',[35] with almost unbelievable force, and from that encounter arises a store of energy and of transformed matter whereby to build, with the aid of mineral salts from the anchoring earth, the biomass which will culminate in a flower. That no one, in 1915, knew quite how this came about was all to Lawrence's advantage. He was the more free to envisage photosynthesis in Heraclitic terms as the means to 'a consummation of all the wandering sky and sinking earth',[36] a vision he would return to in *Mr Noon*:

Do not the watery thread-tender streams run forward to touch the thread-tender fiery beamlets of the sun, in every growing plant and every unfolding flower? . . .

---

[32] From *The Crown*, included in *Reflections*, pp. 262–3.   [33] *Ibid.*, p. 250.
[34] Actually an Afterword, and not published in Lawrence's lifetime.
[35] *Study*, p. 8.   [36] *Reflections*, p. 303.

Before a plant adds one new cell to its growing tip, has it not been the living battle field and marriage bed of fire and water? (p. 186)

Or, in the words of Lady Chatterley's lover: 'flowers are fucked into being, between sun and earth'.[37]

Having thus, with the help of Heraclitus and of *Sonchus arvensis*, clarified the argument of the *Study* in the first two essays of *The Crown*, Lawrence confidently returns in the final essay to his poppy and to another metaphysical framework, that afforded by the Christian Trinity (with which, in the Foreword to *Sons and Lovers*, his philosophical explorations had begun):

The flower is the burning of God in the bush: the flame of the Holy Ghost: the actual Presence of accomplished oneness, accomplished out of twoness. The true God is *created* every time a pure relationship, or a consummation out of twoness into oneness takes place. So that the poppy flower is God come red out of the poppy-plant. (p. 303)

But this rapture of flowering belongs to a fourth dimension. In space-time, petals fall apart, relationships sour. Between the sow-thistle and the poppy, between these two passages of joyous consummation, *The Crown* concerns itself largely with the theme of dissolution. It was a theme to which Lawrence was led in part by the difficulties of his marriage but much more by the horrors of the Great War. Mud and barbed wire are images that arise in these intervening essays, where the writer often appears to be himself bogged down in his struggling thoughts. Once again, because fiction alone can 'get the whole hog',[38] he seeks through fictive characters in action, this time those of *Women in Love* (written in 1916), a clarification such as he cannot achieve by imagery per se, although plant imagery is repeatedly brought into play in the novel.

Birkin, the character who approximates to Lawrence, broods much on dissolution and decay. He sees Gudrun and Gerald as 'pure flowers of dark corruption', an association which Gudrun herself has already made by identifying herself with the plants rising from the 'festering chill' of the lake-bed, and with which she in turn identifies Gerald as he reaches for her sketch of them – 'his hand coming straight forward like a stem'.[39] In contrast, Ursula, who has at this point wandered on as far as the millpond where she finds Birkin, shrinks from the 'evil-smelling fig-wort and hemlock'[40] of its margin. *Her* flowers are the daisies that Birkin casts on

[37] *Lady Chatterley's Lover*, p. 301.   [38] 'Why the Novel Matters' (1925), *Study*, p. 195.
[39] *Women in Love*, pp. 173, 119, 120.   [40] *Ibid.*, p. 124.

to the dark water where they float brilliantly, free from the decay beneath; later he will see her as a Heraclitic dry soul, a rose, 'warm and flamy'.[41] Their love is consummated in a chapter that is the fictional counterpart of Lawrence's passages on the flowering of the poppy and the sow-thistle. It starts with a furious quarrel during which Ursula's will to overpower and possess expresses itself unconsciously in the act of tearing spindleberries – the reader is meant to remember their fiercely discordant colouring – from the hedge and thrusting them into her coat. Reconciliation begins with her proffer of a sprig of heather, such as Ruskin drew and described in *Proserpina* as an exemplar of incipient life. It continues with Birkin looking into Ursula's face 'that was upturned exactly like a flower ... And he was smiling faintly as if there were no speech in the world, save the silent delight of flowers in each other'[42] – another Ruskinian notion. And it comes to climax in Sherwood Forest, because to Lawrence's mind there could be no more fitting marriage-bed than what ecologists call a climax vegetation: the fullest conceivable transformation, that is, of inorganic elements into living tissues: essentially the process that brings the poppy into flower.

Women in Love culminates, however, in the very antithesis of this, in a sub-zero world above the tree line, where the flora, if it has ever existed, is obliterated under the snow; life-giving moisture (we recall the flowing spring in Sherwood Forest) has now become a destructive force. It is a world in which Birkin and Ursula, the life-seekers, are content to play for a time, but which they are soon ready to leave. The death-seekers Gudrun and Gerald stay on, only to tear one another to pieces in a sexual strife that is as destructive as that of the other lovers was creative. At the end, when Gerald is literally a frozen cadaver, the reader's thoughts go back to the image of his shattered condition after his father's death, when he sought out Gudrun and slept with her for the first time: 'he knew how destroyed he was, like a plant whose tissue is burst from inwards by a frost'.[43] When the life-sustaining moisture in the vacuoles of a plant's cells expands into ice, the cell walls burst and recovery becomes impossible.

2

Lawrence's philosophical writings, in both fictional and essay form, reflect his knowledgeable awareness of the life processes at work beneath the appearances of tree or flower. A gardener's way of looking as well as a botanist's, it makes him distinguish, at the beginning of *Sons and Lovers*,

---

[41] *Ibid*, p. 173. [42] *Ibid.*, pp. 312–13. [43] *Ibid.*, p. 345.

between the shade-loving auriculas and saxifrages of the miners' gardens in the lower part of The Bottoms and the pinks and sweet williams of the sunnier upper row. But the miners themselves, whatever their gardening skills, had another way of looking at flowers, which Lawrence defined many years later:

> I've seen many a collier stand in his back garden looking down at a flower with that odd, remote sort of contemplation which shows a *real* awareness of the presence of beauty. It would not even be admiration, or joy, or delight, or any of those things which so often have a root in the possessive instinct. It would be a sort of contemplation: which shows the incipient artist.[44]

At the time Lawrence wrote this he had behind him virtually the whole of an œuvre in which this mode of perception is fully as active as the biological mode with which we have hitherto been concerned, and in which personality is often defined in terms of the possessiveness or non-possessiveness of an individual's response to beauty in the natural world.

The same essay accuses women at large of possessiveness in their response to flowers: with some justice, in that throughout Lawrence's lifetime women of all classes prided themselves upon having fresh flowers – which meant dying flowers – about their persons. Clara, the militant feminist of *Sons and Lovers*, repudiates the expected womanliness of the time when she refuses to pick cowslips on the grounds that she does not want to surround herself with corpses. Against this high-mindedness Lawrence sets what is to him the innocence of Paul Morel's 'you get 'em because you want 'em'[45] and the simple delight of Paul's mother in any offering of flowers. But he knew that there were less innocent forms of appropriation. One of the most insidious was the fanciful transformation of flowers – and animals too, for that matter – into something other than themselves. It was a habit of mind nourished by the early twentieth-century cult of childhood, the determination of writers and artists to give the child what they thought the child wanted: small animals in bonnets or motoring goggles, flowers transformed into fairies, silver birch trees seen as dainty ladies. During the nine-year reign of Edward VII, when so many writers refused to grow up, Lawrence – in succession pupil-teacher, student and schoolmaster – was surrounded by young women teachers who formed a ready readership for the new kind of writing for children, not least because its fantasies were set in the middle-class world to which many of them aspired. Nor was he

---

[44] 'Nottingham and the Mining Countryside', *Late Essays and Articles*, p. 291.
[45] *Sons and Lovers*, p. 259.

himself immune to this way of seeing. In his first novel, *The White Peacock*
(1911), there is nothing to distinguish the floral fancies of the leading
character, Lettie, from those of her brother who tells the tale. It is this
narrator – a thin disguise for the author – who pictures daffodils throwing
back their yellow curls and gossiping together, bunched snowdrops press-
ing up white, mute lips, and a willow poising 'a golden, fairy busby on
every twig'.[46] But in the novels that follow, Lawrence progressively dis-
tances himself from such whimsicalities.

In 1910, Helen Corke, another teacher at Croydon, lent Lawrence her
diary of a five-day stay the previous summer on the Isle of Wight in the
company of a married man who, shortly after his return home, took his
own life. Lawrence, who had been holidaying elsewhere on the island
during the same hot August days, made these events the subject of *The
Trespasser*, his second (and least-read) novel, interpreting them to imply
that what destroys the man in the affair is the impossibility of his ever
overcoming the woman's self-sufficient immaturity (an interpretation to
which he may have been led by his own strong desire for Helen). In the
novel, the brilliant coastal flora that was Lawrence's own vivid memory of
the island serves as an index to the couple's incompatibility. Siegmund and
Helena both fantasise about the wild flowers all round them, but he does so
from a kind of desperate reaching after a response to his feelings, imagining
that 'the full-mouthed scabious and the awkward downcast ragwort'
looked at him 'with the same eye of tenderness', whereas Helena 'dwelled,
as she passed, on all tiny, pretty things; on the barbaric yellow ragwort and
pink convolvuli', amusing herself with the notions that one was tousled
because the fairies had failed to brush and comb it and that the other
furnished the fairies with their telephones. 'She clothed everything in
fancy'[47] – belittling and prettifying fancy that is the measure of her inability
to respond to her lover's need for her total commitment. The novel is over-
written, but lays claim to being a serious study of what happens when one
character in a relationship is incapable of being *sérieuse*.

Lawrence's third heroine, Miriam in *Sons and Lovers*, is nothing if not
serious-minded, but her response to the beauty of flowers is even more of
an appropriation, because through it she attempts to draw Paul into her
way of seeing, and so take possession of his very soul. Led by her to look at a
wild rose bush at dusk, he turns aside as if pained, unable to share in the
spiritual communion she seeks. 'They seem as if they walk like butterflies,

---

[46] *The White Peacock*, p. 155.   [47] *The Trespasser*, pp. 134, 75.

and shake themselves', is his attempt to free the flowers from the religiosity of her vision of them, 'some incurved and holy, others expanded in an ecstasy'.[48] Later, as their relationship sours, he erupts into rage at the sight of Miriam lavishing 'fervid kisses' upon daffodils: "Can you never like things without clutching them as if you wanted to pull the heart out of them?"[49] For distinct though it is from the trivialising fancies of Lettie or Helena, Miriam's appropriation of flowers betrays a falsifying imagination.

The truly imaginative way of seeing flowers is Mrs Morel's, and it manifests itself very early in the novel, before Paul is born, when a drunken Morel thrusts her out of doors. At first, as her mind races through every stage of the quarrel, she is blind to all about her. Then fear at her plight – it is cold and she is in the eighth month of her pregnancy – forces upon her an awareness of her surroundings. She hurries to the front of the house, where the scene of the moonlit valley into which the rows of cottages descend floods in upon her consciousness: a scene unified, like so many of Wordsworth's, by light, and a scene alive with 'presences' that, again like Wordsworth, she apprehends through more than one sense:

The tall white lilies were reeling in the moonlight, and the air was charged with their perfume, as with a presence. Mrs Morel gasped slightly in fear. She touched the big, pallid flowers on their petals, then shivered. They seemed to be stretching in the moonlight. She put her hand into one white bin: the gold scarcely showed on her fingers by moonlight. She bent down, to look at the bin-ful of yellow pollen: but it only appeared dusky. Then she drank a deep draught of the scent. (p. 34)

To this intense realisation of the flowers there now succeeds a loss of self-awareness – as when Wordsworth's 'light of sense / Goes out' – in which her consciousness of the child in her womb is the last thing to fade: 'the child too melted with her in the melting-pot of moonlight, and she rested with the hills and lilies and houses, all swum together in a kind of swoon' that leaves her restored and healed, as her response to other flowers in the garden shows: 'She touched the white ruffles of the roses. Their fresh scent and cool, soft leaves reminded her of the morning-time and sunshine'.[50]

Weariness, anger and fear soon return. But Mrs Morel has experienced the apartness of beauty, and the power of that apartness to deliver the beholder from selfhood while renewing his or her essential self, in a way that contrasts not only with the possessiveness of other women in Lawrence's early novels, but also with Lawrence's own insidious form of

---

[48] *Sons and Lovers*, p. 196.   [49] *Ibid.*, p. 257.   [50] *Ibid.*, pp. 34, 35.

possessiveness in his early poetry and fiction – a Symbolist manipulation of the green world. '"Don't those flags smell strong in the evening?"' a woman in the early story, 'The Old Adam', remarks to an 1890-ish young man. He replies with a quotation from the French lyric he has been reading and then drawls an English paraphrase: 'A peculiar, brutal, carnal scent, iris.'[51] Likewise, in a poem written about the same time, the 'faint, sickening scent of irises' that rises from a vase on the classroom table sends the speaker's mind back to their marshy habitat where he once saw the 'you' of the poem, her face overcast with the reflected colour of the kingcups she had gathered: a memory embittered – cut across, as it were, by the scent of irises – on account of her submissiveness in their subsequent lovemaking, which has left him both resentful of her passivity and remorseful at what he knows must to her have seemed brutality. The poem, 'Scent of Irises', is painfully confessional, dense with feelings about Jessie Chambers that, when recollected in tranquillity, created in *Sons and Lovers* both the kingcup episode preceding the 'test' that Miriam fails and, very shortly afterwards, the scene in which Paul goes out into the garden at night before returning to tell his mother that he intends to break with Miriam.

What has drawn Paul outside on this last occasion is the scent of madonna lilies that he experiences as a stealthy 'prowling'. He must cross a 'barrier' of them to reach the field from which he watches the moon set; even so, he senses them panting and calling behind him until another smell intervenes, the 'raw', 'coarse', 'brutal' scent of irises. The reader readily associates this awareness of the light and dark flowers with Paul's dual realisation that he has to break free of Miriam's emotional demands and that to do so will be an act of cruelty. But the same reader has been in this garden before Paul's birth, a fact that ensures that the lilies are also associated with Mrs Morel. In giving way to his mother's resistance to Miriam, he could be attempting to re-enter the womb – and that, we are told, is not the way to be born again; the 'grasping hands' of the irises are as suggestive of her hold on him as they are of Miriam's. At the same time the soft falls and erect styles by which these last flowers reveal themselves to Paul's touch – 'At any rate he had found something' – indicate his need for direct sexual experience, free of emotional claims, such as Clara can offer him. So his announcement is a Pyrrhic victory for Mrs Morel; aware that 'the male was up in him, dominant',[52] and not wanting to see him too clearly, she takes off her glasses.

---

[51] *Love among the Haystacks and other Stories*, p. 75.   [52] *Sons and Lovers*, pp. 337–8.

Powerful as the passage is in its management of the flowers' significances, the reader may feel that in comparison with the earlier moonlit scene it works them overhard. Indeed there are hints within the passage that Lawrence was becoming uneasy with the symbolism that weighs down such poems as 'Snap-dragon', poems in which the meddling intellect too often tampers with the pure act of realisation. The habit was not easy to shake off. In *Women in Love* as first written, the fact that a daisy is a 'company' of tiny florets sets Birkin off in mad pursuit of analogies:

'Well, then, there you are,' he said. 'The daisy is a perfect concord, circling round the Invisible, circling in rings in their proper order, the yellow ones palpitating with the Presence, absorbed in praise, the white ones transmitting the Glory, the green sepals like Hierarchies sheltering the Mystery, and the leaves and the grass around are the Magnitudes and Powers. What more do you want, for heaven?'[53]

There is more than a whiff of self-mockery here, and it grows stronger in the final version, in which Birkin turns the flower into 'the golden mob of the proletariat, surrounded by a showy white fence of the idle rich', before conceding 'It's a daisy – we'll leave it alone.'[54] It can safely be left alone because, in the fabric of the narrative, the bright little cotillion of flowers floating on the dark stream has already done its work, unaided by any exegesis. It has moved Ursula with that sense of a beginning – 'as if something were taking place'[55] – which verifies the truly creative and imaginative perception of natural beauty.

Two factors in Lawrence's own life strengthened this association between the experience of the beautiful and the sense of life remade. One was precarious health. He survived at least six life-threatening illnesses. At the beginning of the twentieth century, each such illness meant weeks in bed, as it does for Paul Morel:

Paul was in bed for seven weeks. He got up white and fragile. His father had bought him a pot of scarlet and gold tulips. They used to flame in the window, in the March sunshine, as he sat on the sofa chattering to his mother. The two knitted together in perfect intimacy. Mrs Morel's life now rooted itself in Paul.[56]

Artless-sounding, this paragraph carries a heavy charge of irony. In the crisis of his illness, Paul has 'realised' his mother as he will never realise his father. The love and concern expressed in the warm, affirmative colours of the growing plants go unacknowledged. They serve only as background to a bonding that, while it has brought Paul back from the brink, threatens

---

[53] *The First 'Women in Love'*, p. 117.   [54] *Women in Love*, p. 131.
[55] *Ibid.*, p. 130.   [56] *Sons and Lovers*, p. 171.

the son with domination and the father with exclusion. Roots can be invasive. But (Lawrence continues) this rooting of her life in Paul in place of his dead brother has, in her sister's view, 'saved' Mrs Morel – a word that points to the second factor contributing to that lifting of the heart Lawrence so often experiences in his perception of flowers: his Evangelical upbringing, with its emphasis on the importance of feeling oneself to have been born again.

This tradition of spiritual renewal together, maybe, with past experiences of physical recovery, helped him climb out of the deep trough of his fortunes, in which he all but drowned in the winter of 1917 to 1918. By then, *The Rainbow* had been banned and its author reviled; no publisher would accept *Women in Love*; and on the suspicion of spying, Lawrence and his German-born wife had been ordered to leave Cornwall, where his gardening skills had enabled them virtually to live off the land. Even floral diagrams in an old botany notebook appeared sinister in the eyes of the police, who continued their surveillance throughout the winter as the pair found what accommodation they could with the help of friends in and around London. Lawrence's letters of the time reveal much bitterness. At the beginning of April he wrote to his friend Catherine Carswell, who was pregnant, 'I feel as if I had a child of black fury curled up inside my bowels. . . We will both pray to be safely delivered.'[57]

Their prayers were answered. Three weeks later, Lawrence is able to tell Catherine 'We'll come through by a gap in the hedge if not by the gate' – a turn of phrase that recalls *Look! We Have Come Through!*, the proof of earlier resurgences and pledge perhaps of later ones, which had been published in the preceding dark November. Now, exceptional weather began to deliver him from despair, so that he felt the scent of cowslips to be 'a communication direct from the source of creation – like the breath of God breathed into Adam'.[58] It was a brilliant spring and, for Lawrence, a prolonged one. Bluebells were fully out in Berkshire when he and Frieda moved north from there to Derbyshire and watched their colour flood its upland woods. 'Let us hope we can all start off afresh', he writes to Catherine on learning of her safe delivery. In anticipation of the birth he had already written a celebratory poem, 'War-Baby', in which the biblical grain of mustard seed stands for their joint resurgence – 'As for our faith it was there / When we did not know, did not care' – for in Catherine he could recognise a resilience that matched his own. After the death of her first child, she had fought a long legal battle for the annulment of her

---

[57] *Letters*, vol. III, p. 231.   [58] *Ibid.*, p. 241.

marriage to a demented and violent husband, before a happy second marriage and now the birth of a son gave her life back to her.

Some special celebration was called for, and although, in the parlance of the time, Lawrence had not tuppence to rub together, he contrived to send Catherine what she called an exquisite present: twenty or more species of wild flowers, kept fresh in a moss-lined shoe box. A floral guide in minute writing was enclosed; Catherine was to recall that it described each plant – 'making me see how they had been before he picked them for me, in what sorts of places and manner and profusion they had grown, and even how they varied in the different countrysides'.[59] There were rock roses, which a covering letter calls 'pure flowers of light', milkworts, wood-avens, aconites, forget-me-nots, mountain violets such as had turned the patch of ground round the Lawrences' cottage into a Fra Angelico meadow, and a piece of woodruff – 'we call it new-mown-hay'.[60] That tribal 'we' comes from Lawrence's flower-hunting boyhood. But he also saw these flowers with the contemplative eye he was to attribute to Nottinghamshire miners: men like his father for whom, returning from night shift 'through the dewy fields in the first daybreak'[61] every flower must have been as much a flower of light as were the 1918 flowers to Lawrence himself after his darkest years. The exuberance of that spring, which he tried to pack into a shoe box, was to stay in his memory through years of travel and serve, in his last novel, both as symbol and setting for the remaking of two damaged lives.

The 1918 spring and that of the following year – less memorable because it was shorter and because he was too weak after post-war influenza to enjoy it – were Lawrence's last experiences of 'an English spring'. He makes Connie Chatterley mock the proprietary turn of this phrase; but like most expatriates he grew homesick when April came round. His plan to return to England in March 1925 was frustrated by a serious illness, in which tuberculosis first declared itself. An autumn visit, and another in the late summer of the following year, helped him familiarise himself anew with the Midlands landscape. But when he began to write *Lady Chatterley's Lover*, he had to fall back on memories from the first two decades of the century for his depiction of spring in an English wood.

The feat of memory is considerable. Lawrence not only recalls a great number of plants and the exact order of their flowering, but endows Connie Chatterley with his own sharp and delicate enjoyment of their appearance – celandines 'pressed back in urgency and the yellow glitter of themselves',

---

[59] Catherine Caswell, *The Savage Pilgrimage* (1932), p. 107.   [60] *Letters*, vol. III, p. 248.
[61] 'Adolf', *England, my England and other Stories*, p. 201.

'cottony' young cowslips 'still bleared in their down', wild daffodils shaking 'their bright, sunny little rags' – and often of their scent as well: daffodils have 'a faint, tarry scent', violets smell 'sweet and cold, sweet and cold', wood anemones give off a faint odour of apple blossom.[62] Clifford Chatterley's sensibility works differently. Hyacinths must be taken out of his room because their scent is 'a little funereal' and when Connie hands him a sprig of woodruff its fragrance of new-mown hay recalls for him 'the romantic ladies of the last century'.[63] In an earlier version these were ladies from a novel by Fogazzaro, for Clifford can usually lay his hand on some literary substitute for the living plant. The wood anemones that Connie sees as 'wide open as if exclaiming with the joy of life'[64] are to him unravished brides of quietness, while violets are sweeter than the lids of Juno's eyes. 'I don't see a bit of connexion with the actual violets' is Connie's steely comment, for she detects in Clifford's bookishness his lack of what the novel's first version calls the 'soft, frail tendrils of perception and true intelligence'.[65]

Clifford's incompatibility with all that Lawrence makes woodland represent is brilliantly exposed when, holding forth on the supremacy of the technically empowered ruling class, he steers his mechanised wheelchair into the undergrowth, leaving a trail of havoc as 'the wheels jolt over the wood-ruff and the bugle, and squash the little yellow cups of the creeping-jenny'.[66] Then the engine breaks down, and Clifford's ensuing struggle to get it going, rather than submit to being pushed by Mellors, results in a massacre of bluebells. In the end however natural bodily energy prevails over mechanical energy. Likewise in the end, the life of nature regenerates in its full springtime vigour, giving the lie to Mellors's earlier despair, modelled on Lawrence's own wartime despair, at the evil he felt emanating from the world of greedy mechanisation: 'Soon it would destroy the wood and the bluebells would spring no more. All vulnerable things must perish under the rolling and running of iron.'[67]

So too it had seemed to Connie in February, when she sat on a dead stump and listened, against a background of colliery noises, to Clifford's praise of the partly felled wood as the heart of old England. But when she returned alone in March she sat with her back to a young fir tree 'that swayed against her with curious life'; and as she follows Clifford's wheelchair on this destructive May outing she notices that 'Even the snaggy, craggy oak-trees put out the softest young leaves, spreading thin, brown

[62] *Lady Chatterley's Lover*, pp. 165, 182, 86, 93. [63] *Ibid.*, pp. 98, 186. [64] *Ibid.*, p. 93.
[65] *Ibid.*, p. 91; *The First and Second Lady Chatterley Novels*, p. 87. [66] *Lady Chatterley's Lover*, p. 184.
[67] *Ibid.*, p. 119.

little wings like young bats-wings in the light.'[68] If, in the forget-me-not episode, Connie is improbably (and uncomfortably) tricked out with sprigs of young oak, the reason is that Lawrence simply cannot forgo the story's most persistent emblem of regeneration, the overhead leafing that succeeds to the pell-mell blossoming beneath. On her return to the wood the day after she and Mellors have first made love, she seems to feel in her body 'the huge heave of the sap in the massive trees, up, up to the bud-tips, there to push into little flamy oak-leaves, bronze as blood'.[69] Later, after the pair have experienced the height of their happiness, she sits seemingly listening to Clifford reading Racine's passionate tirades, but actually 'gone in her own soft rapture ... like the dark interlacing of the oak wood, humming inaudibly with myriad unfolding buds'.[70]

The surprising thing is that the encounter that has given rise to this reverie has not taken place under oak trees, but in a flowerless plantation of conifers such as Lawrence, on his last visits to England, would have noticed were replacing the deciduous woodland felled for trench timber during the war by landowners like Clifford's father. To Connie, as she hurries through it with her bunch of 'recklesses' (auriculas), it appears menacing, and she cries out in fear when Mellors suddenly bars her way. Yet what begins with associations of rape ends in supreme happiness: the lovers climax together, leaving Connie with a feeling of adoration for Mellors and with the hope that she has conceived. That all this should happen on a bed of dead branches has its own metaphoric force: the phoenix rises anew. If the spring flowers abounding at so many other places in the story are here excluded, it is because they are not to be reduced to metaphor. The connection between their vitality and that of the lovers is something altogether more real, an interrelatedness that lies at the heart of the forget-me-not episode and is conveyed most clearly in the second of the novel's three versions. There, Connie arrives at the gamekeeper's hut in 'the quick pattering of June rain'[71] and has got a fire going by the time he joins her. On impulse, she runs out naked into what has become a downpour; he pursues and catches her and 'in the middle of the path, in the pouring rain, went into her, in a sharp, short embrace'.[72] They return to the shelter in order to dry themselves at the fire, and it is at this point that the flowers are brought, literally, into play, as the lovers begin to decorate one another's bodies.

Once again Lawrence is reaching for an expression of affinity that will transcend metaphor. Lovemaking and blossoming are both a

---

[68] *Ibid.*, pp. 86, 184.   [69] *Ibid.*, pp. 121–2.   [70] *Ibid.*, p. 138.
[71] *The First and Second Lady Chatterley Novels*, p. 457.   [72] *Ibid.*, p. 459.

coming-into-being through the elemental process that pre-Socratic thinkers saw as the creative union of fire and water; the flowers that 'stop out-doors all weathers'[73] have, like the lovers, reached their climax through the conjunction of rain and shine. But here interrelatedness takes a further form. The flowers are named one by one, not only in recognition of the distinct identities that they, in common with the man and the woman, have achieved in their flowering, but also to evoke the individual brilliance of colour and form that Connie has been made aware of on her way to the hut: bluebells, guelder roses and campions glowing in the rain, forget-me-nots 'knee-deep, all with wet faces'.[74] All, in their lesser degree, represent the shock of the beautiful that is conveyed by Connie running in the rain and by the firelight playing on the nude bodies. The episode is intensely visualised. 'There she was'[75] is an invitation to stand back and see Connie, tricked out with primroses and bryony, as in a Renaissance Triumph of Flora: a withdrawal to, as it were, the other side of the easel (Lawrence had begun to paint again) that comes as a relief from the reader's over-involvement with one or other of the protagonists in their earlier encounters. If there is rather too much of a sex fantasy about the chase, it serves none the less to associate the scene with the erotic element in painting, calling to mind a Poussin bacchanal, or rather – since her lover here appears to Connie as 'the wild man of the woods whom she remembered in old German drawings'[76] – the nymphs and satyrs that Altdorfer transferred to his northern forests.

Sadly, this contemplative and pictorial quality has all but vanished from the final, published version, in which the centre of consciousness has shifted to Mellors at his most resentful and so at his most ready to defy verbal taboos. As a result, the tone becomes hectic and sometimes hectoring. In this rewriting, it is Connie who initiates the game with flowers as part of an attempt to exorcise the bitterness that prevents her lover taking any pleasure in the thought of the child that is expected. There is a ritual note too in the dance that has replaced her run through the rain, while the elaborate flower-decking that occurred after the return to the hut is turned into a mock marriage ceremony, the coronal of John Thomas and Lady Jane.[77] Few readers are happy with these elaborations and with the change of tone.

---

[73] *Ibid.*, p. 460.   [74] *Ibid.*, p. 457.   [75] *Ibid.*, p. 461.   [76] *Ibid.*, p. 460.

[77] Popular euphemisms for the genitalia, which Lawrence at one time thought of using as the title of the novel.

Why, asked Ada Lawrence, did Middleton Murry, in his study of her brother,

want to convey to the public the impression of a self-tortured and frustrated man, with no glimpse of the other side? I know of no other person capable of such real happiness as D. H. Lawrence when in a bluebell wood.[78]

Both Lawrences, of course, existed, and Murry's all but dominates the *Lady Chatterley's Lover* most of us know. But it was Ada's Lawrence-in-a-bluebell-wood who, in the novel's second version, came closest to rounding out his œuvre with the depiction of a wholly right relationship confirmed by the beauty of the natural world.

3

Lawrence's botanical travels began in Croydon. When Jessie Chambers failed to send him some promised violets, he sent her a coals-of-fire box of almond blossom, which he was seeing for the first time: 'You said you would be my Persephone – you would not', but now 'Persephone has passed through the town' and he can visualise Jessie beneath almond boughs in the company of girls from 'the happy lands, / Provence, Japan and Italy'.[79]

Nothing, however, had prepared Lawrence for the botanical excitement that he experienced, along with all his other turmoil of feelings, when he first travelled abroad in the summer of 1912. An attempt to describe his first alpine meadow breaks down into 'oh, flowers, great wild mad profusion of them, everywhere'.[80] A few weeks later he is on his way across the Alps and surrounded by the mountain flowers of late summer:

There are millions of different bells: tiny harebells, big, black-purple mountain harebells, pale blue, hairy strange creatures, blue and white Canterbury bells – then there's a great blue gentian, and flowers like monkey-musk. The Alpine roses are just over – and I believe we could find the Edelweiss if we tried.[81]

Once he and Frieda are over the Alps and settled beside Lake Garda, there follow the first encounters with the transalpine flora: 'wild little cyclamens' in October; 'great handfuls of wild Christmas-roses' in November; and then, the marvels of an Italian spring –

[78] Quoted by Neville, *A Memoir*, p. 202. [79] 'Letter from Town: the Almond Tree'.
[80] *Letters*, vol. I, p. 413.
[81] *Ibid.*, p. 441. The four alpine species of bellflower referred to here could be the species known in English as: fairies' thimbles; bearded bellflower; Scheuchzeri's bellflower; and great bellflower. All will figure in *The Captain's Doll*.

There are little grape-hyacinths standing about, and peach-blossom is pink among the grey olives, and the cherry-blossom shakes in the wind. O my sirs, what more do you want?[82]

These descriptions were for the few people who were in the know about Frieda and who would recognise that Lawrence's excitement over the flowers he was seeing for the first time was all of a piece with his certainty as a lover that 'The world is wonderful and beautiful and good beyond one's wildest imagination.'[83] Frieda in a prospect of flowers is the theme of the sequence of poems, 'All of Roses'. Although the Bonnard-like vision of her in 'Gloire de Dijon' takes its title from a long-familiar garden rose, the starting point of the sequence was the moment when Lawrence discovered that wild roses in Bavaria were of a warm, deep colour. He was looking for the first time at *Rosa gallica*, the *rose de Provence* that had inspired so much of Europe's love poetry, and it followed from this that the sequence as it was published (to Frieda's pride and pleasure) in January 1913, was a lover's tribute in the tradition of Catullus, Ronsard and Schiller.

When, however, Lawrence in 1917 came to put together the poetry of this time for the collection he called *Look! We Have Come Through!* he made changes in these poems, changes that cast a shadow of anxiety over their happiness. In part these reflect the different man he felt himself to have become by 1917. But they also turn what had been a wedding bouquet for Frieda into a more honest record of what their relationship and their situation had been in 1912. From being warm and red, the roses by the Isar are now seen as dark and wild, and instead of blending with them in an embrace the lovers become aware of the glacier-cold water beneath –

> And glimmering
> Fear was abroad. We whispered: 'No one knows us.
> Let it be as the snake disposes
> Here in this simmering marsh.'   ('River Roses')

There were many snakes in this Eden. Lawrence could be morose and guilt-ridden – mother-haunted, Frieda felt – while she for her part was subject to almost intolerable pressure from both her husband and her German family to end what they saw as an escapade. Above all she pined for her children. Globe flowers are among the flowers that, according to Lawrence's letters, make him almost cry for joy, but as, in 'She Looks Back', their 'lovely pale-gold bubbles' swarm across a meadow towards the

---

[82] *Ibid.*, pp. 462; 478; 536.   [83] *Ibid.*, p. 414.

sunset, he knows they are drawing Frieda's thoughts westwards towards England.

A bigger test of the relationship came when the pair left Bavaria and made their way, partly on foot, across the Alps. Ten days after he had written his letter about the profusion of bellflowers, Frieda made Lawrence stop on a mountain path in order to tell him that while he and Bunny had been botanising, Bunny's travelling companion had 'had' her in a hay-hut. It is hardly surprising that Lawrence, in 'The Crucifix among the Mountains' and the poems he wrote about the journey, is almost silent on the finds he and Bunny made, although the unfinished and highly autobiographical *Mr Noon*, written eight years later, offers a glimpse of Bunny 'scrambling up or scrambling down the ravines, for a yellow violet or a bit of butterwort'.[84] In the novel, the admission of infidelity is met with swift forgiveness. This satisfies neither party; heaviness and darkness descend on the man, leaving his soul 'acid and hard'.[85] Only in 1922, when a holiday in the Austrian Tyrol at the same time of year brought back memories of the 1912 journey, did Lawrence perceive what now appeared to him to be a better response than Gilbert Noon's 'convulsion of selflessness';[86] and the perception gave him the theme for one of his best novellas, *The Captain's Doll*.

This tale of the Scottish war veteran Alexander Hepburn and his one-time mistress, the German aristocrat Hannele who has survived post-war inflation by making and selling dolls, culminates in the two of them joining an excursion to a Tyrolese glacier. At first their path mounts through a narrow ravine where the sinister effect of the rocks and of the 'ferocious water' below them is repeated by the wild flowers; by, for instance, 'the hairy mountain-bell, pale-blue and bristling' that 'stood alone, curving his head right down, stiff and taut'.[87] Tourists with edelweiss in their hats swarm up and down this deep romantic chasm, shouting 'Bergheil' at one another. Hannele shares their romantic afflatus, but Hepburn, himself stiff, taut and bristling, hates it, and the two quarrel. Yet when they emerge from the ravine onto the open alp above he begins to respond with delight to his surroundings and in particular to the flowers: some of them the same, others new:

wonderful harebells, big and cold and dark, almost black, and seeming like purple-dark ice: then little tufts of tiny pale-blue bells, as if some fairy frog had been blowing spume-bubbles out of the ice: then the bishops-crosier of the stiff,

---

[84] *Mr Noon*, p. 205.   [85] *Ibid.*, p. 259.   [86] *Ibid.*, p. 277.
[87] *The Fox. The Captain's Doll. The Ladybird*, p. 129.

bigger, hairy mountain-bell: then many stars of pale-lavender gentian, touched
with earth-colour: and then monkshood, yellow, primrose yellow monkshood and
sudden places full of dark monkshood. That dark-blue, black-blue, terrible colour
of the strange rich monkshood made Hepburn look and look and look again. How
did the ice come by that lustrous blue-purple intense darkness? – and by that royal
poison? – that laughing-snake gorgeousness of much monkshood. (p. 133)

We are seeing through the eyes of Hepburn, who is 'happy in that upper
valley',[88] open and glaciated like his native landscape and abounding in
flowers reminiscent of Scotch bluebells. But anger persists, in the dark
Alpenglocken and the dark monkshood that is a veritable touch-me-not
plant, poisonous in every part. So he and Hannele (who picks none of
these, but the high-mountain species of what is in effect *her* Bavarian
national flower, the gentian) proceed to 'have it out' by airing past resent-
ments: hers at his disappearance after his wife's death, his at her having sold
the doll that she once modelled upon him. In the fitful sunlight and beside
a stream from the melting snow 'crying its birth-cry',[89] there is some
clearing of the air. But as the pair resume their ascent the valley closes in
again, the rain pours down, and the large bellflowers hang 'dark and with
that terrible motionlessness of upper mountain flowers', while under the
dripping rock-face 'the white and veined flowers of the Grass of Parnassus
still rose straight and chilly in the shadow, like water which had taken on
itself white flower-flesh'.[90] The quarrel breaks out afresh; Hannele decides
that Hepburn must be bullying her into loving him and resolves for her
part that she will accept nothing less than the declaration of *his* love.

The 'curious dark, masterful force that supplanted thought'[91] in
Hepburn at this point is, however, something quite different from romantic devotion. Its nature begins to define itself as the terrain opens out once
more, this time into a broad stony valley blocked at its upper end by the
glacier. The same flowers grow here, 'even more beautiful' but even more
closely associated, in the way they are described, with the fields of ice above:
the bellflowers 'almost black and ice-metallic', the big cups of the Parnassus
grass 'terribly naked and open to this ice-air'.[92] Implicit in them, and in the
exhilaration that Alexander (Lawrence is now using Hepburn's conquering
forename) has begun to feel, is the naked truth of self-recognition, though a
self-recognition that comes on the very brink of self-annihilation; we are on
the thin dividing line between the organic life of the plants and the
inorganic world of snow and ice. The theme is underlined by Alexander's
foolhardy but self-affirming scramble onto the cusp of the glacier's tongue

---

[88] *Ibid.*   [89] *Ibid.*   [90] *Ibid.*, pp. 135; 136.   [91] *Ibid.*, p. 138.   [92] *Ibid.*, p. 141.

and by the thought that there comes to him – 'Never a warm leaf to unfold, never a gesture of life to give off.'[93] He has come very close to such annihilation in the romantic falsehood of his marriage and in his desolation of spirit after his wife's death. For this reason, once the two are back at the road-head (Hannele having picked more flowers on the way 'and put them in her handkerchief so they should not die'[94]), he proposes marriage in the terms of his new-found self-awareness. Instead of offering romantic adulation, he demands 'honour, and obedience: and the proper physical feelings'[95] in return for his undertaking to love and to cherish. Loyalty is worth more than love as that emotion is popularly conceived.

This was Lawrence's own position by 1921, a stand he now perhaps felt he ought to have taken on that other mountain path in 1912. But *The Captain's Doll* is very much more than *l'esprit de l'escalier* delayed by a decade. It is a rich and subtle study of a relationship, no less in the way its mood is skilfully steered between the absurd and the tragic than in its handling of a range of motifs which all relate to its central idea: the lie of the land, the weather, the mannered artefacts that are dwarfed by the landscape, the tourists' absurd 'Bergheil!' (a failure in the recognition of the Other such as 'Grüss Gott' or even 'Guten Tag' bestows), and above all what the mountain flowers are made to tell us. These flowers are something less passive than symbols. They communicate. *Utterance* is a word Lawrence in his post-war writing frequently associates with flowers, and in *The Captain's Doll* the alpine plants speak to the condition of both characters. They help to deepen Hepburn's resolve to be his own man, but they also warn him of how close he is to spiritual extinction; they tell Hannele both of his inviolability and of her need for him, something that she must not let die. The mountain flora is a discovery for them in both senses of the word: they are seeing these flowers for the first time, but the flowers themselves have revelations to make.

Revelation – the word's religious overtones are cogent – is something Lawrence seeks again and again from the flowers of the Italian lakes and coasts: 'the flowers', he was to write in 1927, 'that speak and are understood, in the sun round the Middle Sea'.[96] The mythical implications of names such as asphodel and narcissus suggest the kind of revelation he awaited. During his pre-war sojourn in Italy, however, it was slow in coming, impeded perhaps by his own excitement of discovery. 'They are little living myths that I cannot understand', he wrote of the autumn cyclamens

---

[93] *Ibid.*, p. 143.   [94] *Ibid.*, p. 144.   [95] *Ibid.*, p. 150.   [96] 'Flowery Tuscany', *Sketches*, p. 225.

by Lake Garda, and the hellebores that succeeded them were no less enigmatic – 'flowers of darkness, white and wonderful beyond belief'.[97]

In wartime England, however, at the time when the Mediterranean spring would have been in full colourful cry, the early spring blossoms which had given Lawrence such pleasure in Italy appear as 'ghastly first-flowers, / Which are rather last-flowers!' 'Craving for Spring' is a yearning, in the darkest days both of the war and of Lawrence's fortunes as a writer, for a sap-driven renewal of the life that, in Donne's phrase, is shrunk to the bed's feet; and the pledge of that renewal will be the deep strong colour of the first violets:

> Oh, if it be true, and the living darkness of the blood of man is
>   purpling with violets,
> if the violets are coming out from under the rack of men, winter-
>   rotten and fallen,
> we shall have spring.
> Pray not to die on this Pisgah blossoming with violets.
> Pray to live through.
> If you catch a whiff of violets from the darkness of the shadow of man
> it will be spring in the world,
> it will be spring in the world of the living;
> wonderment organising itself, heralding itself with the violets,
> stirring of new seasons.

John Clare, as we have seen, responded in this way to the first violets after a winter spent in the company of the insane. It has also to be remembered that Clare was insane himself; and 'Craving for Spring' as a whole, with its frenzied rejection of wintry flowers, reminds us how close Lawrence came to alienation in 1917. Crocuses such as those he had delighted in at Gargnano – 'pale, fragile, lilac-coloured flowers with dark veins, pricking up keenly like myriad little lilac-coloured flames among the grass, under the olive trees'[98] – are now 'death-veined exhalations ... issue of corruption, nourished in mortification' and the pleasure it gives him to tread them down is another disturbing echo, this time of the rage at 'evil' flowers that seized Ruskin when he was on the edge of a breakdown.

But Lawrence came through. We have seen that the English spring of 1918 afforded him Pisgah-sights that he remembered for the rest of his life, and in 1919, back in Italy, he seemed to re-enter the Promised Land. 'Living in Sicily after the war years', Frieda wrote, 'was like coming to life again.'[99] In *The Lost Girl*, written during the following spring, the wonderment

---

[97] *Twilight in Italy*, p. 154.   [98] *Ibid.*, p. 110.   [99] *Not I, but the Wind . . .* (1934), p. 94.

Lawrence had felt in 1913 at his first sight of wild crocuses, and that he had savagely perverted in 1917 by turning them into *fleurs du mal,* organises itself into Alvina's reverence before the same flowers. 'Wonderfully fragile on their stems of sap', with deeper markings 'running up their cheeks ... like the clear, proud stripes on a badger's face', they open in sunlight into 'great five-pointed, seven-pointed lilac stars, with burning centres, burning with a strange lavender flame', so that she wants to 'bend her forehead to the earth in an oriental submission, they were so royal, so lovely, so supreme';[100] a submission that is only one stage of her attentiveness to the sequence of spring flowers, from February's crocuses to May's gladioli, as they 'came out and uttered the earth'.[101]

That utterance is what Lawrence is straining to hear in 'Cypresses', which was written in Tuscany in 1920 and is one of the poems on fruit, flowers and trees that form the first part of his finest volume of verse, *Birds, Beasts and Flowers* (1923). What he seeks from the slim dark trees is a revelation about the 'wavering men of old Etruria'; plants ought to be able to speak of a lost past because, as the *sine qua non* of human life they have been here longer than we have. But the Etruscans left no legends for the living to reinterpret. It was otherwise with the Greeks in Sicily, and the fresh meanings that Lawrence finds in Greek myths are the sure sign of his post-war resurgence. In his early poems, the Persephone legend is a story of winter's tyranny, bequeathed him by the line of English poets who took their cue from Milton's unforgettable lines about gloomy Dis and Ceres' pain, while *Look! We Have Come Through!* blends Persephone–Frieda's escape to flower-packed meadows with the legend of Orpheus leading Eurydice to freedom. In *The Lost Girl,* however, the comfortable middle-aged doctor whom Alvina abandons is hardly a winter-king. That role is played by Ciccio when he carries her off to his mountain village, and icy as it is, the astonishing wealth of flowers that springs from its soil has the effect of binding her to it and to him forever. Lawrence has stood the legend on its head, as he does in a poem that has for springboard his discovery, in Demeter's own island, of deep-purple anemones – 'Little hells of colour, caves of darkness ... Hell rearing its husband-splendid, serpent heads.'[102] Dis-Pluto is here the real giver of flowers, Persephone the wilful wife who periodically runs home to mother. Lawrence is reaching back behind Milton's northern dread of winter to a Mediterranean understanding that plants need cold and darkness for their survival or propagation. Demeter, as the High God tells her both in the

---

[100] *The Lost Girl,* p. 332.   [101] *Ibid.,* p. 335.   [102] 'Purple Anemones'.

Homeric hymn and in Ovid, simply did not know when her daughter was well off.

Again in Sicily, and fuelled by the same energy of perception, Lawrence at last seized upon the mythical significance of another flower, which had eluded him in 1912 and still eluded Alvina when she wept over 'the last of the rose-coloured Alpine cyclamens, near the earth, with snake-skin leaves, and so rose, so rose, like violets for shadowiness'.[103] This time, Lawrence creates his own myth. Prehistoric man and woman, when they first part the hair from their eyes, see the beauty of the Sicilian landscape and, at their feet, 'tiny rose cyclamens between their toes, growing / Where the slow toads sat brooding on the past'.[104] As a metaphor for the round, exquisitely mottled ('frost-filigreed . . . snail-nacrous') leaves of cyclamens, 'slow toads' is an imaginative leap beyond the 'snake-skin leaves' of the prose passage, and so corresponds to the mental leap taken by these Pelasgic figures, who have begun to move out of the waters of unawareness in which they were, amphibian-like, submerged. Their new alertness is suggested by the flowers 'Folding back their soundless petalled ears' like young, slim greyhounds; an alertness which will lead on to the perception of human beauty – implicit in the 'women at a well, the dawn-fountain' – and its expression in the sculptures that will be fashioned from the limestone of 'sea-blanched Mediterranean stone-slopes' –

> Greece, and the world's morning
> Where all the Parthenon marbles still fostered the roots of the cyclamen.
> Violets,
> Pagan, rosy-muzzled violets
> Autumnal
> Dawn-pink,
> Dawn-pale
> Among squat toad-leaves sprinkling the unborn
> Erechtheion marbles.

Violets? Yes, because as with Alvina (an Eastwood girl), exotic discovery must be linked to familiar experience. This is Lawrence's way of setting his signature to the poem's close and so of validating the universal import of the tale he has told – in short, of making it mythical: he is one with the prehistoric pair whose dawning sense of the beautiful is the pledge of all future creativity.

Something similar occurs in the collection's other perfect poem about flowers, written some three months later when Sicily's rusty-black almond

---

[103] *The Lost Girl*, p. 332.   [104] 'Sicilian Cyclamens'.

trees erupted into blossom. Lawrence here writes as if the almond were a transalpine plant, an exile in the sun-baked island. That its original home was in southern latitudes had been known to him since 1909, when he first saw Persephone's girdle left in a London street. None the less he chooses to think of the tree as retaining from its diaspora a memory of 'sun-gentler lands', in order the better to identify his exiled self with the tree's disclosure of the living world's power of rejuvenation:

> storming up,
> Strange storming up from the dense under-earth
> Along the iron, to the living steel
> In rose-hot tips, and flakes of rose-pale snow
> Setting supreme annunciation to the world.   ('Almond Blossom')

Rising over the ground bass of reiterated monosyllables that define the event itself – 'steel', 'heart', 'earth', 'snow' – are biblical harmonies that reveal a significance neither of Lawrence's own making nor taken from Greek legend, but at the heart of the Christian myth as he understood it. Aaron's blossoming rod (the underlying idea of the novel Lawrence was trying to write at the time) is the archetype which not only brings together the Passion and the Resurrection, 'the Cross sprouting its superb and fearless flowers', but links the Creation story – 'the tree of life in blossom' to the apocalyptic promise, 'Behold the Bridegroom cometh':

> And the Gethsemene blood at the iron pores unfolds, unfolds,
> Pearls itself into tenderness of bud
> And in a great and sacred forthcoming steps forth, steps out in one stride
> A naked tree of blossom . . .

'Have you not seen, in the wild winter sun of the southern Mediterranean, in January and February, the rebirth of the almond tree, all standing in clouds of glory?' Lawrence asked in the epigraphs he added, three months before his death, to each group of poems in *Birds, Beasts and Flowers*: 'Ah yes! Ah yes! Would I might see it again!'

Early in 1922, Lawrence decided to leave the country that had done so much to restore him to life as man and artist. One reason for his departure was the Italian political ferment that he mocks in the last of the 'Flower' poems, a not-too-serious protest against the Sicilian communists' choice of flower emblems which gives him the chance to celebrate the royal, non-egalitarian splendours of scarlet hibiscus and of 'The dragon-faced, / The anger-reddened, golden-throated salvia'. From a society that he held to have become unworthy of such magnificence, Lawrence took himself off to the United States by a slow easterly journey, broken by sojourns in

Sri Lanka (then Ceylon) and in Australia. The poet who had written 'Hibiscus and Salvia Flowers' might have been expected to revel in the flamboyance of Ceylon's plant life. But in the event, the island's heat overwhelmed him, and beyond the 'queer noise of tall metallic palms'[105] its vegetation had nothing to say to him.

Nor, at first, had the 'sun-refusing leaves' of Australian eucalyptus. When Lovat, the central character in *Kangaroo* (written in an eight-week stay on the coast south of Sydney), prepares to leave after a brief involvement with Australian post-war politics, he is still unable to get beyond the alien, unlighted and unenlightening aspects of cabbage palms and tree ferns and gum trees. But it so happens that the point when Lawrence–Lovat stops straining to listen, the bush speaks out, in the swift onset of the New South Wales spring. It does not, however, deliver any message from old gods; it speaks simply of itself, of plentitude, of fantastic variability. The final chapter of *Kangaroo* is a heady celebration of that plentitude. Lovat and his wife drive over the crest of the Illawara escarpment, and discover marvel upon marvel in the virgin bush beyond. It is all to the good that they cannot name any of the plants with certainty and that Lovat can make only tenuous links between their outlandish flowers and the botanic families with which he is familiar, for this means nothing can distract them from the sense of revelation. They plunder freely and, back in their temporary home, sit eating boiled eggs in a house filled with wattle-bloom, a scene that recalls a friend's comment on Lawrence and Frieda at table in a room full of foxgloves: 'as is their custom when they love anything, they make a sort of fiesta'.[106] Inside the novel's world, Lovat is in effect celebrating recovery from a long alienation; externally to it, Lawrence's wonderment before the Australian spring does a little to right the balance of a book that has become violently distorted by the long 'Nightmare' chapter reliving his wartime experiences.

Utterances from a remote past such as Lawrence did not expect to hear in New South Wales came to him in the antiquities of Mexico. But they were not leaf-fringed legends; he does not appear to have been aware of the importance of flowers in Aztec and pre-Aztec ritual, and in *The Plumed Serpent* (1926) tropical vegetation supplies little more than local colour. It was in New rather than Old Mexico that Lawrence found his spiritual home in America, and there, on the ranch given to Frieda Lawrence in the

[105] *Letters*, vol. IV, pp. 233–4.
[106] E. W. Tedlock (ed.), *Frieda Lawrence: the Memoirs and Correspondence* (1964), p. 106.

spring of 1924, the landscape and its life-forms spoke out loud and clear. They did not however all deliver the same message.

When Lawrence, in the last year of his life, recalled the many kinds of natural beauty he had witnessed, he remembered wild tulips in Tuscan cornfields, English bluebells at dusk, mimosa among the grey-green Australian foliage – 'But for a *greatness* of beauty I have never experienced anything like New Mexico.'[107] The breath-taking prospect of desert and mountains from Kiowa Ranch furnished a run of bravura paragraphs towards the end of *St Mawr*, the novella he wrote shortly after he had settled in. Once again, a piece of writing that is almost obsessively misanthropic in tone is counterbalanced at the close by a powerful and brilliant description of non-human nature which, we are to understand, heals and restores a central character who has fled the hurts inflicted by European society. But in *St Mawr* the portrayal of that natural world is more complex than it was in *Kangaroo*. The Australian bush had offered pure escape; Kiowa Ranch had to be managed. When, five years later, Lawrence remembered himself standing and looking 'over the desert to the blue mountains away in Arizona, blue as chalcedony, with the sage-brush desert sweeping grey blue in between',[108] he recalled that he had a hoe in his hand. At the time of writing *St Mawr*, he was wielding the hoe a good deal, for like the characters in the story he was discovering how unremitting was the struggle to keep the wilderness at bay. 'The very flowers came up bristly, and many of them were fang-mouthed, like the dead-nettle.'[109] 'Bluebells' in New Mexico proved to be an invasive species of snapdragon, and the frail wild tulips of Italy were replaced by flaunting scarlet and yellow blossoms that throttled the young alfalfa. The spokesman, as it were, for this rampant wild life was the giant pine towering over the ranch's log cabin, a guardian from a 'pre-sexual primeval world ... where each creature was crudely limited to its own ego, crude and bristling and cold, and then crowding in packs like pine-trees and wolves'.[110]

The reader may, at this point, be pulled up by the thought that pine trees are no more sexless than wolves, and that a pre-sexual world would be, at best, a sea swarming with the forebears of plankton; in short that what Lawrence is giving us is a projection of the viewer's emotions onto other forms of life. This becomes even more evident if we compare this account, in the story, of the tree (which *Mornings in Mexico* shows to have been indeed something of a personal totem) with his celebration of it in the

[107] Edward D. McDonald (ed.), *Phoenix: the Posthumous Papers of D. H. Lawrence* (1936), p. 142.
[108] *Ibid.*   [109] *St Mawr and other Stories*, p. 148.   [110] *Ibid.*, p. 145.

essay, 'Pan in America', in which there is no ventriloquism: the pine is its own tree. But out of his recognition of its otherness comes Lawrence's sense of its interpenetration with his own life, his recognition that 'its raw earth-power and its raw sky-power, its resinous erectness and resistance, its sharpness of hissing needles and relentlessness of roots, all that goes to the primitive savageness of a pine tree, goes also to the strength of man'.[111] Such communion, rather than communication, with other life-forms was something that Lawrence found he shared with the New Mexico Indians. The discovery makes him deeply responsive, elsewhere in the same essay, to their secret sympathy with trees, as, in other essays written about this time, he is to the songs and dances which, the Indians believed, 'stimulate the tremulous, pulsating protoplasm in the seed-germ, till it throws forth its rhythms of creative energy into rising blades of leaf and stem'.[112]

In having his central character in *St Mawr* so aware of an underlying savagery, Lawrence knows that he in danger of making a solipsistic use of the pathetic fallacy. So he calls an independent witness. The point of view from which, for the most part, the reader is made to see the ranch is not that of its buyer, the world-weary, embittered emigrée Lou, but that of the New England wife of the man who sells it. Conditioned by her upbringing to hear sermons in stones, and in trees too, she responds with an Emersonian lifting of the heart to the grandeur of the distant landscape. But when she turns to the life-forms immediately surrounding her, to the pack rats and the strangling weeds, the message she receives from this 'world before and after the God of Love'[113] is that it has no benevolent creator. Defeated, she withdraws; Lou hears and accepts the message, and buys the ranch.

Lawrence has buttressed his argument with a clever narrative device. Yet in the end the same simple delight as he felt at the coming of an Australian spring undermines his own purposes. New Mexico's flora is a Darwinian battlefield. But the battle is fought under brilliant banners, and the painter's relish for colour combines with the botanist's eye for forms of growth to give us the herb honeysuckle's 'cleanest fire colour, hanging in long drops like a shower of fire-rain', or another flower's 'sparking, fierce red stars running up a bristly grey ladder'; until, forgetting significances and intimations, he stands rapt in the discovery of 'the moth-still, ghost-centred mariposa lily with its inner moth-dust of yellow'[114] balanced on its invisible stalk. A shout of beauty drowns the ventriloquist's voice as it had already done in the Australian bush. Once again, Lawrence makes a fiesta.

[111] *Phoenix*, p. 26.   [112] *Mornings in Mexico* (1927), p. 106.
[113] *St Mawr*, p. 149.   [114] *Ibid.*, pp. 148; 149.

Back again in Europe – for good as it turned out – and freed from the compulsive quest for revelations of the primeval, but faced instead with the 'revelation in flowers'[115] that, according to Frieda, was the spring of 1927, Lawrence writes his most eloquent celebration of the Mediterranean flora. In 'Flowery Tuscany' an almost incantatory repetition of such legendary names as anemone and asphodel at the start of the essay, together with talk of their 'significance', lead us to expect myths and messages. But here Greek mythology gets cavalier treatment. After Lawrence has brought the grape-hyacinth to life in all its fine detail, the thought that it is the flower of the many-breasted Artemis comes almost as an irrelevance, while the mythic origins of the Venus' tears anemone, abundant everywhere ('how the poor lady must have wept')[116] is only a footnote to his attempt to render in words the colour of the Adonis' blood species:

How a colour manages to be perfectly strong and impervious, yet of a purity that suggests condensed light, yet not luminous, at least, not transparent, is a problem. The poppy in her radiance is translucent, and the tulip in her utter redness has a touch of opaque earth. But the Adonis-blood anemone is neither translucent nor opaque. It is just pure, condensed red, of a velvetiness without velvet, and a scarlet without glow. (pp. 232–3)

Oil painting, with its problems of translucence and opacity, is by now as important an activity to Lawrence as is his writing. Moreover his re-discovery this spring of this and the other flowers whose appearance he recounts in a finely orchestrated sequence (listen, one finds oneself saying, for the entry of the violets) was made in the company of a painter friend, who marvelled, as Jessie Chambers had once done, at how much he knew. Anemones, in his sixth Italian spring, have grown as familiar as cowslips once were, so that he no longer strains after revelations but is content to revel in the sense of a shared vitality. This sense of communion, like that he once felt with the pines and the sprouting corn of New Mexico, has been prepared by the age-long inhabitant of the country; the Tuscan peasant, 'feeling his way sensitively to the fruitfulness of the earth, has moulded the earth to his necessity without violating it'.[117] So it is natural for Lawrence to see closed-up crocuses as the tepees of an Indian encampment, and, once the sun has caused them to open, for him to enter into their fullness of life as completely as the bee that 'stands on his head, kicking slowly'[118] inside a blossom. Repetition, his most dangerous stylistic habit, here becomes the pulse of the flower's existence:

[115] '*Not I, but the Wind...*', p. 177.   [116] *Sketches*, p. 233.   [117] *Ibid.*, p. 226.   [118] *Ibid.*, p. 230.

You cannot believe that the flowers are really still. They are open with such delight, and their pistil-thrust is so red-orange, and they are so many, all reaching out wide and marvellous, that it suggests a perfect ecstasy of radiant, thronging movement, lit-up violet and orange, and surging in some invisible rhythm of concerted, delighted movement. You cannot believe they do not move, and make some sort of crystalline sound of delight. If you sit still and watch, you begin to move with them, like moving with the stars, and you feel the sound of their radiance. All the little cells of the flowers must be leaping with flowery life and utterance. (p. 230)

'Utterance' because, in the end and without Lawrence straining after any message, the rapid flowering and fading speak to his condition. But they do not speak, as flowers traditionally do in poetry, about mutability and mortality. 'Flowery Tuscany' ends in a contrast between the northerner's tragic concept of life as a lighted interval in perpetual darkness and Mediterranean man's instinctive feeling that light is the final absolute:

We can think of death, if we like, as of something permanently intervening between us and the sun: and this is at the root of the southern, underworld idea of death. But this doesn't alter the sun at all. As far as experience goes, in the human race, the one thing that is always there is the shining sun, and dark, shadow is an accident of intervention. (p. 138)

4

The tolling reiterations of one word, 'oblivion', in the poems Lawrence wrote during the last months of his life seem to refute his assurance, in the conclusion to 'Flowery Tuscany', that 'in the sunshine, even death is sunny'. Yet the shadows that give a title to one of the most finely shaped of these last poems are still accidents of intervention. Successively they are night, the dark of the moon, the winter solstice, and the sickness that, while it has made the poet's life 'only the leavings of a life', can still yield place to

> . . . snatches of lovely oblivion, and snatches of renewal
> odd, wintry flowers upon the withered stem, yet new, strange flowers
> such as my life has not brought forth before, new blossoms of me –

which are living proof that

> I am in the hands of the unknown God,
> he is breaking me down to his own oblivion
> to send me forth on a new morning, a new man.

'Oblivion' has more than one meaning in these poems, but annihilation is not one of them. At the start of 'Shadows' it is simply the good night's sleep that was a rare blessing for someone in Lawrence's condition, a blessing in which he put his faith that he could go on writing. God's *own* oblivion is, however, something other than human sleep, just as God for Lawrence, in these 'strange, new flowers' that he produced in his last months, is quite other than an anthropomorphic Creator who conjures a being into existence with a 'hey presto! scarlet geranium!'[119] Rather it is the dark of the Deity, an expectancy of matter that 'becomes at last a clove carnation' because

> The lovely things are god that has come to pass, like Jesus came.
> The rest, the undiscoverable, is the demiurge.

There is a play here on 'rest' (God at rest) and also on 'pass': each avatar of 'The Body of God' (of which these are the concluding lines) passes away in what, in 'God is Born' Lawrence calls 'the great aeons of accomplishment and débâcle', during which, as part of the endless transformation of species, the narcissus lifts its five-point stars from the hitherto flowerless world of mosses and ferns to witness, like all else that is evolved, that there is 'no end to the birth of God'.

It follows that the 'new man' who emerges at the end of 'Shadows' from God's own oblivion may be, over and above the creative self restored by rest, an entirely new and different being. Yet the assertive force of the repeated first person pronouns calls up something more: the idea of individual survival. Can it be, Lawrence asks at the end of his draft of 'The Ship of Death', that the lapse into pure oblivion is also 'procreation'? In the finished 'Ship of Death' that evolved, along with other poems, from the draft, he seems to elaborate this notion, but actually is continuing to hold it at bay; in consequence the little ship (of readiness, acceptance?) provisioned by the soul, although at one moment it has been 'entirely gone', sails home, and the soul 'steps into her house again'. We are back, that is, not with a paradisal immortality, or evolutionary transformation, or transmigration, or even reincarnation, but with a literal awakening to a daylight that may, or may not, be the pledge of any of these:

> Swings the heart, renewed with peace
> Even of oblivion.

A similar quickening has been described before, in similar words. 'His heart seemed to break out of its limits, and take a larger swing' Lawrence wrote of Gilbert Noon's first sight of wild gentians – 'so blue, so much more than heaven blue' – as he had himself seen them for the first time in

---

[119] 'Red Geranium and Godly Mignonette'.

1912, when it seemed to Frieda that 'the gentian yielded up its blueness, its very essence, to him'.[120] Now, in September 1929, he was so ill that Frieda at times feared that an enormous bunch of gentians was the only thing still alive in his room. But 'Glory of Darkness' implies a response to the flowers as vital as that of 1912:

> How deep I have gone
> dark gentians
> since I embarked on your dark blue fringes[121]
> how deep, how deep, how happy!
> What a journey for my soul
> in the blue dark gloom
> of gentians, here in the sunny room!

The lines can imply that the journey has taken many years, during which Lawrence has gone deep in his exploration of the human desire for a consummate union, as well as in his exploration of consummate natural beauty, and has interrelated the two in a way that he will recall in a yet later poem, 'Flowers and Men':

> All I want of you, men and women,
> all I want of you
> is that you shall achieve your own beauty
> as the flowers do.
>
> Oh leave off saying I want you to be savages.
> Tell me, is the gentian savage, at the top of its coarse stem?
> Oh what in you can answer to this blueness?

Primarily, however, the first 'Glory of Darkness' is an immediate response to the flowers under his gaze: a painterly delight at strong colour in sunlight. Yet when Lawrence returns to the theme – still, it would seem, in the presence of the gentians and in the same 'sunny room' – apprehension takes the place of this happy contemplation. Now the flowers point the way to the under-world, and it is 'so dark / in the dark doorway'. He continues with what sounds like a reply to some utterance, some revelation from the flowers:

> Oh, I know –
> Persephone has just gone back
> Down the thickening thickening gloom
> Of dark blue gentians to Pluto . . .

---

[120] *Mr Noon*, p. 109; '*Not I, but the Wind . . .*', p. 33

[121] Deep blue, tall and fringed, these appear to be *Gentianella ciliata*, widespread in southern Germany. Lawrence was back in Bavaria, at Rottach.

'Oh I know' can be affirmative: yes, the Persephone legend and the natural cycle it mythologises reassure me that there is a resurrection. But as the picture builds up of a thickening gloom, of 'all the dead', of a path made by the 'cold, cold' mountain gentians, 'Oh I know' begins to feel like an impatient 'Don't tell me', and the allusion to Persephone the forlorn wish that Lawrence was to add as epigraph to his earlier flower poems: 'Oh Persephone, Persephone, bring me back from Hades the life of a dead man.'

This contradiction between the aesthetic pleasure felt in one version of 'Glory of Darkness' and the sense of a disquieting revelation felt in the other – both of them ways of experiencing the actual flowers – is resolved when these two tentative poems are subsumed in 'Bavarian Gentians'. The catalyst proves to be Lawrence's third and perhaps most instinctive way of looking: his botanical vision, his empathy with a plant's distinguishing habit of growth and his awareness of its life-processes. The unique way a gentian's ribbed, erect corolla flares back abruptly into points gives rise to the torch image, in its turn empowering the poem to take off in an oxymoronic blaze of darkness which eclipses the sunshine – now no more than 'white day'. Here as in Lawrence's earliest poems, white is the colour of death-in-life, and blueness – the heart of the flame – is life-in-death. And as his imagination engages in this way with the flowers, the tone of the poem becomes sumptuous and celebratory, and the verse rhythm takes a longer, a Whitmanesque swing, reminiscent of 'Come lovely and soothing death...' For unlike those of Lawrence's last poems that appear to be concerned with dying but turn out to be largely about remission, 'Bavarian Gentians' does actually confront death. It exists in two versions, and if the second of these has any edge over the more familiar one, it is in its greater self-awareness: the lingering shade of fear in the Everyman question, 'whom have you come for, here in the white-cast day?' that gives way to the resolute 'let me guide myself with the blue, forked torch of a flower' and finally to the personal stance of the concluding lines:

> Give me a flower on a tall stem, and three dark flames,
> For I will go to the wedding, and be a wedding guest,
> At the marriage of the living dark.

A lifelong empathy with plants has made it possible for Lawrence to see that life's flowering does not originate in Persephone's escape to the fields of Enna but – as the Greeks knew – in the embrace of Pluto: the living dark which is the source of all life, not least that of the poetic imagination.

CHAPTER 7

Poetry and photosynthesis

Any reader of poetry who lived through most of the 1900s was bound from time to time to feel that the close relationship between poetry and plant science, which had held ever since Linnaeus, was in danger of being severed. To begin with, the poets who dominated the earlier part of the century declined to write about the green world. Next, botany as the study of whole organisms began to lose its attraction for scientists and their backers. Then, in the century's closing decades, the very plants themselves began to vanish.

Fortunately, disappearance does not always imply extinction. One of England's rarest plants is called the ghost orchid, not just because it has the palest of flowers and no green parts, but also because of the spook-like way it vanishes for years from a particular spot and then re-appears 100 metres away. Cold and dry weather may discourage buds from developing, but the coral-like root can throw out long underground runners in search of better conditions and in the hope of better springs. It had not however surfaced in England for some years, and was giving cause for concern, when Michael Longley sought to conserve it in a terse lyric:

> Added to its few remaining sites will be the stanza
> I compose about leaves like flakes of skin, a colour
> Dithering between pink and yellow, and then the root
> That grows like coral among shadows and leaf-litter.
> Just touching the petals bruises them into darkness.[1]

After four lines of notebook exactitude (though a classicist perhaps should not have spoken of leaves on a plant called *Epipogium aphyllum*), the last line rides a power-surge of feeling, combining as it does regret for a species that may have gone for good with a warning image of the way human heedlessness threatens the rest of the biosphere. By the closing years of the

---

[1] *Selected Poems* (1998), p. 123.

century, many of Longley's readers were aware of and had acted upon that warning. They were helped by the fact that botany, expelled at mid-century by the prongs of biochemistry and molecular biology, had returned through the back door as plant ecology. As for Modernism's abandonment of the natural world, Longley's own work and that of other poets that I consider, if all too briefly, in this final chapter, show them to have triumphantly re-entered the plant kingdom.

I

In the 1920s and 1930s, 'nature poet' was virtually a term of derision. Many explanations for this are on offer. Once Darwinism had the backing of Mendel's re-discovered genetics, there was no longer any possibility of viewing nature as benign to man, in the way that it had been for most nineteenth-century poets. Also played out was the non-moral aestheticism that had replaced an earlier moral earnestness about nature; readers were satiated with the *fin de siècle* beauty of lilies and roses. Modernism, as represented by T. S. Eliot's generation, was essentially an urban movement; if any flower could be found in its back streets, it was a madman's dead geranium. Moreover, as poets' reading of Freud and Jung caused them to shift the poetic focus from the phenomenal world to a multiplicity of internal worlds, those streets became an Unreal City. And although the succeeding generation of poets prided themselves on their return to the external and immediate, they were too taken up with the advances of technology and the impasse of rival ideologies to go about the woodland in search of wild cherry trees. Above all, nature poetry was a casualty of war, and in particular of the First World War; by 1916, Neo-Georgian pastorals bore an unseemly irrelevance to the slaughter that was taking place in Flanders.

There were of course writers, notably Lawrence, whose work made them exceptions to this general abandonment of the natural scene. Thomas Hardy's second career, as novelist reverted to poet, coincided with Robert Frost's first collections. Edward Thomas was made a poet by the war, and Edmund Blunden went back to country concerns after writing powerful war poetry. But while the 'sentry of dark betonies, / The stateliest of small flowers on earth'[2] observed by Frost and Thomas together may linger with the reader, the concern of these poets is primarily with the life of

[2] Edward Thomas, 'The Sun Used to Shine'.

the farming year, the unchanging rhythms of which they contrast with the upheavals of the political world. Changing farming methods, however, have nullified the belief that an old horse drawing a harrow and smoke rising from a bonfire of couch grass 'will go onward the same / Though Dynasties pass'.[3] When last did any of us smell the 'sweet bitter reek' of burning couch grass that Ivor Gurney believed to have been 'dear to the Roman perhaps'?[4]

To a minor degree the tradition of the poet–botanist was kept alive by Geoffrey Grigson, and that of the botanising parson–poet by Andrew Young. Both, however, are more widely remembered for their prose writings: Grigson for the treasure chest of plant names and plant lore that he called *The Englishman's Flora*, and Young for *A Prospect of Flowers* which, as the title from Marvell hints, is largely a consideration of poets' botanising, and in which he neatly deflates the portentousness of Tennyson's lines about the flower in the crannied wall – 'But was that a way for a poet to start a Contemplation Upon Flowers, to tear one up by the roots?'[5] (A less overblown subject for contemplation than 'what God and Man is' would have been the resourcefulness with which the fruits of ivy-leaved toadflax – which Young believed to be the plant in question – twist on their stalks and, as it were, thrust their seeds back into the crannies.)

During the first half of the twentieth century, then, poetry about the green world became infrequent, not to say rare. This makes all the more notable the appearance in the 1940s of a group of poems that, it has been said, 'deserve to cling to future anthologies like Marvell's "Garden" or Wordsworth's poem about the daffodils'.[6] A mere baker's dozen in number, they owe their being to a childhood that was, quite literally, roses all the way. Their writer, Theodore Roethke, grew up inside a vast greenhouse, or more accurately a chain of greenhouses, where his father provided the warmth, light, nutrients and skilful handling that caused roses and carnations, in defiance of the Michigan winter outside, to bloom as in the Garden of Eden. Like Eden, too, this Paradise was soon lost. When Roethke was in his early teens his father sold his share of the business to a brother whose mismanagement of it led shortly afterwards to his

---

[3] Thomas Hardy, 'In Time of "The Breaking of Nations"'.

[4] Gurney's post-war poem 'Brown Earth Look' is a kind of rejoinder to Hardy's wartime one. The exhaustion of the labourer who has been digging out couch grass brings to the poet's mind the struggle for life in starving Europe.

[5] *A Prospect of Flowers* (1945), p. 102. A predecessor in this field was Vernon Rendall: *Wild Flowers in Literature* (1934).

[6] Louis Martz, 'A greenhouse Eden', in Arnold Stein (ed.), *Theodore Roethke: Essays on the Poetry* (1965), p. 27.

committing suicide, just before Otto Roethke's own hard death from cancer. Twenty years on from these traumatic events, his son began to write what are known as the greenhouse poems.[7]

It is perhaps because this world was so finally lost by the 1940s that the most impressive poem in the sequence is about an occasion when the enterprise came close to foundering. 'Big Wind' recalls a winter storm that not only threatened the huge structure but also caused its water supply to fail. Family and employees worked all night, keeping the boilers going with liquid manure and stuffing gaps in the panes with burlap –

> But she rode it out,
> That old rose-house,
> She hove into the teeth of it,
> The core and pith of that ugly storm,
> Ploughing with her stiff prow,
> Bucking into the wind-waves
> That broke over the whole of her,
> Flailing her side with spray,
> Flinging long strings of wet across the roof-top,
> Finally veering, wearing themselves out, merely
> Whistling thinly under the wind vents;
> She sailed into the calm morning
> Carrying her full cargo of roses.

Like the company of a ship bearing wartime supplies, the greenhouse workers comprise a tightly controlled society. A Prussian perfectionist is at the helm: 'all night watering roses, his feet blue in rubber boots' or transplanting seedlings with 'a single twist of the thumbs, a tamping and turning'.[8] Otto Roethke's dedication and dexterity (good virtues for a poet to inherit) are felt throughout the sequence. The Prospero of this glassed-in island, he is no less autocratic than Shakespeare's character, so that at one time his son, resentfully working for his pocket money by crawling to weed beneath the concrete benches, is playing Caliban and at another, as he dangerously surveys a wider world from the greenhouse roof, is Ariel anticipating his freedom. But he remains under the spell of the magician who is able to resurrect such seemingly dead matter as stem-cuttings: 'Their intricate stem-fur dries; / But still the delicate slips keep coaxing up water.'[9] The same cuttings are re-visited in a second poem; and now the poet's

---

[7] Biographical facts are drawn from Allan Seager, *The Glass House: the Life of Theodore Roethke* (1968). Quotations are from *Collected Poems* (1966).
[8] 'Transplanting'. [9] 'Cuttings'.

feelings have shifted from wonder that cut tissue can put out new growth to empathy with the reborn plant:

> This urge, wrestle, resurrection of dry sticks,
> Cut stems struggling to put down feet;
> What saint strained so much,
> Rose on such lopped limbs to a new life?
>
> I can hear, underground, that sucking and sobbing,
> In my veins, in my bones I feel it, –
> The small waters seeping upward
> The tight grains parting at last.
> When sprouts break out,
> Slippery as fish,
> I quail, lean to beginnings, sheath-wet.   ('Cuttings, later')

The adult questioning with which the poem began has made way, as in a trance, to the open consciousness of a young child for whom the life around is not yet distinct from his own, and has finally regressed, in those remarkable closing lines, to the infant's slither into neo-natal life, symbol-ised by the cutting's visible 'take'.

The greenhouse provides conditions that not only conjure life from the seemingly lifeless but also give fragile seedlings the security to grow into plants that culminate in 'The whole flower extending outward, / Stretching and reaching'.[10] Everything burgeons in this artificial warmth; even in the dark cellars bulbs break out of boxes, etiolated shoots dangle and droop. Floriculture at the time was nothing if not organic – 'what a congress of stinks!' – so that not only plants but fungal and bacterial forms of life as well 'pulse with the knocking pipes' and the very soil 'kept breathing a small breath'.[11] Yet the perfect blooms that are the end product of all this cherishing are hardly visualised. For one thing, they are above the child's head. Much later, in a collection posthumously published in 1964, Roethke recalls how his father lifted him up

. . . high over the four-foot stems, the Mrs Russells, and his own elaborate hybrids,
And how those flowerheads seemed to flow towards me, to beckon me, only a
     child, out of myself.   ('The Rose')

But from this distant perspective, recollections are perhaps too rose-tinted: 'what need for heaven then / With that man and those roses?' The green-house poems of the 1940s are, one feels, more faithful to experiences that

---

[10] 'Transplanting'.   [11] 'Root Cellar'; 'Forcing House'.

were at the time a blend of pleasure and awe, so that in the original sequence the presence of the flowers, like that of Roethke's father, can be disturbing in a way that recalls Wordsworth's experience of low breathings after him. Far from seeking an embrace, as some of the other flowers that sway towards him appear to be doing, the epiphyte orchids lean down 'adder-mouthed' from their containers –

> And at night,
> The faint moon falling through whitewashed glass,
> The heat going down
> So their musty smell comes even stronger,
> Drifting down from their mossy cradles:
> So many devouring infants!
> Soft luminescent fingers,
> Lips neither dead nor alive,
> Loose ghostly mouths
> Breathing.   ('Orchids')

Scents like these are more than odours: they are the aura of each plant, confirming its presence as an individual life; thus carnations, in the poem so titled, gain their place in the poet's memory by their exhalation of

> A crisp hyacinthine coolness,
> Like that clear autumnal weather of eternity
> The windless perpetual morning above a September cloud.

In its original, 1948, edition, *The Lost Son*, of which these greenhouse poems form the first part, ends with another sequence, comprising four longish poems that bear witness to the attack of mania Roethke suffered between the writing of the two groups. Each of these later poems opens with frenetic images that intensify and darken in the central section but then give place to a sense of release and reintegration: the turning point every time is an escape from the madhouse to the greenhouse. In the first, which is also the title poem, the poet recalls hiding all night among the flowers until, in the chilly dawn, a 'scurry of warm' signalled that his father had arrived and opened the steam-cocks, with the result that the child could become part of the plants' joyous and reviving response to light and heat. Similarly in the fourth section of the next poem, Roethke exorcises his mind's disarray by conjuring up the banked lilies and cyclamens of that ordered world – 'The leaves, the leaves become me! / The tendrils have me!' The third poem is set in the outdoors of a later stage in growing up, and here the moment of revelation takes the form of a defining consciousness that enables him to see 'the separateness of all things'. Finally, in the last movement of the

fourth poem, the Traherne-like trance of the greenhouse existence passes
into an adult serenity that links past happiness to the present contentment
of a life brought under control, imaged as the handling of a small boat.
The poem ends with the reward of this maturation: the 'contained flower'
of art.

> To have the whole air!
> The light, the full sun
> Coming down on the flowerheads,
> The tendrils turning slowly,
> A slow snail-lifting, liquescent;
> To be by the rose
> Rising slowly out of its bed,
> Still as a child in its first loneliness;
> To see cyclamen veins become clearer in early sunlight,
> And mist lifting out of the brown cattails;
> To stare into the after-light, the glitter left on the lake's surface,
> When the sun has fallen behind a wooden island;
> To follow the drops sliding from a lifted oar,
> Held up, while the rower breathes, and the small boat
>   drifts quietly shoreward;
> To know that the light falls and fills, often without our knowing,
> As an opaque vase fills to the brim from a quick pouring,
> Fills and trembles at the edge yet does not flow over,
> Still holding and feeding the stem of the contained flower.

This is a haunting passage, but it is also haunted. Eliot's influence was
not easy to escape at the time, and Roethke, in these ambitious longer
poems, often succumbed to the lure of the older poet's imagery and
rhythms. In contrast, the actual greenhouse poems are wholly original in
substance and style. Their unique purity, immediately recognised by
Kenneth Burke ('Ted's gong struck then, when he hit that greenhouse
line'[12]) made Roethke's reputation as a poet in what was only his second
publication. Over and above their intrinsic quality, the subject matter of
these poems appealed to critics and general readers alike; the feeling that
the vegetable world was a poet's natural habitat persisted, in defiance of
Modernist prejudice.

   If in the first part of the twentieth century, nature poetry was very widely
proscribed by the Modernists, another cultural movement was soon to
wreak havoc upon another staple of earlier poetry: the association of
women with flowers. Compared to the first and mainly political women's

---

[12] Quoted by Seager, *The Glass House*, p. 144.

movement, the wave of 1960s feminism was seismic in its effect. In the field of letters, not only were as many women as men writing noteworthy verse, they were also handling themes and motifs traditional to love poetry in a directly confrontational way. Two that they tackled with special zest were women as recipients of the gift of flowers, and women imaged as themselves flower-like. Sylvia Plath's 'Tulips' comes to mind as a striking example of the former. But I want to pause here over another feminist poet's handling of the herself-a-fairer-flower theme, for the reason that a comparison of her poem with another written forty years earlier serves virtually to catapult us into the changed social world that confronted poets in the second half of the century.

William Carlos Williams was unusual among Modernists in that he had no prejudice against nature poetry and in fact had a fine eye for botanic detail. This may help explain the popularity of the poem he wrote in the 1920s that begins

> Her body is not so white as
> anemone petals nor so smooth – nor
> so remote a thing. It is a field
> of the wild carrot taking
> the field by force . . .

'Queen Anne's Lace', the title of Williams's poem, is the American name for the wild carrot, which is distinguished from all other white umbellifers by having, at the centre of the cluster of white florets that makes up each of the plant's flower-heads, a single deeply coloured floret.[13] The function of this eluded Charles Darwin and is still unexplained. 'We speculate, following Darwin (1888), that the dark central floret may now be functionless and possibly represents a trait that has persisted long after its original function has been lost', write two modern investigators[14]. So in a poem called 'The Knot', written in 1965, Adrienne Rich was at liberty to imbue it with a startling personal meaning:

> In the heart of the queen anne's lace, a knot of blood.
> For years I never saw it,

---

[13] In the common language that divides us, the British sometimes use the name 'Queen Anne's lace' for the plant more widely known as 'cow parsley'. The discrepancy led Sarah Maguire, in her anthology *Flora Poetica* (2001), which is arranged in botanic families, to present the two poems here discussed as referring to different plants.

[14] E. Lamborn and J. Ollerton, 'Experimental assessment of the functional morphology of inflorescences of *Daucus carota* (Apiaceae): testing the "fly catcher effect"', *Functional Ecology* 14 (2000), p. 445.

years of metallic vision,
spears glancing off a bright eyeball,

suns off a Swiss lake.
a foaming meadow; the milky way;

and there, all along, the tiny dark-red spider
sitting in the whiteness of the bridal web,

waiting to plunge his crimson knifepoint
into the white apparencies.

Little wonder the eye, healing, sees
for a long time through a mist of blood.

The full significance of that casual 'For years I never saw it' only strikes home
when we get to 'the bridal web' and connect this image of billowing lace with
the title. The speaker was, for years, blinded by a dazzling, romantic concept
of marriage. Her disenchantment seizes upon the tiny red flower surrounded
by lacy whiteness to create an image as disturbing as the one Shakespeare
gives Leontes when he has him say, 'I have drunk and seen the spider.' Rich's
'foaming meadow', however, suggests that the effectiveness of 'The Knot'
owes more to a more recent poet: to the inspiration – only provocation
might be the better word – of further lines in Williams's poem:

Each flower is a hand's span
of her whiteness. Wherever
his hand has lain there is
a tiny purple blemish. Each part
is a blossom under his touch
to which the fibres of her being
stem one by one, each to its end,
until the whole field is a
white desire . . .

What would have struck readers, in 1925, as a mildly daring description of
sexual arousal, in 1965 makes Rich see red, on account of its masterful tone
and its calm assumption that gratification is the man's gift. Added to which,
the insistence on whiteness would have jarred upon her sensibilities as a
campaigner for Black civil rights – a reminder that feelings about race as well
as gender could, in the turbulent 1960s, impinge on the most unlikely
material. But anger at what is in Rich's eyes the elder poet's male chauvin-
ism is uppermost, and it joins with the frustration she herself experienced
in a conventional marriage to create a very powerful poem. Even an

unsympathetic reader has to admire her incisive handling of the floral motif (whereas Williams does not quite know what to do with it) and the way that her rhythmic and lexical control of her bitterness makes it possible for her to transcend it in the final lines and so restore balance to the poem's ending.

2

As the twentieth century advanced, some poets at least found new uses for the age-old connection between women and flowers. But very few indeed of them sought to connect flowers with God, even though that conjunction had been a staple of poetry since the Middle Ages and had been supremely expressed as recently as 1918, in sonnets of Gerard Manley Hopkins that had been held back for half a century. One voice that for upwards of sixty years from the 1940s on sustained the carol of creation, and especially the part in it of growing things, was that of Richard Wilbur. But in what often seemed the worst of times there were few to share even his muted certainty that, in the end, all manner of things shall be well. For if we are so rash as to try to define the dominant temper of a whole hundred years, what distinguishes the twentieth century from all others is not this or that social revolution or technological advance, but its record of unremitting violence. Total war, genocide and terrorism made it, in the words of one historian, 'the most murderous century of which we have record'.[15] From Passchendaele to Srebrenice, the names of its killing fields have engraved themselves deep in the Western consciousness.

A poet wanders into an unimproved meadow in June, his or her mind full of some private emotion that may conjoin with that roused by the field's flowers, and if his or her awareness of these presences is perceptive enough the result of this conjunction is, as Browning said of another creative art, not a third chord, but a star: nebulous at this stage, but capable of contracting into a poem. But what if the thoughts the poet brings are of Auschwitz or Hiroshima? The difficulties that then arise are well illustrated in a poem of the 1960s, one of fifteen 'Flower Poems' that formed part of Jon Silkin's *Nature with Man* (1965). Silkin appended to the volume a short essay explaining that his method was to take a close look at each plant and, in making its appearance and habit 'substantial', to suggest to the reader certain correspondences with humans and their predicaments. There is, he adds, no question of an anthropocentric replacement, of one element

---

[15] Eric Hobsbawm, *Age of Extremes: the Short Twentieth Century, 1914–1991* (1995), p. 13.

sliding over the other. 'I am trying to find some common denominator that will pull together these two kinds of life.'[16]

This promises an interesting attempt to deal afresh with the pathetic fallacy. But the poems themselves, though highly praised at the time, have not worn well. One reason for this may be implicit in the poem in question, which is called 'Milkmaids' (another name for *Cardamine pratensis*, or lady's smock) and is rather different from the rest in that it is based not on an affinity but on a confrontation. It gets off to a good start by calling up the plant's light vigour of leaf, stem, and finally flower –

> From each undomestic
> Flare, four petals; thrown wide; a flexible
> Unplanned exuberance.

The plants are 'twice free'[17] because their tender and wild strength enables them to 'wander' – presumably, seed themselves – across open fields until they are halted by barbed wire and, beyond it, the sight of starving men. Aghast at the prisoners' suffering, the flowers, in Silkin's own paraphrase 'absorb the experience of the human beings and are changed . . . so deeply that this change is inherited by their children'.[18]

This confrontation, seen as causing 'total distress' to the flowers, leaves the reader also in some distress. To link the grim historical facts of the Nazi final solution to 1960ish fancies about plant awareness is, on the face of it, so inept that we begin to search for a sub-text that will offer an escape from our unease. The sub-text I would suggest is this: what Silkin, who was born in 1933, calls the 'untrammelled consciousness' of the flowers is actually that of a young Jew who is just leaving childhood when the full horror of the extermination camps becomes known: revelations that leave him a victim to survivor's guilt – the debilitating twentieth-century malady, irrational and irremediable, that is to overshadow the remainder of his work. 'I speak of the six million / and do not shave' he writes nearly forty years later in a poem about a blossoming tree. For whatever the power of the plant's 'incipience of fruit' to 'make plump / the maidenly flowers',

> to what is torn,
> wrenched, shot or beaten, it can bring
> nothing,

and as the light on the flowers fades, 'what droops away / is beauty as consolation'.[19]

---

[16] *Nature with Man* (1965), p. 54.   [17] *Ibid.*, p. 45.   [18] *Ibid.*, p. 56.
[19] *Testament without Breath* (1998), p. 21.

This repudiation of the beautiful was already evident in the 1967 Flower Poems. What, they ask, have the hard, teeth-like flowers and fat, sheathe-like leaves of lilies-of-the-valley 'to do with beauty?' Or the 'yellow brutal glare' of the dandelion's 'small, coarse, sharp petals?'[20] When readers complain, as I have heard them do, that for all his painstaking, cerebral descriptions Silkin's flowers are not *there*, they are really saying that enjoyment is missing. 'Stern as a pin' (to make use of his own odd characterisation of a harebell), Silkin looks at each flower with a grim determination to discover human analogies, but hardly ever with loving and informed insight into the processes that have brought it into being. For such an insight, empowering its possessor to relate his experience of green nature to his no less first-hand experience of living in murderous times, we have to turn to an Irish poet who is at the same time a born naturalist: Michael Longley.

Longley is a field botanist of the traditional kind, and in 'Alibis' he shows that tradition to be socially complex:

> My botanical studies took me among
> Those whom I now consider my ancestors.
> I used to appear to them at odd moments –
> With buckets of water in the distance, or
> At the campfire, my arms full of snowy sticks.
> Beech mast, hedgehogs, cresses were my diet,
> My medicaments badger grease and dock leaves.
>
> A hard life. Nevertheless, they named after me
> A clover that flourished on those distant slopes.[21]

The lines recall the gentlemen plant-hunters of the previous century – William Hooker perhaps in Iceland, Joseph Hooker in the Himalayas – but the speaker finds his alternative self in those who waited on them and who knew plants primarily as food or medicines. Clare comes to mind; and the concluding lines may touch on Crabbe who, it will be recalled, regretted *not* having a species of *Trifolium* named after him. Longley resembles these two poet–botanists in another way: he likes to use the odd flower as a bookmark. One such, its 'calyx, filament, / Anther staining' his pocket flora, typifies the way that just handling the book brings back searches in sodden pastures, where a sudden glimpse leads on to the

---

[20] *Nature with Man*, pp. 40, 38.   [21] *Poems 1963–1983* (1985), p. 104.

dual pleasures of recognition and of naming the find by a traditional and euphonious name:

> Where bell and bugle,
> A starry cluster
> Or butterfly wing
> Convey me further
>
> And in memory
> And hands deposit
> Blue periwinkles,
> Meadowsweet, tansy.[22]

This poem, 'Flora', is for Longley unusually simple, but then so is its subject, the single-minded happiness of the flower-seeker. A deeper dimension is given to this happiness in the third part of 'Spring Tide', which describes a flower foray on the coast of County Mayo, when the ebb of a spring tide offers the poet the chance to explore otherwise inaccessible dunes and flats:

> The spring tide has ferried jelly fish
> To the end of the lane, pinks, purples,
> Wet flowers beside the floating cow-pats.
> The zig-zags I make take me among
> White cresses and brookweed, lousewort,
> Water plantain and grass of parnassus
> With engraved capillaries, ivory sheen:
> By a dry-stone wall in the dune slack
> The greenish sepals, the hidden blush
> And a lip's red veins and yellow spots –
> Marsh helleborine waiting for me
> To come and go with the spring tide.[23]

With a botanist's feeling for plant communities, Longley notes common plants alongside less common ones such as the grass-of-parnassus that quickens his pleasure into a descriptive phrase or two, until he reaches a dune slack – a boggy patch between sand-hills, possessing its own small but distinctive flora. What happens next is less a description than an act of recognition, as the one indigenous orchid that (it has been said) meets everybody's expectation of what an orchid should look like reveals itself feature by feature. But at this point too, as Neil Corcoran has noted, 'the line-break and the cumulative syntactical sway of the penultimate line dramatise both longing and disappointment: not "Marsh helleborine waiting for me," alas, but "Marsh helleborine waiting for me / To come

---

[22] *Ibid.*, p. 121.   [23] *Ibid.*, p. 156.

and go with the spring tide.'"[24] In their inaccessible retreat the orchids, for all their comparative rarity, have a security that the poet does not enjoy. If he is not to suffer the jellyfishes' fate in reverse, he must watch the tide that waits for no man. Somewhere around too is the Dickensian euphemism of going out with the tide, for Longley's stripped-down lines repeatedly make us aware of what is left out.

Poems such as these account for Longley being typecast by readers of his earlier collections as a nature poet; a labelling updated by the environmental concerns he has since shown in, for example, his introduction to a book on the flowers of County Clare's botanic Eden, the Burren:

On my most recent visit to The Burren I wrote the names of the plants into my notebook as usual, a fresh page for each location. This time the names arranged themselves rhythmically, as though to release their power into prayers or spells. Campion, samphire, milkwort, lavender – these at Pol Salach. And on Black Head, crowberry, juniper, saxifrage, willow. Prayers for what is irreplaceable. Spells muttered in the shadow of exploitation and destruction.[25]

The destruction overshadowing the Burren is the harm that mass tourism could do to its unique flora. But at the time these words were written in 1991 a more immediate destructiveness was threatening the poet's own habitat, which is and always has been Belfast. From 1969 (the date of his first collection) to the Good Friday Agreement of 1998 which instigated a fragile peace, Ulster and its chief city in particular were torn apart by atrocities on both sides of the Protestant–Catholic divide. If Longley's work is approached from another direction than that of his 'botanical studies' – say, that signposted by his recent re-assemblage of some sixty poems under the title *Cenotaph of Snow* – he appears a poet much possessed by violent death, whether of the victims of the Spanish Civil War, the Blitz, the Holocaust or the Troubles. Other poems pay homage to the combatant poets of two world wars. Others again are translations from Homer, whose *Iliad* is for Longley 'the most powerful of all war poems as well as being the greatest poem about death',[26] and these need no more than an evocative title –'Butchers', say, for Homer's account of the massacre of Penelope's suitors and maids – and such a small change as 'bog-asphodels' for Homer's flowers of the underworld, to enable the reader to connect

---

[24] 'My botanical studies: the poetry of natural history in Michael Longley', in Alan J. Peacock and Kathleen Devine (eds.), *The Poetry of Michael Longley* (2000), p. 108.

[25] E. Charles Nelson, *The Burren: a Companion to the Wildflowers of an Irish Limestone Wilderness* (1991), p. vii.

[26] *Cenotaph of Snow: Sixty Poems about War* (2003), Introduction.

them with more recent violence: in this case, the 500 and more murders carried out in the 1970s by the Shankill Road Butchers.

So if on the one hand Longley's knowledge of the Burren's flora issues in a poem addressed to Our Lady of the Fertile Rocks (a concept that, coming from a 'Protestant' poet, is itself something of an anti-sectarian challenge), on the other hand it shapes 'The Ice Cream Man', which is about a particularly ruthless Belfast killing:

> Rum and raisin, vanilla, butter-scotch, walnut, peach:
> You would rhyme off the flavours. That was before
> They murdered the ice-cream man on the Lisburn Road
> And you bought carnations to lay outside his shop.
> I named for you all the wild flowers of the Burren
> I had seen in one day: thyme, valerian, loosestrife,
> Meadowsweet, tway blade, crowfoot, ling, angelica,
> Herb robert, marjoram, cow parsley, sundew, vetch,
> Mountain avens, wood sage, ragged robin, stitchwort,
> Yarrow, lady's bedstraw. bindweed, bog pimpernel.[27]

The third and fourth lines of this poem register, and reproduce in the reader, both the poet's shock at the murder and his anxiety for his young daughter, whose delighted recitations of ice-cream flavours it has silenced. Childhood seems left behind in the act of bringing, as a tribute to the shopkeeper, one of those cellophane-wrapped bunches of florists' blooms that pile up at every scene of sudden urban death – saddest of all conjunctions between flowers and violence. So the rest of the poem sets about replacing the memory of this ritual with images from a different Ireland. 'I named for you' can mean both 'I told you about' and 'I recited on your behalf': the litany of wild flower names is both a distraction of the child's thoughts and a prayer or at the very least a spell aiming to protect her, so that the names fall into the incantatory rhythm (though now in alexandrines, not pentameters) that he speaks of in the prose passage already quoted. Some of the names comfort by their familiarity, others by their hint of agreeable tastes, others by their suggestion of healing properties. 'Loosestrife' acquired its English name in the sixteenth century as a translation of Pliny's *lysimachia*, 'an end to strife', and this surely is the poem's wider plea, behind its concern for the mental harm a terrorist act may have done to one child.

There is no amen to the prayer. Sentimentality is avoided by an inconclusiveness that may suggest a dying-away into despair, though it could also hint at the certainty of there always being more flowers to follow. Nor does

---

[27] *Gorse Fires* (1991), p. 49.

Longley sentimentalise the culture of that other Ireland the flowers come from. Peasant life produces its own atrocities in the cruelty that ignorance and prejudice visit upon the vulnerable, and especially upon children. In the last decades of the last century there was added to our awareness of living in overtly violent times a growing disquiet over hidden abuses within the family or the clan. There are two victims of such ill treatment in 'Self-heal',[28] which begins with a woman recalling her attempt, as a young girl, to befriend a boy who is stunted in mind and body:

> I wanted to teach him the names of flowers,
> Self-heal and centaury; on the long acre
> Where cattle never graze, bog asphodel.

But the process is slow, and the poem names no more flowers until the speaker recalls the day she

> pulled a cuckoo-pint apart
> To release the giddy insects from their cell.
> Gently he slipped his hand between my thighs.

Unprepared and shocked, the girl runs to tell 'them'. The boy is savagely punished, and in consequence himself becomes brutalised into a tormentor of animals.

Of the four flowers named here, two are linked, and the other two have each a double poetic function. 'Cuckoo-pint' (pintle, penis) was long ago so named by the 'they' who would have seen the girl's action of exposing the spadix in the spathe as proof of their belief that she was 'leading him on', although for her the action is as innocent as is her use of the name. And there is a further irony in 'release'. None of the victims has been liberated: not the hidebound community, nor the girl now burdened with guilt, nor the boy whom she sees, at the poem's close, as having himself become

> the ram tangled in barbed wire
> That he stoned to death when they set him free.

Suddenly we see the significance of the villagers, insensitive to other vulnerabilities, protecting their cattle from the bog asphodel. This plant, the beauty of which Longley has celebrated in a recent poem,[29] is a danger to livestock. Its specific name is *ossifragum*, and in Donegal it is 'cruppany grass', because it is believed to give sheep cruppany, or bone stiffness.[30] In

---

[28] *Poems 1963–1983*, p. 163.   [29] *Snow Water* (2004), p. 12.
[30] *The Englishman's Flora*, p. 429. The toxin has recently been shown to cause obstruction of the animal's gall-duct.

the same way the girl's kindness, morally beautiful in its origin, leads to two lives suffering irreversible damage. Mercifully, there is far more healing than venom in the plant world, and the very act of recall that constitutes the poem represents the self-heal of the title. But because that does not of itself suffice, self-heal is conjoined with centaury. Nature, even an agnostic poet concedes, has to be allied to grace as well as to art; it is necessary to bring together 'verse / And herb, plant and prayer, to stop the bleeding'.[31] In Ireland, centaury, traditionally a bitter but curative herb, is also a bene-dictory plant, sacred to the Virgin.[32]

The curative properties of plants, until lately humans' chief hope of healing, are thus the link between Longley's botanical pursuits and the thirty years of fratricidal violence (his own phrase)[33] that coincided with much of his poetic career. In 'Bog Cotton', he conjoins both with his admiration for the poets of two world wars by calling the white down of this sedge 'a desert flower' in a direct address to Keith Douglas, whose 'Desert Flowers' had contrasted the sporadic though deadly violence of the Western Desert campaign in 1943 with the mass slaughter symbolised by the profuse poppies of Flanders. Between his recall of each of these greater conflicts and its poet-victims, Longley 'makes room' for his own emblem of the Irish Troubles:

> (It hangs on by a thread, denser than thistledown,
> Reluctant to fly, a weather vane that traces
> The flow of cloud shadow over monotonous bog –
> And useless too, though it might well bring to mind
> The plumpness of pillows, the staunching of wounds,
>
> Rags torn from a petticoat and soaked in water
> And tied to the bushes around some holy well
> As though to make a hospital of the landscape –
> Cures and medicines as far as the horizon
> Which nobody harvests except with the eye.)[34]

The passage powerfully conjures up the hopelessness that must often have assailed those who lived through Ulster's three decades of violence. They could see no end to the injuries inflicted on the province; there was incessant talk of reconciliation, but always a reluctance to take the risks involved. Yet the parenthesis (in which we can perhaps detect the recall of

---

[31] *Poems 1963–1983*, p. 159.
[32] *The Englishman's Flora*, p. 297. Is it coincidental that Gerard, whom Grigson quotes, says that centaury opens 'the stoppings of the liver, gall and spleen'?
[33] *Cenotaph of Snow*, Introduction.   [34] *Poems 1963–1983*, p. 167.

another war poet admired by Longley, David Jones)[35] *does* close, and on the knowledge that the landscape in fact abounds in curative herbs: a knowledge that enables Longley to transcend near-despair by remembering the example of Isaac Rosenberg who, in 'Break of Day in the Trenches' thought of the fallen as countless poppies, before putting a real one, a little dusty, behind his ear.

When peace of a kind was achieved on Good Friday, 1998, Longley commemorated it in 'At Poll Salach',[36] a four-line poem with a pointedly Yeatsian sub-title, 'Easter Sunday, 1998', that brings together all the characteristics of this poet–botanist at his mature best: a lapidary terseness; delicate handling of a personal relationship; a muted self-irony; the sense of a dear peculiar place; and a descriptive precision that is heightened if we remember that the fen violet of the Burren turloughs is a pale sky-blue in colour:

> While I was looking for Easter snow on the hills
> You showed me, like a concentration of violets
> Or a fragment from some future unimagined sky,
> A single spring gentian shivering at our feet.

3

Ted Hughes's way of looking at growing things is in many ways the antithesis of Michael Longley's. Far from being antidotes to violence, the plants in his poetry as often as not embody it: every thistle is 'a revengeful burst / Of resurrection'.[37] 'Snowdrop', in his second collection (*Lupercal*, 1960), is typical:

> Now is the globe shrunk tight
> Round the mouse's dulled wintering heart.
> Weasel and crow, as if moulded in brass,
> Move through an outer darkness
> Not in their right minds,
> With the other deaths. She, too, pursues her ends,
> Brutal as the stars of this month,
> Her pale head heavy as metal.

Despite the title, it looks at first as if animals will dominate here as they tend to do in most of Hughes's early 'nature' poems, where if plants occur at all they are seen in zoomorphic terms: sycamore leaves are lizards

---

[35] *In Parenthesis* (1937). [36] *The Weather in Japan*, p. 17.
[37] 'Thistles'. Quotations are from *Collected Poems* (2003).

spreading enormous ruffs, a holly tree recoils 'like a squid into clouds of protection'.[38] But when, after a delay that helps to suggest the effort involved, the snowdrop does appear, it is the most alive thing in the poem; in contrast to the dormouse in torpor and the predators kept going by a zombie-like hunt for food, the flower is making its supreme bid for existence, pushing through the hard ground with a thrust comparable, *pari passu*, to that of a rocket engine.

The violence for which Hughes's early poetry was often adversely criticised is in fact energy, and not only energy conceived in metaphysical terms as a Blakean eternal delight, although Blake's tiger prowls through these early volumes. First and foremost it is energy as physical fact, the energy that has dominated scientific thinking ever since it was quantified in 1905: the energy that holds entropy at bay in 'Crow Hill', where, in the austere Yorkshire landscape,

> Between the weather and the rock
> Farmers make a little heat

– the heat of the farm animals which 'hold off the sky' and, by their trampling, help the inanimate forces that turn rock to soil.

> What humbles these hills has raised
> The arrogance of blood and bone,
> And thrown the hawk upon the wind,
> And lit the fox in the dripping ground.

Marvellous lines: but something is missing from this celebration of life's resistance against elemental odds. Those 'pigs upon delicate feet' need feeding if they are to tread the soil and manure it into the bargain. The transfer of energy can only begin at one point: with the primary producers that pass it on to the plant-eaters, great and small, and so to the top consumers, hawk, fox and – man eats pig – humans (processes in which denizens of the other kingdoms, fungal and bacterial, also play their part).

The missing factor appears in a poem written some four years later, the ambiguously titled 'Still Life'. The outcrop stone of the moor is seen as 'miserly' of itself, confident that it can guard its bulk to the end of time –

> It expects to be in at the finish.
> Being ignorant of this other, this harebell,

---

[38] 'Sunday Evening'; 'Trees'.

That trembles, as under threats of death,
In the summer-turf's heat-rise,
And in which – filling veins
Any known name of blue would bruise
Out of existence – sleeps, recovering,

The maker of the sea.

This final image takes us to the interface of the animate and inanimate: life's beginning in the sea, personified perhaps as a blue-skinned avatar of the Creator. But more simply and immediately it is the power of even so fragile-seeming a plant to share in vegetation's work of breaking down rock into soil; a process paralleled in the destruction of derelict factory walls by nettle, bramble and sycamore (the last, though decapitated, growing 'five or six heads, depraved with life') that Hughes finds has begun when he returns to his native valley in *Remains of Elmet* (1979):

Before these chimneys can flower again
They must fall into the only future, into earth.

('Lumb Chimneys')

Around the time this was written, Hughes put his harebell to a more exact use than he had done in 'Still Life', by contrasting its perfect fitness to its environment with the doomed existence of another creature that could not adapt. The Irish elk survived the last Ice Age only to be made extinct by subsequent changes in the vegetation. One theory is that as scrub became upland bog the elk (really a deer) could not obtain from its grazing sufficient calcium to build both its bones and its gigantic horns ; and since the latter continued to be sexually selected for, the rest of its physiology weakened. It is not perhaps too fanciful to feel the animal's faltering vitality in the spaced-out closing lines of the poem:

The waters of Elk have gone.

The bog-cotton drank them.

And now the memorial of Elk
Is the harebell

Feeding downwind.   ('Irish Elk')

That final image of the flowers bent to the ground on wind-pliable stalks is not only visually pleasing; it conveys the idea of security (downwind, you scent a predator before it scents you), a security not shared by the great deer, for all its armature.

But the greatest security of living things lies of course in their power to reproduce, a power the Irish elk ultimately lost and which is the theme of another poem that contrasts stone and flower. This time, the stone of 'time-blackened cathedrals' stands for what Hughes sees as a life-denying religion, which in the end proves as vulnerable as are stone outcrops and derelict masonry before the onslaught of self-replicating life. The plum-blossom as it opens its

> Volcanoes of frailty –
> Mouths without hunger but to utter
> Love, love to each other

is reducing past, present and future to

> Luckless snow-crystals
> In the silent laughter
> Of these raw barbarians, these burning hairy mouths.
>
> ('Plum Blossom')

The snow image, however, works two ways; one touch of frost, and the volcanoes of frailty could be quenched. Hughes grew up in an ice-scoured landscape that imparted to him a vivid awareness that he lived in an interglacial period. In 'Heather', the dominant plant of the Yorkshire moors, ground into existence – in a brilliant use of a biblical image – between the upper millstone of harsh weather and the lower millstone of thin coarse soil (millstone grit), listens apprehensively 'For the star-drift / Of the returning ice'. Meanwhile, the sun is shining, bees are gathering the heather's nectar, people are out enjoying themselves; life literally *goes on* by means of a continual transfer of energy through the ecosystem. If the grouse (we remember they feed on young heather shoots) are active, so are the 'gunshots', while other secondary consumers in the food chain are hinted at in the nectar being 'keen as adder's venom' (a hot day brings out vipers) and, more exotically, in the 'grizzly bear-dark pelt' of the heather-clad skyline, the contours of which suggest the browsing of herbivore flocks. Real or imaged, all this activity is a passing on of vigour: the very opposite process to the ice sheet's annihilation of plant life.

Hughes's liveliest celebration of the part vegetation plays in sustaining the web of life comes in poems written with child readers and listeners principally in mind. 'Hay', 'Barley' and 'The Golden Boy' are about the significance grasses hold for man and beast. These are songs of triumph: genuine harvest hymns. When the Golden Boy's 'murderers' slay, grind, bake, slice and finally eat him (in lines that cry out to be said in unison), they know they are receiving the gift of life. A similar delight in plants' power to clothe the earth, though this time in a form that would bring less joy to haymakers, inspires 'Lucretia' (1978):

> The buttercup lifts her wing-cases
> From between the claws
> Of the retracting glacier.
>
> Still she shakes out, on her crane stilt,
> With her green core of tough subsistence,
> Venturing over the bog.
>
> So Lucretia has overtaken Englishness
> The angler golden to the knees
> The steeple at anchor on the river of honey
>
> Just as she did the trekking weight of the mammoth
> That jolted her cup
> And set her pollens smoking.

'Overtaken' (in the third stanza) causes a moment's puzzlement before we realise that it is used in the sense of 'being come upon suddenly', as when we are overtaken by darkness. Only here the landscape is overtaken by the flowers' luminosity; and it helps at this point to know that the light-bearing name Lucretia belongs to a five-year-old American, well able to break down English reserve and replace it with the nexus of feelings represented by the enchanting imagery of the next two lines – which, paradoxically, conjure up an essentially English rural scene. But the most striking thing about the poem as a whole is its success as a piece of plant portraiture: something new for Hughes who, one suspects, had been trained early by his gunshot elder brother to look out for anything that moved, and had in consequence paid small heed to flowers unless they brought themselves to his notice by an animal-like vigour or tenacity. Now he pauses with delicate exactitude over the hard, sharp sepals as they release the gleaming petals and over the leggy stalks bearing the close knot of fruits that, together with the pollen-bursts (of which Thomas Hardy also made effective use), ensure that future buttercup cohorts will possess the field.

It is tempting to associate such a late flowering with the emergence 'from world of blood to world of light'[39] that Keith Sagar finds in the poet's work

---

[39] Keith Segar, *The Laughter of Foxes; a Study of Ted Hughes* (2000), chapter 4.

around this time. The transition was not however a smooth one. Two years on, there appeared a poem in which the floral structure of the Madonna lily, familiar from countless Annunciations, provokes a volley of deeply disturbing images – a woman's flared cheekbones, the 'mouthings' of her embrace and then her 'shameless and craving' vagina, which in turn becomes the passage to a birth, the expectation of which is, for the poet, a torturer's branding-iron –

> And life cannot peel naked enough
> Hurt cannot open deep enough
> To quench it.

Whatever the distress underlying a poem as powerful as Shakespeare's sonnet on the expense of spirit in a waste of shame[40], the crisis passed, and the skills represented by 'Lucretia' rather than by 'Lily' furnish the light-hearted evocations of feminised flowers in *Flowers and Insects* (assembled in 1986 in cooperation with Lucretia's artist father and dedicated to a now adolescent Lucretia), and which, in the same collection, run riot in 'An Almost Thornless Crown': the newly appointed Laureate's first offering to his sovereign.

Hughes is indulging himself in this volume. A poem such as 'Cyclamens in a Bowl' is full of exclamatory delight at the flowers' translucent beauty – 'a winged Hallelujah! ... Letting the God-light glow through'. Yet a moment's recall of Lawrence's Sicilian cyclamens brings the realisation that Hughes's poem, for all its verve, is not really getting anywhere. It is the 'nature' poems of his early collections and of the landscapes to which he returned in 1979 after a decade of mythologising, that are *sérieux* with the weightiness of the poet's ecological awareness. The best poems in the 1986 collection are those that combine that awareness with his pleasure in flower-personality: the 'Big Poppy' for example, her tattered finery still able in August to allure the bee uttering his 'thin / Sizzling bleats of enjoyment' but soon (pollination achieved), to be shed in order that all the plant's resources may be concentrated on the poppy-head seed-box. Like the snowdrop, she pursues all-important ends and only when these are accomplished does the poet indulge his new-found art of flower portraiture, recalling her huge flop of petal, 'Her big, lewd, bold eye, in its sooty lashes', and her hairy athletic leg 'in a fling of abandon'.

---

[40] See Elaine Feldstein, *Ted Hughes: the Life of a Poet* (2002), p. 234, and related note.

4

'I seek a poetry of facts' declared Hugh MacDiarmid in 'Poetry and science' (1943). In the oddly prosy style he adopted when writing 'standard' English, the leader of the Scottish literary renaissance urged poets to look at flowers, not only with an identifying attentiveness that could reveal their minute beauties, but also with

> the botanist's knowledge
> Of the complete structure of the plant
> (Like a sculptor's of bone and muscle)
> – Of the configuration of its roots stretching under the earth,
> The branching of stems,
> Enfolding of buds by bracts,
> Spreading of veins on a leaf.[41]

The failure of many poets, so grievous to MacDiarmid, to 'know *about*' things, as distinct from 'knowing' them, could be illustrated from a favourite of Green anthologists, Swinburne's 'The Sundew', in which a brief glimpse of something 'yellow-green / And pricked at lip with tender red' that the poet appears to mistake for the sundew's flower prompts a flow of sub-Wordsworthian reflections upon, among other things, Nature's benignity towards a helpless plant. If only anthologists would replace these muddled musings by instead giving us Amy Clampitt's plunge into the mud to investigate what she calls 'The Sun Underfoot among the Sundews'[42]: a poem built on our shared knowledge that the sticky drops on the leaves which give the plant its name ensure that, far from being in need of care and protection as Swinburne imagines, it can well fend for itself by trapping insects. The twentieth-century poet's delight in this 'ingenuity', and the beauty that results from it, a spectacle now rare on this side of the Atlantic –

> an underfoot
> webwork of carnivorous rubies,
> a star-swarm thick as the gnats
> they're set to catch, delectable
> double-faced cockleburs, each
> hair-tip a sticky mirror
> afire with sunlight

– makes her poem a worthy substitute, despite its mischievous reference to the 'roundabout refusal to accept responsibility / Known as Natural

---

[41] *The Complete Poems* (1983), vol. I, p. 630.   [42] *Collected Poems* (1997), pp. 16–17.

Selection', for the poem on *Drosera rotundifolia* that Charles Darwin said he could write, but never did.

That every schoolgirl knows the sundew to be carnivorous is the result of twentieth-century educational reforms: changes which, in Britain, began the year after MacDiarmid's plea was published, and which, in Western society generally, soon guaranteed to all some training in active and informed observation of the natural world. Not every horse drank of course; but those who were resistant to school biology often yielded later in life to the expository skills of the century's great scientific popularisers. C. P. Snow's accusation that literature paid too little attention to science was outdated almost as soon as he made it in 1959.

In one respect, poets of the second half of the last century showed themselves, if anything, over-eager to profit from the life sciences. Because they live by language, poets have an insatiable hunger for new words such as scientific terminology provides in abundance. In particular, from about 1960 onwards, poetry absorbed a whole botanical lexis. A rapid trawl through an anthology or two brings on board: inflorescence, corolla, nectaries, perianth, bromeliad, calyx, gymnosperm, rachitic, chlorophyll, pollinia, pistillate, taxonomy, pinnate, filament, xeric, chromosome . . . But even as one compiles such a list, most of the contexts have begun to fade from the mind. The memorable poems are those whose writers are able to say all that they want to say about the life of plants without recourse to a specialised vocabulary. Judith Wright, for example, when she comes upon a lonely specimen of *Phaius australis* (another wetland species, although of swamps, not bogs)[43] asks

> for whose eyes
> does this blind being *weave*
> *sand's poverty, water's sour,*
> *the white and black of the hour –*

and so puts into the twelve common words I have italicised the processes that have gone to the orchid's making: its establishment in the poorest soil, its translocation of water and mineral salts, its photosynthesis by day and its continuing respiration by night. In so doing, she clears the way to her central concern, which is the vulnerability of whatever is wrought intricately and with great toil, in nature no less than in art. There are said to be no more than some 200 individuals of this plant left in the wild, and the

---

[43] Wright's title, 'Phaius Orchid' (*Collected Poems, 1943–1985* (1994), p. 88) does not name the species. It could be *Phaius tankervilleae*, which is scarcely less endangered in Australia than *P. australis*.

poet knows that the site (to use Michael Longley's metaphor) which her poem provides for them cannot last forever: 'Here like the plant I weave / your dying garland, time'.

Botanical terminology may have been there for the poets' picking, but botanical concepts were to prove increasingly elusive, as a result of the changes that traditional plant science underwent in the middle of the last century. For D. H. Lawrence's generation botany, whether pursued in the field, the greenhouse or, with the aid of the light microscope, in the laboratory, was an evidential science, based for the most part on what was directly observable. This meant it hardly counted as science at all for the physicists who were transforming our concepts of matter in those opening decades of the century. Ernest Rutherford is said to have dismissed it as a form of stamp collecting. And it was not long before the new physics, together with the new understanding of organic chemistry that it instilled, laid the foundations of the new discipline of molecular biology. All that was known, for example, about the mechanism of photosynthesis at the time of Lawrence's death in 1930 was that, given certain conditions, carbon went into plants and oxygen came out. This was as much as Coleridge had known, and put to brilliant rhetorical use, over 100 years earlier.[44] Yet by 1960 Melvin Calvin and his co-researchers, using radioactive tracers, had worked out nearly every biochemical step in the complex pathways linking the two events. And this was but one of the advances made in the 1950s; the most important for the life sciences being, of course, the discovery in 1953 of the DNA molecule's functional design. Among all these heady revelations about bonding atoms and molecules, however, one non-chemical bond was in danger of being broken. Poets, who for two centuries had responded to the rich variety of plant life revealed by botanists and to their insights into plant structures and processes were now faced, in effect, with the demise of these studies as they had known them. Perceptions that had once been common ground between writers and plant scientists appeared to have no place in modern laboratories, where the vital perceptions were those of Geiger counters scanning macerated plant tissues.

Yet the discoveries of biochemists and molecular biologists might have been expected to meet responses from poets similar to those that the New Philosophy elicited from John Donne and his followers in the seventeenth century: a blend of intellectual satisfaction in the logic of biochemical pathways with aesthetic satisfaction in their beautiful orderliness, to match the blend of thought and feeling that underlies much Metaphysical poetry.

[44] In Appendix C of *The Statesman's Manual* (1816).

So why have poets fought shy of the New Biology? The reason cannot just be that its processes are invisible to the unaided eye (and mostly to the aided one as well). The creative imagination has always been ready to take up the challenge of bringing whatever lies beyond sensory perception within the compass of the senses, and scientists have met writers and artists halfway by their own picturings and analogies. Indeed the double helix is in danger of becoming a sculptural cliché.

What really made molecular biology and its vigorous relation, genetics, together with the biochemistry that underpinned both, so inaccessible to poets and their readers has been dramatically summed up by one biologist and historian of science as *Death of Life*:[45] a title that can superficially be taken to refer to the threatened extinction of such subjects as whole-plant botany and zoology, but relates more profoundly to the way the younger disciplines have blurred the traditional distinction between the living and the non-living. After 1953, no biologist could be a vitalist. And poets, though for the most part they no longer conceive of 'life' as some physical or spiritual additive, are all vitalists at heart – for the reason, I have suggested, that their instinctive response to another organism is life's recognition of itself. There was little to substantiate such recognition in a science that presented development, growth and reproduction as the outcome of inexorable physical laws. As a source of inspiration to poets, the life sciences appeared after 200 years to be running dry. But even as this happened, another youthful science was riding to the rescue.

One of today's most distinguished geneticists, Nicolas Harberd, to whom (along with his research team) we owe a series of remarkable discoveries about the regulation of growth in plant cells, recently began to feel that his investigations were losing momentum. Reminding himself that he was a biologist because he loved life, he got on his bike to look for a living specimen of thale cress, the small weed that, bred in tens of thousands, provided his laboratory material; and then, having found one in a country churchyard, entered whole-heartedly into its life-cycle, as it clung to existence in defiance of slugs, rabbits and the East Anglian winter, up to the time its seedlings were ready to replace it. Though Harberd's journal of these events, *Seed to Seed* (2005), does not over-simplify the story, one is left with the impression that his laboratory research really did profit from this transformation of himself into a field naturalist. His experience also offers a paradigm for the revitalisation of poetry about the natural world by ecology: the branch of biology regarded for many years, after its emergence

---

[45] Stanley Shostak, *The Death of Life: the Legacy of Molecular Biology* (1998).

a century ago, as natural history that had become too big for its boots, but which in the landmark year 1953 came of age as a science with the publication of Eugenie Odum's *Fundamentals of Ecology*, and is valued today as the science that can tell us what has gone so terribly wrong with an order of things that once seemed inviolable.

Twentieth-century poets were among the first to protest at humankind's pillaging and poisoning of the natural world. Returning to town by a Michigan logging road (itself a memorial to the destruction of a whole ecosystem) with a load of moss for lining cemetery baskets, the young Theodore Roethke felt he had 'pulled the flesh from the living planet'.[46] Later on, at the height of what was so strangely called the green revolution, Geoffrey Grigson had an advocate of the new farming practices tell Ceres that henceforth she could expect 'no sprinkling of bright weeds' in her crops.[47] No bright weeds, no nectar-seeking insects; no insects, no birds; no birds, a silent spring: after the publication in 1962 of Rachel Carson's book with that title, environmental concern rapidly became environmental angst. Eighteen-year-olds stopped signing up for university courses in botany, however re-named, and turned to courses in ecology in the faith that these would help them to save the planet.

At the outset of this study, I expressed concern that the current confusion between environmentalism, a way of thinking that amounts with many to an ideology, and ecology, a body of knowledge, has resulted in the former even appropriating the latter's name. But though there is no inherent relationship between the two, and though the findings of ecology can be made to serve the purposes of exploiters as well as of conservationists, it is largely as the result of our distress at the despoiling and destruction of habitats that many people have at least a broad grasp of ecological ideas.[48] Biophilia remains a driving force, but whereas in the long reign of botany it took the form of a feeling for the organism, since the rise of ecology it has taken the form of a sense of the whole: of the relationships, that is, of organisms with their surroundings and with each other and the changes over time of those relationships (harmonious to the systems ecologist, often discordant to the populations ecologist) as they are governed by the flow of energy and the cycling of matter.

So poet–botanists of the past have been succeeded by poet–ecologists; not a very numerous company by comparison with the host of

---

[46] 'Moss-Gathering'.   [47] *Collected Poems, 1963–1980* (1982), p. 95.
[48] Television producers deserve acknowledgement here, whatever private feelings we may entertain about exploitation by camera. In particular David Attenborough rounded off his various biological series with one (*Planet Earth*) that superbly, and irresistibly, communicates the ecological vision.

poet–environmentalists, but a distinguished one, and it therefore seems to me that the most fitting way to bring to a close this book on poets of the green kingdom is to share with the reader my enjoyment of an ecological poem such as could only have been written in our own time – and incidentally one by a poet who has sometimes said hard things about the trendier forms of environmentalism.

In the tradition of John Clare, who claimed to give a voice to everything, Les Murray, who started his working life as a translator, gives voice in *Translations from the Natural World* (1991) to some forty plants and animals in order that they may make their presences known in human language. A few of them – cow elephants, for instance – can already vocalise, although bats' ultrasound strains the poet's ingenuity. Others politely defy translation. 'I could not have put myself better / with more lustre than my presence did', a beetle declares. But all Murray's plants prove loquacious; not surprisingly, perhaps, in the case of 'Sunflowers', since to converse is, by derivation, 'to turn towards', as the *tournesol* turns towards the sun:

> I am ever fresh cells who keep on knowing my name
> but I converse in my myriads with the great blast Cell
> who holds the centre of reality, carries it behind the cold
> and on out, for converse with a continuum of adorers:
>
> The more presence, the more apart. And the more lives circling you.
> *Falling, I gathered such presence that I fused to Star, beyond all fission –*
> We face our leaves and ever-successive genitals toward you.
> *Presence is why we love what we cannot eat or mate with –*
>
> We are fed from attachment and you, our futures draw weight from
>   both, and droop.
> *All of my detached life lives on death or sexual casings –*
> The studded array of our worship struggles in the noon not to lose you.
> *I pumped water to erect its turning, weighted its combs with floury oil –*
>
> You are more intense than God, and fiercely dopey, and we adore you.
> *Presence matches our speed; thus it seems not flow, but all arrivals –*
> We love your overbalance, your plunge into utterness – but
>   what is presence?
> *The beginning, mirrored everywhere. The true indictment. The end all*
>   *through the story.*

The shifting meanings of 'converse' make it possible for Murray in his opening stanza, to hold together two conceptual extremes: a multitude of plant cells, each bearing the same genetic code, that by their reduplications

8 'Common Sunflower' (*Helianthus annuus*), 1986–7, by Yasuhiro Ishimoto. The dense packing of the plant's fruits has earned it the attention of artists, mathematicians and industrial chemists in search of a clean bio-fuel. (Art Institute of Chicago.)

'The studded array of our worship struggles in the noon not to lose you.
I pumped water to erect its turning, weighted its combs with floury oil – '
(Les Murray, 'Sunflowers')

produce the headlong growth of a sunflower plant; and the single 'great blast cell' that the plant in its own terms conceives the sun to be, using 'blast' to imply budding, originating, primordial (a blastoma is the first bunch of cells in an embryo). The plant does not experience the radiation by which the sun makes its presence felt as visible light, but as the warmth (only briefly interrupted by its nightly disappearance 'behind the cold') that renders possible its own inner processes: processes which include the unseen effect of light, in the conversion, by chloroplasts within its green cells, of solar energy into chemical energy. It is this vital conversion that underlies the two uses of 'converse' in an opening stanza which serves as prologue to the conversation – in the conventional sense – that now begins between two entities that are at a vast distance the one from the other, yet whose conjuncture is representative of the process on which all life depends.

Distinguished on the page by a careful use of italics and punctuation, the speakers are further differentiated by speech rhythms that set an eager, even excited, chorus from the 'continuum of adorers' against the gnomic solemnity of the sun's statements. In the second stanza, a new play of meanings erupts: this time on 'presence', as the word's basic sense of 'being present' gathers around itself a number of rich and precise contextual meanings – making one's presence felt, a man of presence, the royal presence, the divine presence, Wordsworthian 'presences' – to convey the arousal, in another being, of an awareness that amounts ('why we love') to a deep emotional response. For the sunflower, the sun's presence is the radiation that has mysteriously increased as the sun itself has contracted: a mystery the sun clarifies in a one-line life-history – 'Falling, I gathered such presence that I fused to star, beyond all fission.' This is so succinct, that it is with shame one offers an awkward paraphrase: 'as the gaseous cloud in which the sun originated condensed, it became so hot that nuclear reactions set in, fusing the hydrogen atoms at its centre to helium and thus releasing the vast energy that causes it to shine as a star'.

In response to this radiation, the growing plant turns to the sun both its leaves and the flower-head from the centre of which 'ever-successive' florets emerge with a timing and a spacing that ensure their exquisite symmetry. These are indeed what Linnaeus called them, genitalia, for in the next stanza, thanks to the quanta of light that have penetrated the leaves, they have borne fruit in a 'studded array' of such abundance that the stem droops under its weight. This heaviness has long fascinated plantsmen – 'three pounds and two ounces' Gerard records of one specimen that he grew in the century of *Helianthus*'s introduction from America – and poets have responded to it in their own fashion, from the epigrammatic wit of Cowley to Tennyson's sonorities. Murray, like Blake, is aware of the effort that its heliotropism costs the plant, and for all his dislike of Romantic symbolism ('sunflower-y' is his term for 'metaphorical'), the falling and then rising movement of the sunflower's two lines in this stanza brings to mind, perhaps intentionally, the weary yearning of 'Ah! Sunflower'.

But the sun in Murray's poem, far from being unattainably remote, is at the pump handle. By causing leaves to transpire, it raises the water with which groups of cells in the plant's stem become turgid in succession, and so 'erect[s] its turning', while the process of photosynthesis creates, from air and water and from elements in the soil to which the plant is attached, the 'floury oil' that weighs down its seed-head. In its triumph at this last achievement, the sun sounds almost dismissive of the detached life of the animal kingdom. Beings that devour plants or pillage their fruit, like those who in turn devour *them*, are mere consumers; only plant and sun together are proud producers, in this case of the oilseed that feeds bird, beast and man. They have also conjoined to produce another food, hinted at in 'combs'. Here used of the egg-box-like depressions that hold the hundreds of sunflower kernels, the word brings to mind that other marvel of Nature's packaging, the comb filled with honey derived from plant nectar. And it is as the result of such insect visitations that the sunflowers have borne fruit. A single word has reminded us of the interdependence of plant and animal existences that is the essence of ecology.

So animal life is back in the picture, which is perhaps why the first line of the final stanza, with its wriggle of bliss in 'fiercely dopey', sounds so like the sun-worship of the happy human sunbather. 'More intense than God', however, makes us pause. When we think of the sun's power to harm – and 'we' are in Australia, at a time when the gap in the southern hemisphere's ozone layer was giving cause for disquiet – intensity scarcely appears a divine attribute. And the final line only increases our puzzlement: surely the sun's answer to the direct question, 'what is presence?' should round out the poem by affirming that for the sun it is the power to create and sustain life. But then, as so often happens with a good poem, the meaning that has eluded us leaps unexpectedly off the page. With a reversion to the basic sense of 'presence', 'being present', the sun admits that its existence and so its influence, is finite. Out in the galaxy, a thousand stars like itself are coming into being, each mirrored in the lens of the infrared telescopes which, in the 1980s, first recorded such births – and what has a beginning must have an end. This is the writing on the wall: 'God hath numbered thy kingdom' is the true indictment. The sun's ending, an inert mass of helium at its core, was inevitable from the first fusion of its hydrogen atoms: an end, we realise, that was also present all through the poem itself as story, ironically in 'ever fresh' and 'ever-successive', more overtly in the themes of falling and death.

Is this a *volte face* – Murray the Catholic turning on the devotees of Gaia, even though in so doing he is undermining all his poem has achieved? No, because the achievement stands; the conclusion draws a line under the poem, not through it. In its imaginative grasp of the forces sustaining life – which includes man as one species of 'detached life' among a multitude – 'Sunflowers' substantiates Jonathan Bate's belief that Murray is 'the major ecological poet currently writing in the English language'.[49] But the very fact of the poem's existence detaches the poet in another sense, as a member

---

[49] Jonathan Bate, *Song of the Earth* (2000), p. 238.

of the sole species with a verbalising consciousness. For Murray the 'centre of reality' remains something other – man, God, God-as-man – than the solar power that brings into being the diversity of life. And though this closing withdrawal is based upon beliefs that only a minority of his readers will share, it serves as a reminder, and for me at this point a timely reminder, that poetry has concerns beyond the natural world; concerns that for most poets will be human rather than divine. But the plant kingdom is a world in which some of the finest poets have been happiest; as I too have been happy to bring the reader to some of its flowers.

Index of persons

Index of plants

aconite, winter, *Eranthis hyemalis* 134, 144, 205
agrimony, *Agrimonia eupatoria* 118, 123
alfalfa, *Medicago sativa* 219
almond, *Prunus dulcis* 209, 217
anemone, *Anemone* species 221
anemone, crown ('Adonis' blood' if scarlet), *Anemone coronaria* 181, 215, 221
anemone, Venus' tears, *Anemone hortensis* 221
anemone, wood, windflower, *Anemone nemorosa* 23, 57, 122, 206, 233
angelica, *Angelica sylvestris* 117, 240
apple, *Malus domestica* 186
archangel, yellow, *Lamiastrum galeobdolon* 122
arrowgrass, sea, *Triglochin maritima* 108, 110
arrowhead, *Sagittaria sagittifolia* 110, 134, 145, 156, 188
arrowroot, Indian, *Curcuma angustifolia* 51
arum, cuckoo-pint, *Arum maculatum* 241
Arum triloba, dragon arum, *Dracunculus vulgaris* 179
ash, *Fraginus excelsior* 40, 102, 115, 131
asphodel, *Asphodelus aestivus* 170, 213, 221
auricula, bears' ears, *Primula auricula* 10, 16, 16 n. 18, 19, 20, 30, 32, 113, 199, 207
avens, mountain, *Dryas octopetala* 240
avens, wood, *Geum urbanum* 205

balsam, *Impatiens* species 57, 117
barley, *Hordeum* species 246
bean, *Phaseolus vulgaris* 109
bean, broad, *Vicia faba* 38
bear's breeches, *Acanthus mollis* 113
beech, *Fagus sylvatica* 112, 143, 237
bellflower, *Campanula* species 211. *See also* harebell *and* fairies' thimbles
bellflower, bearded, *Campanula barbata* 209, 211
bellflower, great, *Campanula latifolia* 209, 211
bellflower, mountain, *Campanula scheuchzeri* 209, 211, 212
betony, *Stachys officinalis* 227

bindweed, field, or trailing, *Convolvulus arvensis* 132, 200
bindweed, large, *Calystegia silvatica* 132, 145, 240
birch, silver, *Betula pendula* 199
bird's-foot trefoil, *Lotus corniculatus* 186
bittersweet, *Solanum dulcamara* 103
blackberry, *Rubus fruticosus* 117
blackthorn, sloe, *Prunus spinosa* 117, 138
bladderwrack, *Fucus vesiculosus* 57
blanket weed, *Cladophora* (an alga) 139
bloodwell *see* gillyflower
bluebell, *Hyacinthoides non-scripta* 131, 169, 204, 206, 208, 209, 219
bog asphodel, *Narthecium ossifragum* 239, 241–2
bog cotton, cottongrass, *Eriophorum angustifolium* 242, 245
bogbean, *Menyanthes trifoliata* 23, 118
bracken, brake, *Pteridium aquilinum* 112
bramble, *Rubus* species 130, 138, 146, 245
brooklime, *Veronica beccabunga* 118
brookweed, *Samolus valerandi* 238
broom, *Cytisus scoparius* 68
bryony, black, *Tamus communis* 132, 171
bryony, white, *Bryonia dioica* 38, 208
bugle, *Ajuga reptans* 206
bugloss, *Anchusa arvensis* 100
bulrush, 'cat-tails', *Typha latifolia* 232. See also fen sedge
burdock, greater, *Arctium lappa* 186
burnet, salad, *Sanguisorba minor* 134
buttercup, crowfoot, *Ranunculus acris*,*R. repens*, *R. bulbosus* 122, 132, 133, 142, 149, 157, 160, 170, 240, 247
butterwort, *Pinguicula vulgaris* 23–4, 137, 211

cabbage, *Brassica oleracea* 195
campion, moss, *Silene acaulis* 42, 47
campion, red, *Silene dioica* 23, 112, 208, 239
canna, *Canna indica* 49, 50–1, 54, 56, 59